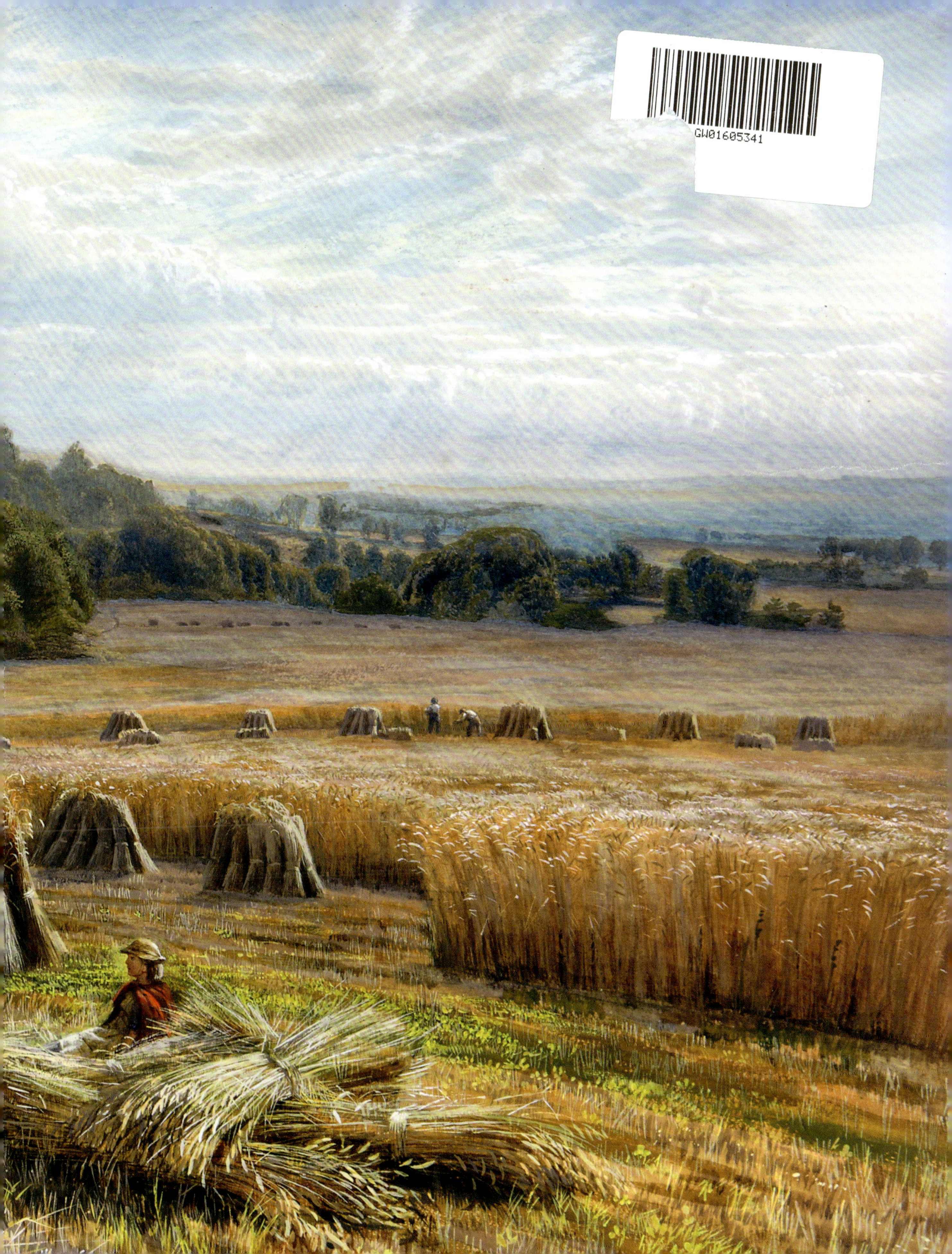

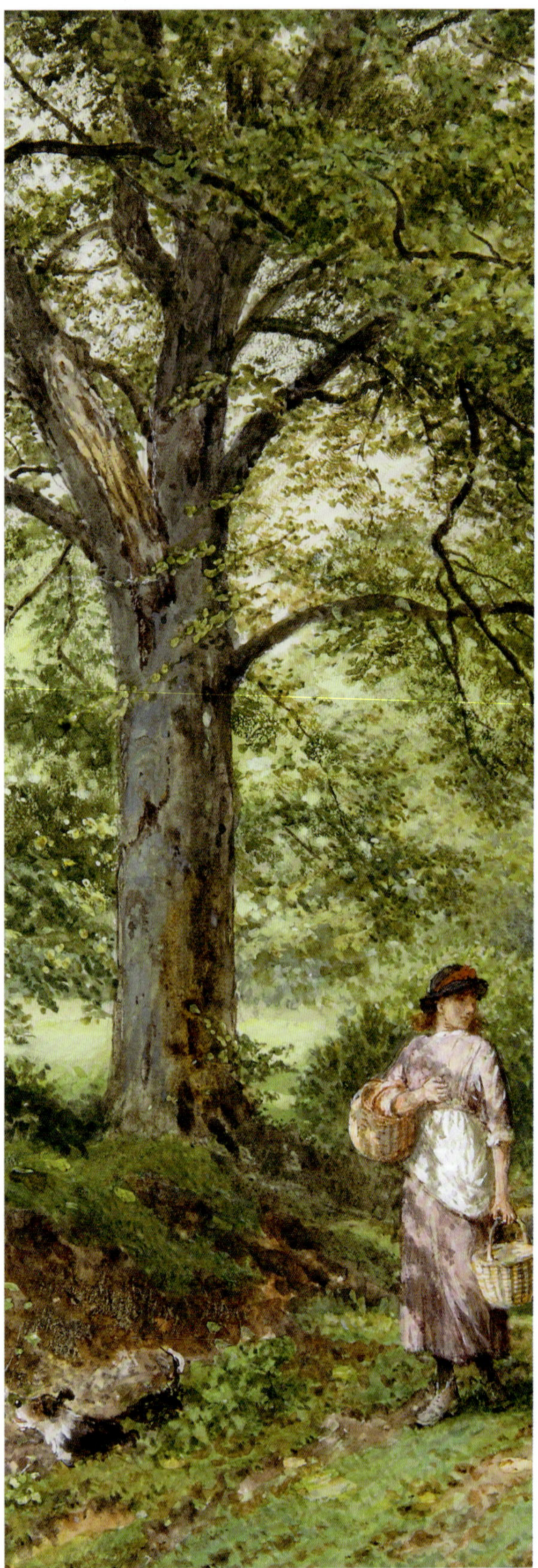

8 & 10 Ryder Street
St James's
London SW1Y 6QB
020 7839 7551
gallery@chrisbeetles.com
www.chrisbeetles.com

ISBN 978-1-905738-99-1

Cataloguing in publication data is available
from the British Library

Researched and written by David Wootton

Edited by Pascale Oakley and David Wootton

Design by Pascale Oakley

Photography by Julian Huxley-Parlour
Reproduction by www.cast2create.com
Colour separation and printing by Geoff Neal Litho Limited

Front cover:
William Henry Margetson, *Spring Love* [66]

Front endpaper:
Edmund George Warren, *High Summer Harvest* [68]

This page:
Birket Foster, *A Surrey Lane* [detail of 70]

Title page:
William Walcot, Women and Children in a Park [78]

Pages 94-95:
John Nixon, *La Belle Liminaudière au Caffée de Mille Collone, Palais Royal, Paris* [4]

Back endpaper:
Constance Frederica Gordon-Cumming,
The Weatherboard, Blue Mountains, New South Wales, Australia [40]

Back cover:
Albert Goodwin, *The Island of the Sounding Cymbals, 'Arabian Nights'* [95]

Chris Beetles Summer Show 2021

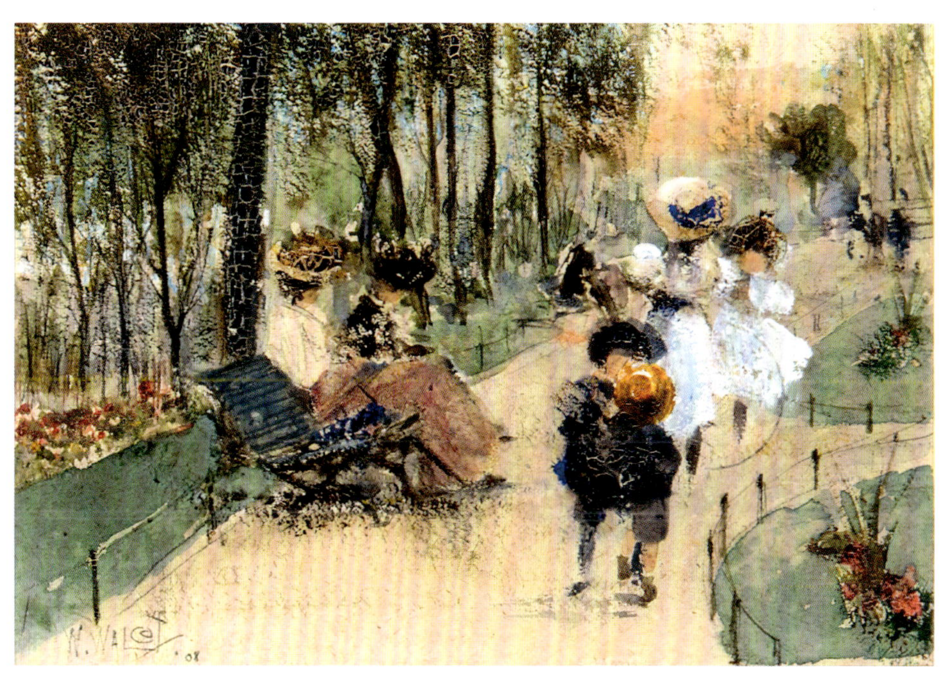

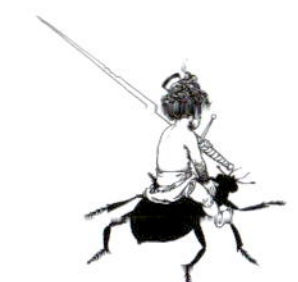

CHRIS BEETLES GALLERY

JOHN DOWNMAN

John Downman, ARA (1750-1824)

John Downman was one of the finest and most popular portraitists of the late eighteenth century, who received the patronage of both members of the royal family and icons of fashion. Working mainly in watercolour and pastel, he specialised in small format images that often depicted the half-length of the sitter in profile or semi-profile.

For a biography of John Downman, please refer to *Chris Beetles Summer Show*, 2020, page 108.

'Handsome, dashing': Maria Brummell, Sister of Beau Brummell

Maria Brummell (died 1854) was one of the three children of William Brummell, private secretary to the Prime Minister, Lord North, and his wife, Mary Richardson, the daughter of the Keeper of the Lottery Office. Her brothers were William (1777-1853) and George (1778-1840), the younger of whom became famous as the dandy and socialite, Beau Brummell.

There is some uncertainty about the date of Maria's birth. Most biographers suggest that she was the eldest child, and born in or before 1777. However, an obituary notice in *The Gentleman's Magazine* in 1854 gives her age at her death as 70, which would make it likely that she was born in 1784. The present drawing is dated 1787, and the child in it certainly looks closer to three than ten years old, so the obituary is probably correct.

Maria grew up on the family's country estate of Donnington Grove, near Newbury, in Berkshire. In 1801, she and Captain George Blackshaw of the Rifle Brigade married in Marylebone, London, and settled at a cottage close to Donnington Grove, though they later moved to Hawthorn Hill, south of Maidenhead. They had two daughters: Anna Georgiana (born 1808), who married the German Baron Heinrich von Maltzahn, and Frances (known as Fanny) (born 1810), who married the Polish nobleman, Konstanty Linowski h Pomian.

Following the death of her husband in Paris in 1815, Maria seems to have shared her time between England and Europe, and probably made Brussels her Continental base. In 1821, she was living at 2 Craven Hill (now Leinster Terrace), Bayswater, next to the theatrical family, the Kembles; Fanny Kemble would describe Maria as 'handsome, dashing' in her *Records of a Girlhood* (1879). In 1840, she was with her brother, Beau Brummell, when he died in Caen, Normandy. She later lived for a time in Florence, and died in Brussels.

1 **Maria Brummell, Sister of Beau Brummell**
Signed and dated 1787
Watercolour
7 ½ x 6 inches
Provenance: The sitter's niece, Georgiana Brummell, Lady Pigott, and by descent, including Mrs Robinson, Dullingham House, Newmarket
Literature: Lewis Melville, *Beau Brummell: His Life and Letters*, London: Hutchinson & Co, 1924, Facing Page 46

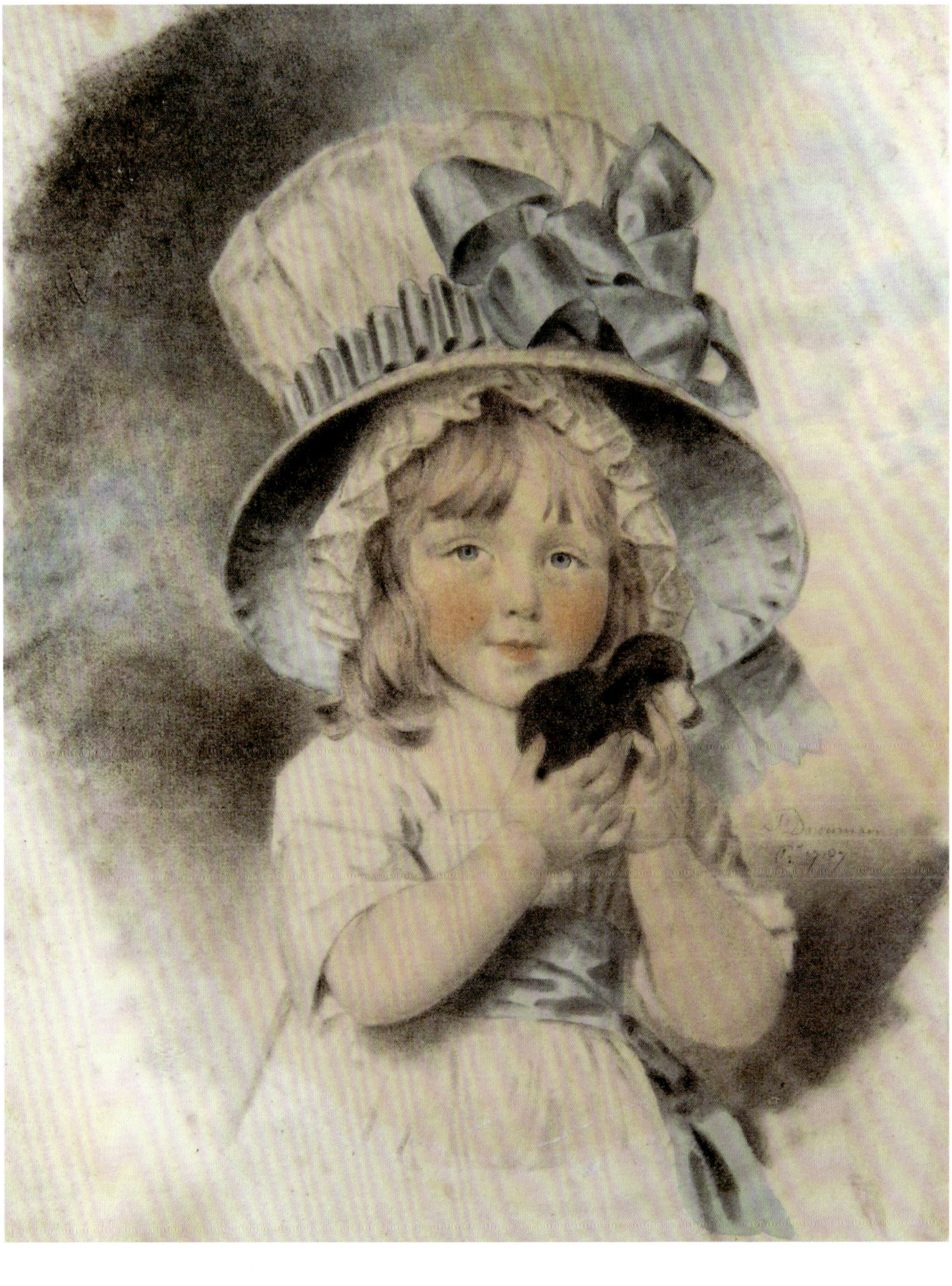

'Young and handsome ... with a good fortune': Miss Ellis as a Young Lady

Mary-Anne Ellis (1778-1855) was the daughter and sole heir of Thomas Ellis of Rolleston, north of Exeter, in Devon. Following his death, she became the ward of Dr Hugh Downman of Exeter, a physician and man of letters, and a relative of John Downman.

In 1799, Mary-Anne Ellis married John Torriano Houlton, who was a Captain in the 1st Wilts Militia, and later a Colonel in the 1st Somerset Militia. Together they would have 14 children. Following their marriage, they lived initially at Mamhead Cottage in the grounds of Oxton House, south of Exeter, which belonged to the antiquary and topographer, the Reverend John Swete. In 1802, they received a visit there from the antiquary and topographer, John Britton, who would recollect the event in his *Autobiography* of 1850:

> [Houlton] was then seated in a delightful villa, Mamhead Cottage, near Exeter, where, with a young and handsome wife, he seemed to be in a sort of terrestrial paradise, with everything lovely and loveable about him. He was a fine specimen of the young gentleman, and had married a young heiress with a good fortune.

The couple soon settled at Houlton's estate of Grittleton, in Wiltshire, which had been bequeathed to him by an uncle, Admiral Houlton. Then, in 1806, on the death of his father, they moved to the estate of Farleigh Hungerford, in Somerset, and set about enlarging Farleigh House in the Neo-Gothic style. The Irish poet, Thomas Moore, was a frequent guest at Farleigh and, in his journal for April 1834, wrote of 'A pretty house, beautiful girls, hospitable host and hostess, excellent cook, good champagne and moselle, charming music: what more could a man wish?'

Farleigh Hungerford would remain Mary-Anne's home for the rest of her life and, though she died in London in 1855, was buried in its cemetery. The Houltons gave up Farleigh House in 1899, when Sir Edward Houlton died with no male heir.

John Downman produced at least four drawings of Mary-Anne Houlton (née Ellis), of which the present example is the second. The first – a half-length – had been produced in 1794, when Downman also drew Mrs Downman, the wife of Mary-Anne's guardian. In 1801, he produced both a pen and ink drawing of Mary-Anne (British Museum) and a double portrait of her and her husband during a visit to Mamhead Cottage.

2 **Miss Ellis as a Young Lady**
Signed and dated 1797
Chalk and watercolour
8 ¼ x 6 ½ inches

Inscribed on an old back label in a contemporary hand
'Mifs Ellis. 1797. Original.
She was a Ward of Dr Downman of Exeter and married
Capn Houlton'

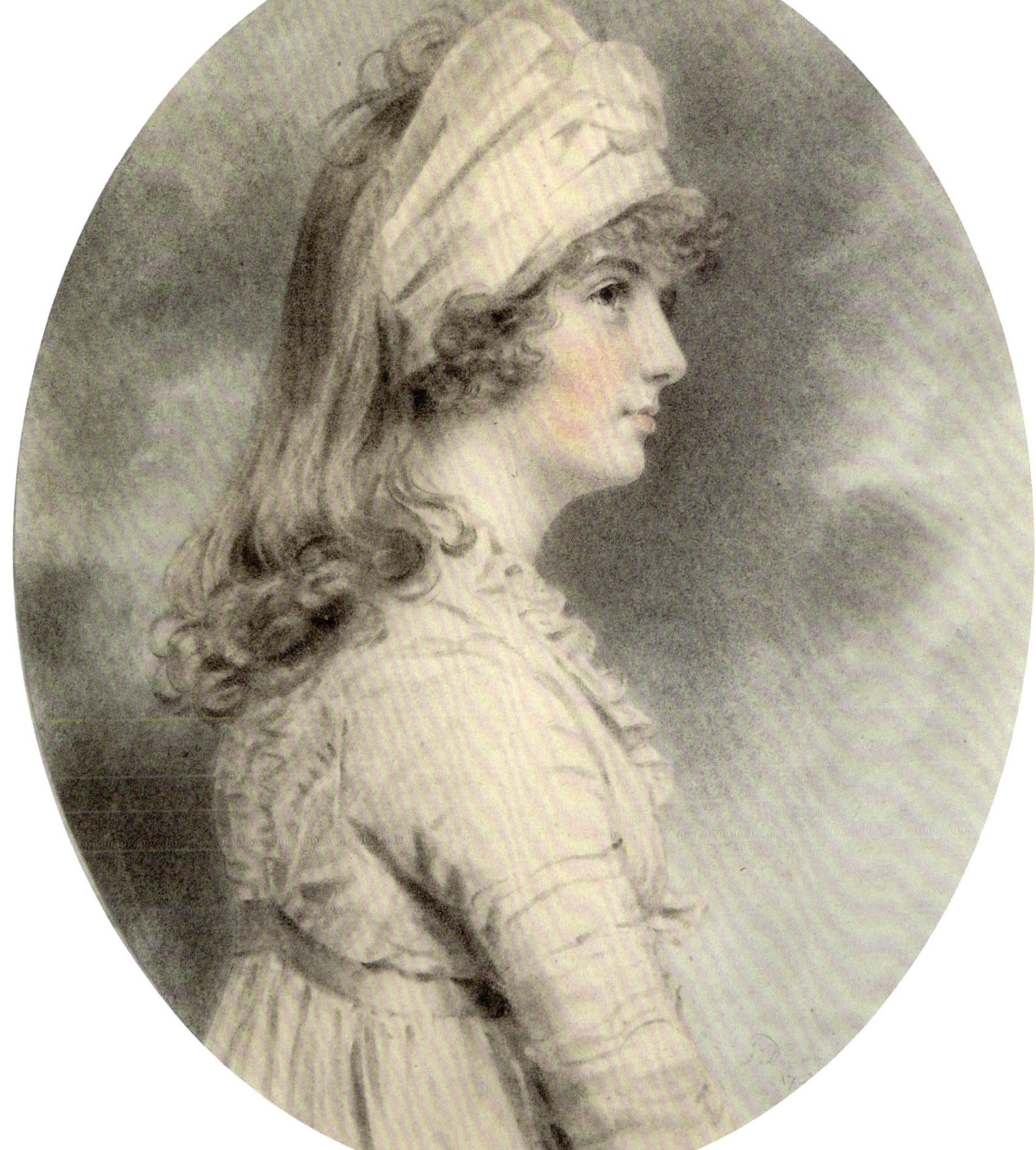

JAMES GILLRAY

James Gillray (1756-1815)

Having developed the skills of draughtsman and engraver, James Gillray established himself as the first professional caricaturist in Britain, and dominated the field. Breaking free of the rigid symbolic language of amateur caricaturists, he employed his rich imagination, and exaggerated the features of his targets, to powerful political ends.

For a biography on James Gillray, please refer to page 96.

Mrs Gibbs the Notorious Street Walker & Extorter

The prostitute, Jane Gibbs, gained a brief period of notoriety in London in the autumn of 1799, when her attempts to extort money from men were exposed. As a result, she became the subject of a number of satirical prints, including the present one.

On Saturday 21 September 1799, Jeremiah Beck was brought to trial at the Old Bailey for highway robbery, having been accused of forcibly stealing the pocketbook of Jane Gibbs, 'a servant out of place', while she was walking in Kensington Gardens on 20 June. The alleged crime had been heard, though not seen, by Stephen Ledyard, a coachman strolling in the gardens, and it was he who caught Beck and escorted him to the magistrate's office in Bow Street, Covent Garden. However, during the trial, Beck's attorney countered the statements of Gibbs and Ledyard, by calling as witnesses several men who, though not present in Kensington Gardens on the day in question, had all been victims of Gibbs, in her attempts to extort money. Her strategy had been to latch on to a man, first by suggesting that she was acquainted with him, then by asking him to return home with her, and eventually pleading poverty. If the man failed to give her money, she would – at over six feet tall – begin to intimidate him, and shout out that it was she who was being robbed. Beck, who was in danger of hanging, was acquitted, while Gibbs had to be escorted from the court for her own protection.

James Gillray was present in the court, and drew and etched this caricature of Jane Gibbs, which was 'sold by all gd book & print sellers' from the Monday. It shows her standing on the witness stand, ready to swear on a copy of the Gospels that is in her hand. It captures both her stature and her physical appearance, her neat dress contrasting with her devious expression, which is emphasised by her squint. The accompanying text is not only descriptive but also cautionary, warning as it does of Gibbs's ability both to affect modesty through her dress and attempt 'her depredations in all parts of the town'. Gillray's portrait soon gave rise to other prints of Gibbs, including one by Isaac Cruikshank and Francis Sansom, which was published by S W Fores.

Despite the exposure, Jane Gibbs continued her delinquent activities. In the October, she appeared before the Bow Street magistrate on the charge of falsely swearing to have been robbed by Mr Evans, an Admiralty messenger – though she was acquitted. Again, her appearance was recorded and publicised in prints by Gillray and others. Then, when she was rearrested just a few days later, she was classified as insane and committed to Bedlam.

3 **Mrs Gibbs the Notorious Street Walker & Extorter**
Hand-coloured etching
10 ½ x 8 inches

Inscribed in plate:
'Caution to the Unwary! –
This Pest of Society is rather of a Tall & Thin form; has a little of the West-Country accent – is, or affects to be hard of hearing; – dresses neat, & appears as a Servant Maid – sometimes as a Quaker, affects a deal of Modesty at first – has no particular Beat or Walk – having attempted her depredations in all parts of the Town

Published Sept' 23rd 1799
& sold by all gd Book & Print sellers in London
Price 6d.

Mrs Gibbs the Notorious Street Walker, & Extorter – Swearing at the Old Bailey to Mr J Beck having Robbed her in Kensington Garden of which charge he was honorably acquitted – multitudes of Witnesses appearing to prove her having made similar Charges against them, in order to extort Money.'

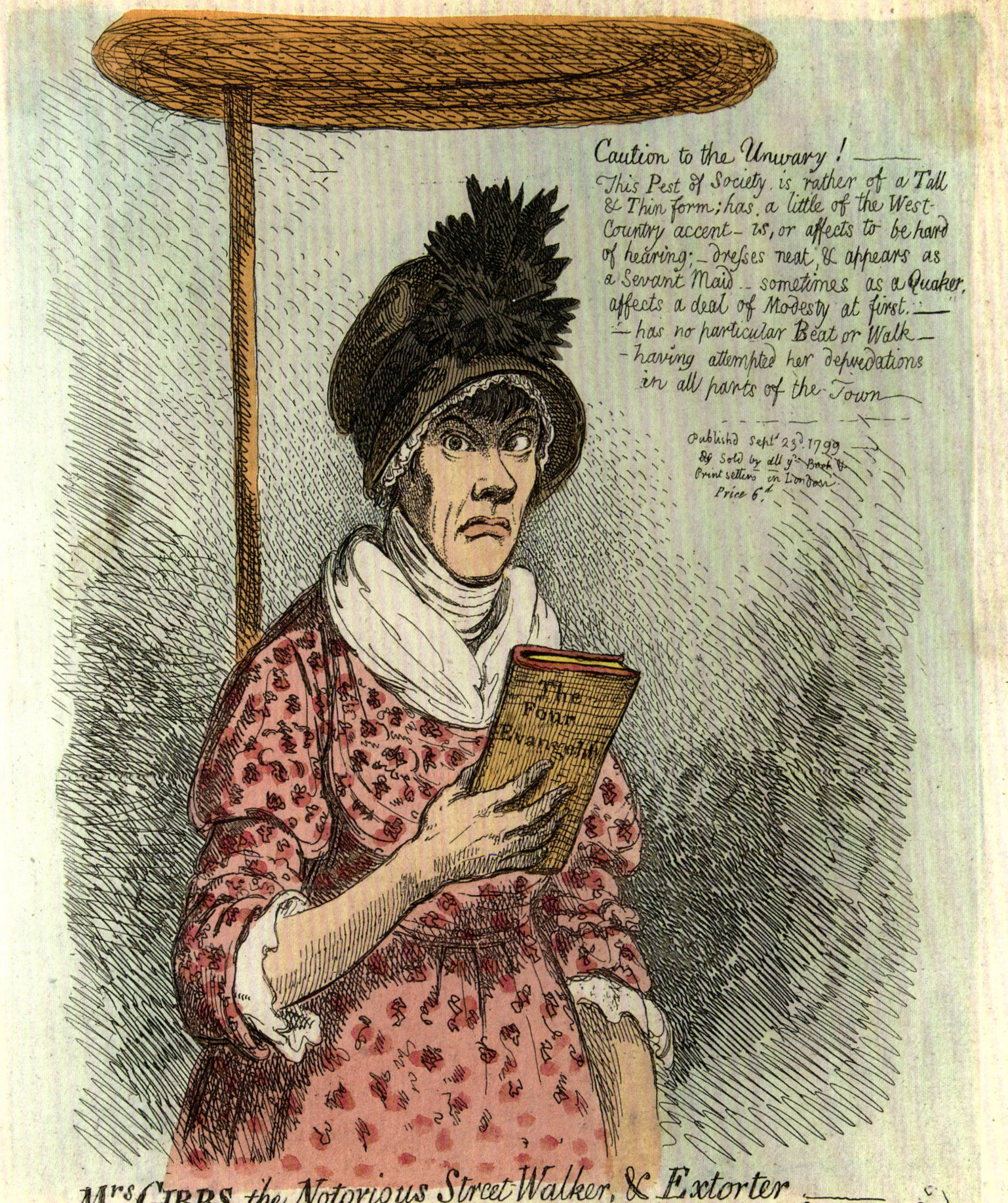

Mrs GIBBS the Notorious Street Walker, & Extorter ——
Swearing at the Old Bailey to Mr. I. Beck having Robbed her in Kensington Garden
of which charge he was honorably acquitted – multitudes of Witnesses appearing to
prove her having made similar Charges against them, in order to extort Money.

JOHN NIXON

John Colley Nixon (before 1759-1818)

One of the most notable amateur artists working in London in the late eighteenth century, John Nixon became best known for his caricatures of urban society.

For a biography of John Nixon, please refer to page 97.

This sober verse, this tranquil strain,
Were it to strive, would strive in vain
That in its couplets should be shown
The Café of the Milles Colonnes.
The pencil gives a better ken
Of its fair Queen – for, ah, no pen
Can paint her glory's grand design,
At least an earth-made pen like mine;
I therefore leave it as 'tis done,
To the rare skill of ROWLANDSON;
By whose enliv'ning, vivid touch,
To which this volume owes so much,
The lady's splendour will survive
When all her graces cease to live,
And the proud mirrors shall no more
Reflect her beauties ten times o'er;
Or when another takes her chair,
Not half so fat, if half as fair.

'Café des Milles Colonnes'
(from William Combe's *The Dance of Life*, 1817)

La Belle Liminaudière au Caffée de Mille Collone, Palais Royal, Paris

[or more correctly: *La Belle Limonadière au Café des Milles Colonnes, Palais Royal, Paris*]

Known as 'La Belle Limonadière' (the beautiful lemonade seller), Madame Romain (born circa 1783) was the celebrated hostess of the Café des Milles Colonnes, which, during Napoleon's Empire and the first years of the Bourbon Restoration, stood on the first floor of 36 Galerie de Montpensier, at the Palais-Royal, in Paris.

Madame Romain and her husband had initially run the Café du Bosquet, which stood close to the Palais Royal in the Rue Saint Honoré. It was there that her beauty had first been noted and had helped attract a large clientele, contrasting as it did with the appearance of her husband, who has been described as small, thin, sallow and one-armed.

In 1807, the Romains took over the Café des Milles Colonnes, in the Palais-Royal, which, since 1784, had contained a shopping and entertainment complex. The café was reached by a beautiful staircase, and its rooms were lined with mirrors, which reflected 30 or more gilt Corinthian columns *ad infinitum*, so giving the establishment its name. Dressed in the height of fashion, Madame Romain presided over the tables from an ornate chair behind a marble-topped desk.

It is said that Napoleon himself was an habitué of the café in its early days. However, from his first exile, on Elba in 1814, it increasingly became the haunt of provincials and foreigners. John Nixon was in Paris during that summer, and produced the present watercolour at the time, along with its pendant, *Madame Véry Restaurateur*. Both were etched by Thomas Rowlandson for publication by Thomas Tegg, and Rowlandson produced his own image of La Belle Limonadière at her desk in the café as an illustration to William Combe's poem, *The Dance of Life* (1817) (of which an extract is printed left).

A refurbishment of the café in 1817 increased the opulence of its interior, and replaced Madame Romain's chair with one that was said to have once been the throne of one of two brothers of Napoleon – either Joseph Bonaparte, King of Naples and later of Spain, or Jérôme Bonaparte, King of Westphalia – both of whom were deposed in 1813.

In 1824, Monsieur Romain died falling from his horse. Two years later, Madame Romain closed the café and entered a convent. The premises were turned into a gaming house.

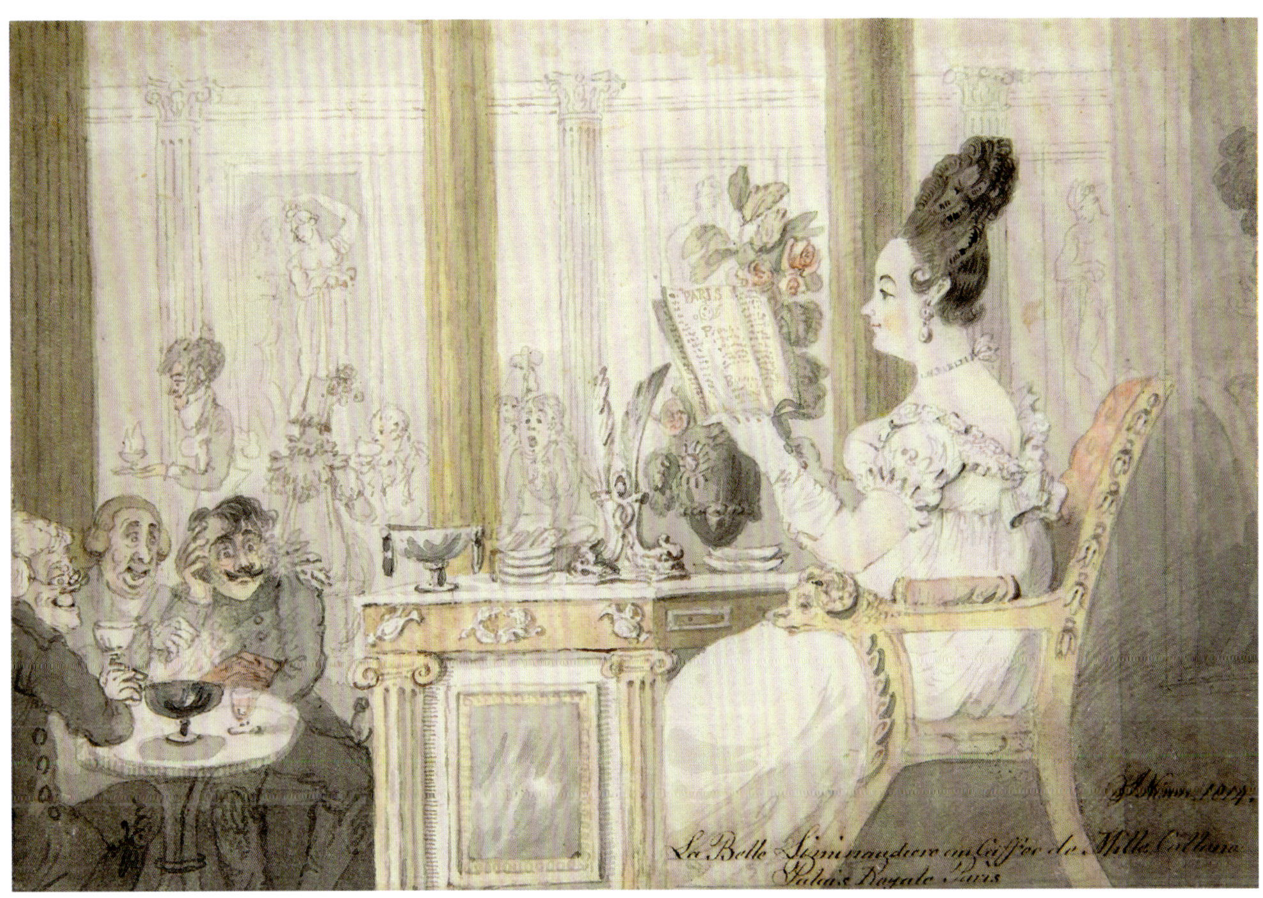

4 La Belle Liminaudière au Caffée de Mille Collone, Palais Royal, Paris

Signed, inscribed with title and dated 1814
Pen ink and watercolour
6 x 9 inches
Literature: Joseph Grego, *Rowlandson the Caricaturist*, London: Chatto and Windus, 1880, Volume II, Pages 272-274

Etched by Thomas Rowlandson, Published by Thomas Tegg, 1814, as a pair with *Madame Véry Restaurateur, Palais Royal, Paris*

THOMAS ROWLANDSON

Thomas Rowlandson (1757-1827)

Thomas Rowlandson raised comic art to a new level by representing the panorama of contemporary life with almost unparalleled fluency – adopting lyricism or incisiveness as best fitted the subject. And, in capturing an abundance of picturesque detail, his work provided a parallel to the novels of Henry Fielding or Laurence Sterne.

For a biography of Thomas Rowlandson, please refer to *Chris Beetles Summer Show*, 2017, page 4.

5 **Money Lenders**
Inscribed with title and 'Pub Novem. 8. 1784 by W H Humphrey No 227 Strand' in plate
Engraving with hand colouring
10 x 14 inches

Published as an etching by William Humphrey, No 227 Strand, London, on 8 November 1784

Money Lenders

Thomas Rowlandson's great Victorian champion, Joseph Grego, describes the present etching in general terms as 'a young nobleman … receiving visits of certain usurers' (*Rowlandson the Caricaturist*, London: Chatto & Windus, 1880, vol 1, page 175). However, later commentators have drawn attention to the Garter star on the nobleman's coat in order to identify him as George, Prince of Wales (the future George IV). George did himself acquire an uncoloured copy of this etching soon after it was published, and Kate Heard, of the Royal Collection Trust, notes that the image 'is thought to be the earliest satire on his increasingly large debts'. She adds that 'In 1784 … he clearly found this image amusing rather than offensive, an attitude reflected in the pose of the borrower in the print, who seems to care little for the debt in which he is miring himself' (*High Spirits: The Comic Art of Thomas Rowlandson*, London: Royal Collection Trust, 2013, page 82). However, while the nobleman may be the portrait of an individual, the moneylenders are generic caricatures of Jews.

6 **Cupid Removing a Thorn from Venus's Foot** (opposite)
Watercolour; 5 ¾ x 8 inches

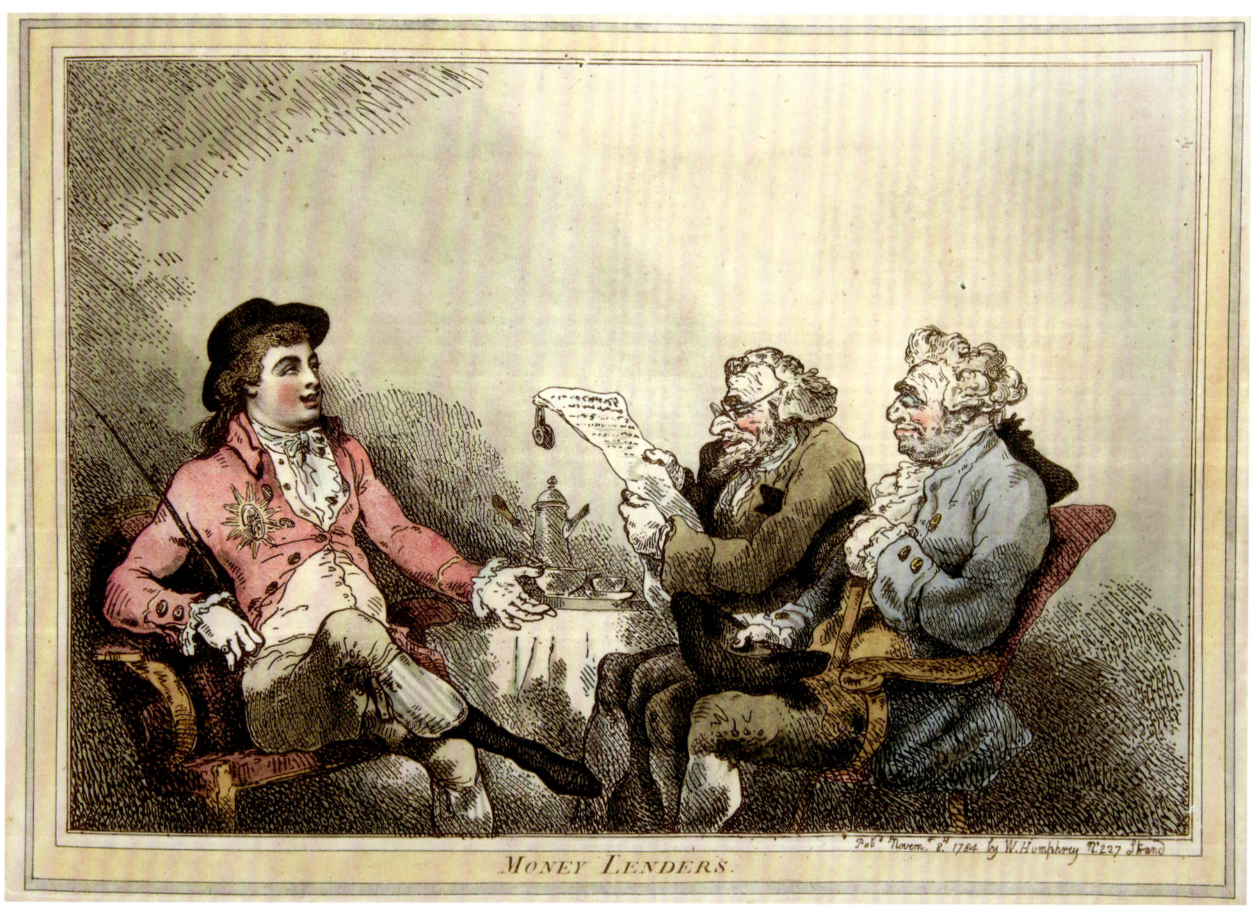

Cupid Removing a Thorn from Venus's Foot

The mythology of the Classical world and the art that it inspired both had a great appeal for Thomas Rowlandson. He was introduced to the study of ancient sculpture while a student of the Royal Academy Schools, and sustained an interest in classical imagery throughout his career, as a result of his enquiring mind and in acknowledgement of the wider antiquarian interests of the time. In turn, he employed Classical imagery as a weapon in his satirical armoury, as the basis of erotic, even pornographic imagery, and in straightforward emulation of its beauty.

The present drawing is an example of that emulation of Classical beauty. Like many of Rowlandson's Classical images, it is based on a print of an old master painting, in this instance Jean-Baptiste Michel's etching and engraving of *Venus and Cupid* by Carlo Maratta (1625-1713). Michel's engraving was published as one of a set of 129 prints entitled *The Houghton Gallery*, which was published by John Boydell between 1774 and 1788, and then gathered in two volumes. (*Venus and Cupid* was Plate 8 of Volume II.) This project was intended as a record of the Walpole collection at Houghton Hall, Norfolk, before it was dispersed – much of it being sold to Catherine the Great, Empress of Russia in 1779. However, the current whereabouts of Maratta's original painting is not known.

In this image, Venus, the Roman goddess of love, reclines on a rock, while her son, Cupid, removes a rose thorn from her foot. Classical poets recounted at least two variants of the origin of the affiliation of Venus to the rose: that it was created when Venus's tears mixed with the blood of her wounded lover, Adonis; and also that, in making a failed attempt to save Adonis, she was wounded by rose thorns, so that her blood turned the white flowers red. Renaissance artists tended to show Venus removing a thorn from her own foot, perhaps inspired by *Lo Spinario*, the famous Hellenistic bronze of a boy doing the same (now in the Palazzo dei Conservatori, Rome). It was only in the eighteenth century that artists regularly showed Cupid taking action, as an extension of the long history of images of Venus together with Cupid.

Other drawings by Rowlandson, in which he explored aspects of the Classical Venus, include *The Bath of Venus* (Fine Arts Museums of San Francisco, CA), *Venus, Anchises and Cupid* (The Metropolitan Museum, New York) and *Venus Crowned by Cupids* (Yale Center for British Art, New Haven, CT). In 1799, he produced a series of four etchings on the subject: *Mars and Sleeping Venus with Putti, Sleeping Venus, Sleeping Venus cuddling a Child* and *Venus and Cupid.* In the same year, he made an etched copy of Titian's *Venus of Urbino* (the original of which is in Le Gallerie dei Uffizi, Florence).

With thanks to Nicholas Knowles for his help in the compilation of this note.

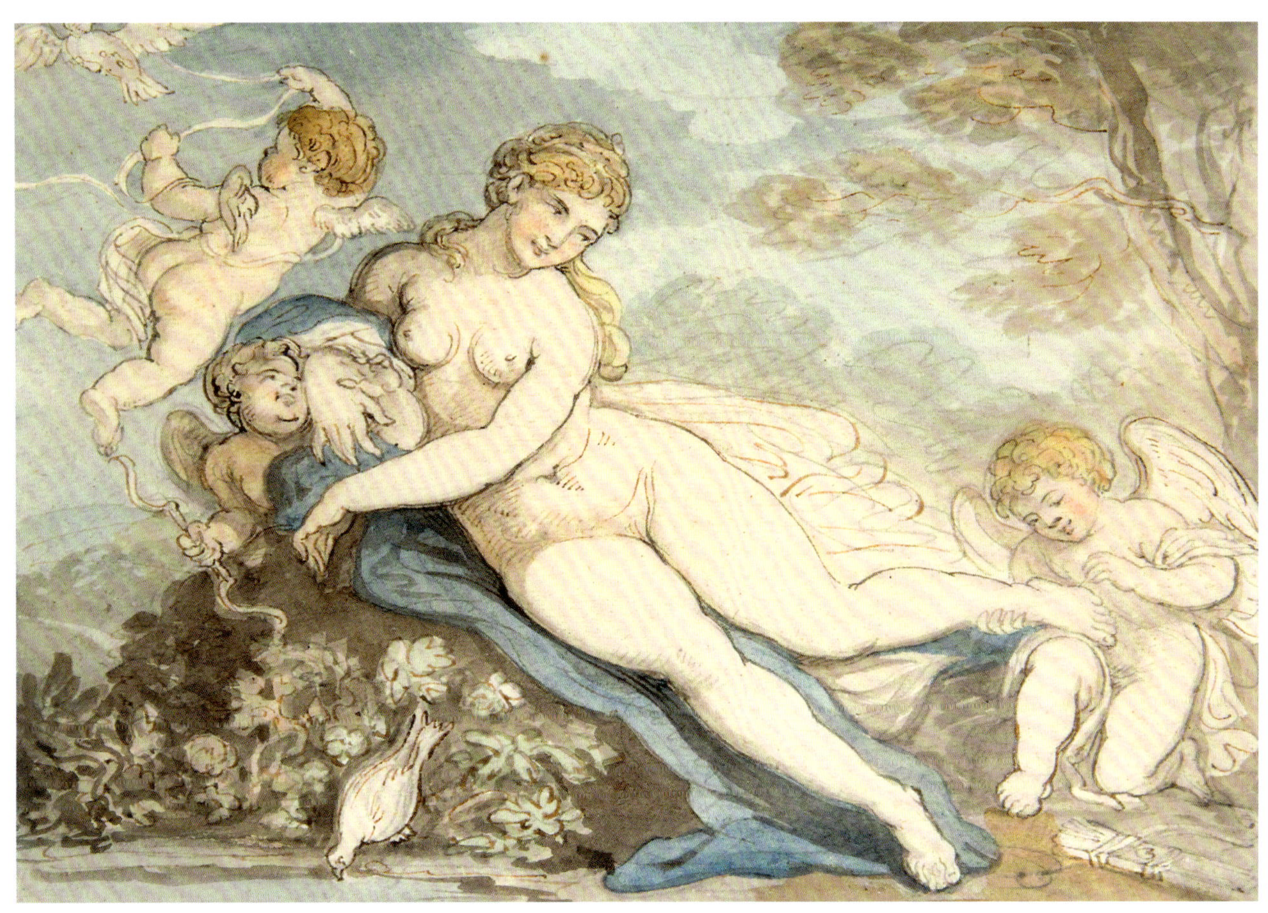

Rowlandson's England

The name of Thomas Rowlandson is almost synonymous with caricature. However, the artist has almost as great a claim to be remembered for his record of the topography and society of late eighteenth and early nineteenth century England. He was also highly aware that he was living in an age of burgeoning tourism. Not only did he make many sketching tours of his own – working up the results into topographical etchings and engravings – but also satirised the activity in *The Tour of Dr Syntax in Search of the Picturesque* (1809-12), his comic images inspiring the accompanying verses of William Combe.

Allowing for a little artistic licence, six of the seven works presented here would fit well into the pages of the pioneering topographical series of books, *The Beauties of England and Wales* (1801-14), of which John Britton – Rowlandson's collaborator on other projects – was the chief author. Thus, some of the following notes quote freely from them.

7 **Greenwich**
Watercolour with pen and ink
5 ¼ x 8 ½ inches

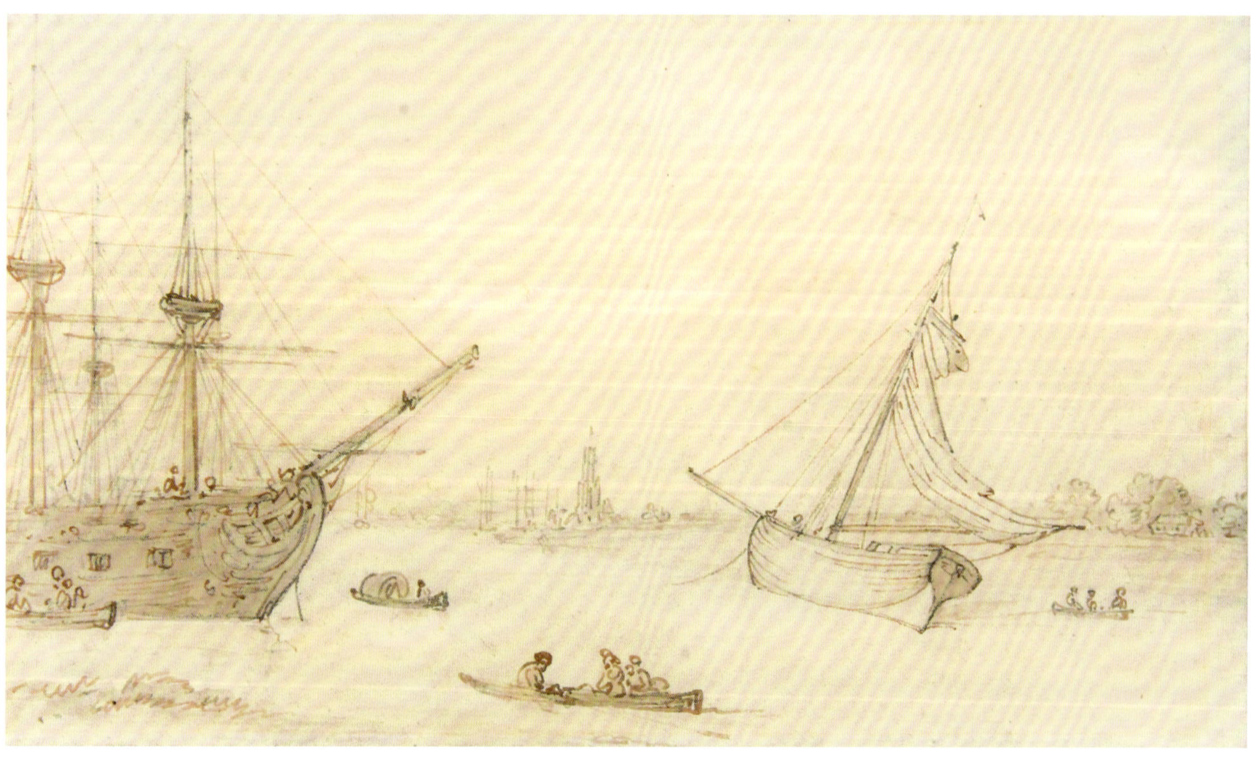

Greenwich and Blackwall

The River Thames was a focus of activity during the time of Thomas Rowlandson, and he was drawn to depict the life and landscapes that he found along it, from Henley to the Estuary. The stretch from Greenwich to Blackwall proved to be of particular appeal, with its mixture of docks, shipyards and halts for pleasure boats.

The present view of Greenwich from the Isle of Dogs focuses on the tower of St Alfege's Church. The domes of the Royal Naval College are a little too distant to register, and the stretch as a whole seems entirely rural. A flavour of the setting is given by Edward Wedlake Brayley in the seventh volume of *The Beauties of England and Wales* (1808):

> Greenwich … is pleasantly situated on the banks of the Thames, which is here from 320 to 360 yards broad, at low water, and proportionately deep. The extensive circuit of the river round the Isle of Dogs, where the capacious West India Docks have been lately formed, has rendered this part of the channel very commodious for shipping from the earliest periods (page 468)

The tower of St Alfege had stood proud since Mediaeval times. However, the remainder of the church had collapsed and had only recently been rebuilt, in the years 1712-14, to designs by Nicholas Hawksmoor, the tower then being refaced and surmounted by a spire in 1730, to a design by John James. It was of patent interest to Rowlandson, who made two detailed drawings of the tower (that are now in the collections of the Huntington Library, San Marino, CA, and the Yale Center for British Art, New Haven, CT).

Around the bend from Greenwich is Blackwall, the docks of which were the subject of many of Rowlandson's studies. The present drawing of busy docks was produced in 1806, in the same year that the artist etched *Perry's Dock, Blackwall*, and it is likely that it too is of Blackwall.

8 **Busy Docks**
Signed and dated 1806
Watercolour with pen and ink
6 ¼ x 9 ¾ inches

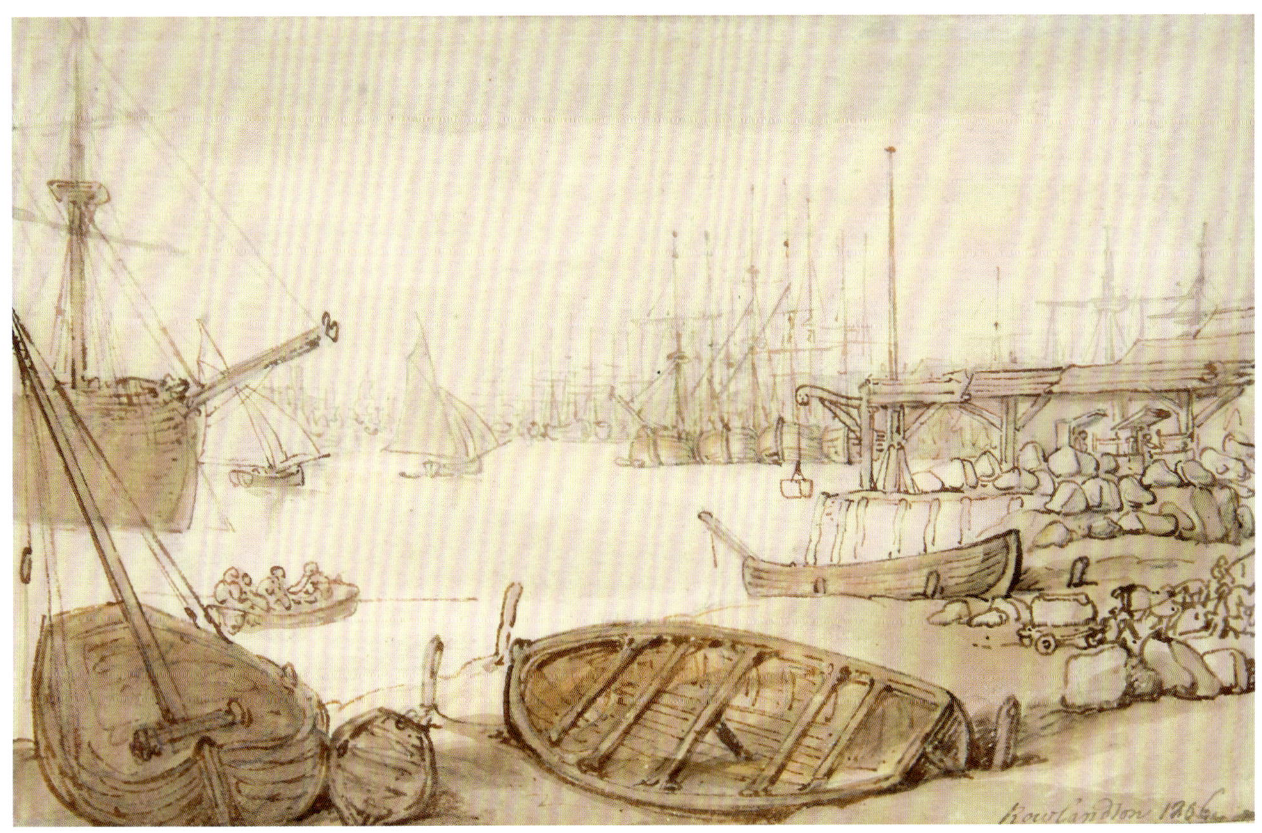

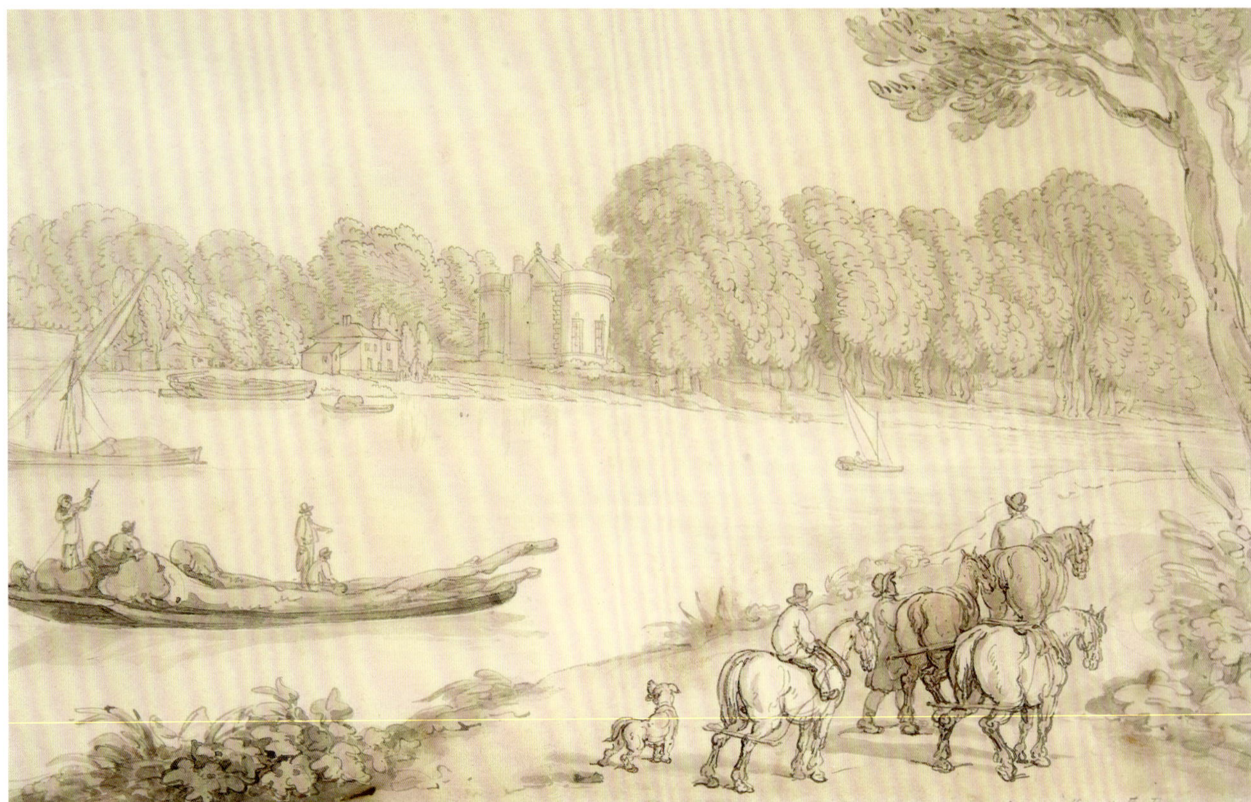

9 **On the Thames**
Pen ink and watercolour
11 x 17 ¼ inches

Village Market (opposite below)
Thomas Rowlandson based the buildings that surround this village market on those at Wokingham, in Berkshire. Most are accurately placed, as is the Ship Inn, which sits at the centre of this image. However, All Saints Church has been moved from the right of the inn to a location behind it in order to create a focus to the composition.

All Saints Church was founded in 1180, but substantially rebuilt in the late fifteenth century in the form shown in this and other of Rowlandson's drawings. However, it was restored and expanded in the mid 1860s by Henry Woodyer, the dormer windows being removed and the east end being rebuilt.

The Ship Inn is a 400-year-old institution, originating as a lodging house and becoming a functioning alehouse and coaching inn in about 1745. The main structure, as shown in Rowlandson's drawings and as it still stands, dates from that time. However, it does retain a half-timbered sixteenth-century wing. The building retains a very distinctive large flank chimney with three shafts, which stands out at the centre of Rowlandson's drawings.

Rowlandson based the present drawing on a more purely topographical one in the collections of the Morgan Library & Museum, New York, which is described as *Hamlet and Church with Scaffolding on its Tower*. Rowlandson has inscribed this 'Oakingham' in the bottom right, Oakingham being a corruption of the Saxon name Wokingham that was in use by the late eighteenth century.

Other versions of the view include *Village with Cart and Figures* (British Museum), *A Village Scene Outside a Church* (The Yale Center for British Art) and *Country Fair for Hiring Servants* (sold by the Chris Beetles Gallery to a private collection).

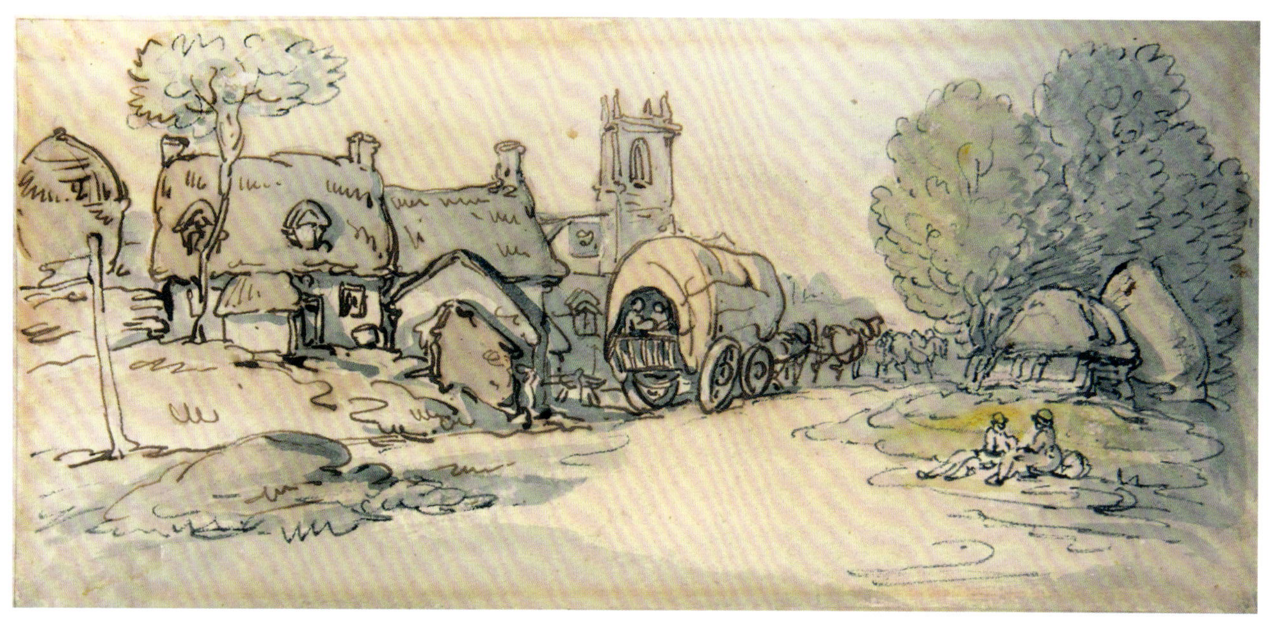

10 Waggoners in the Village (above)
Sketch of a post chaise and passengers on reverse
Watercolour with pen and ink
4 ½ x 9 inches

11 Village Market (below)
Pen ink and watercolour
8 ½ x 11 ½ inches

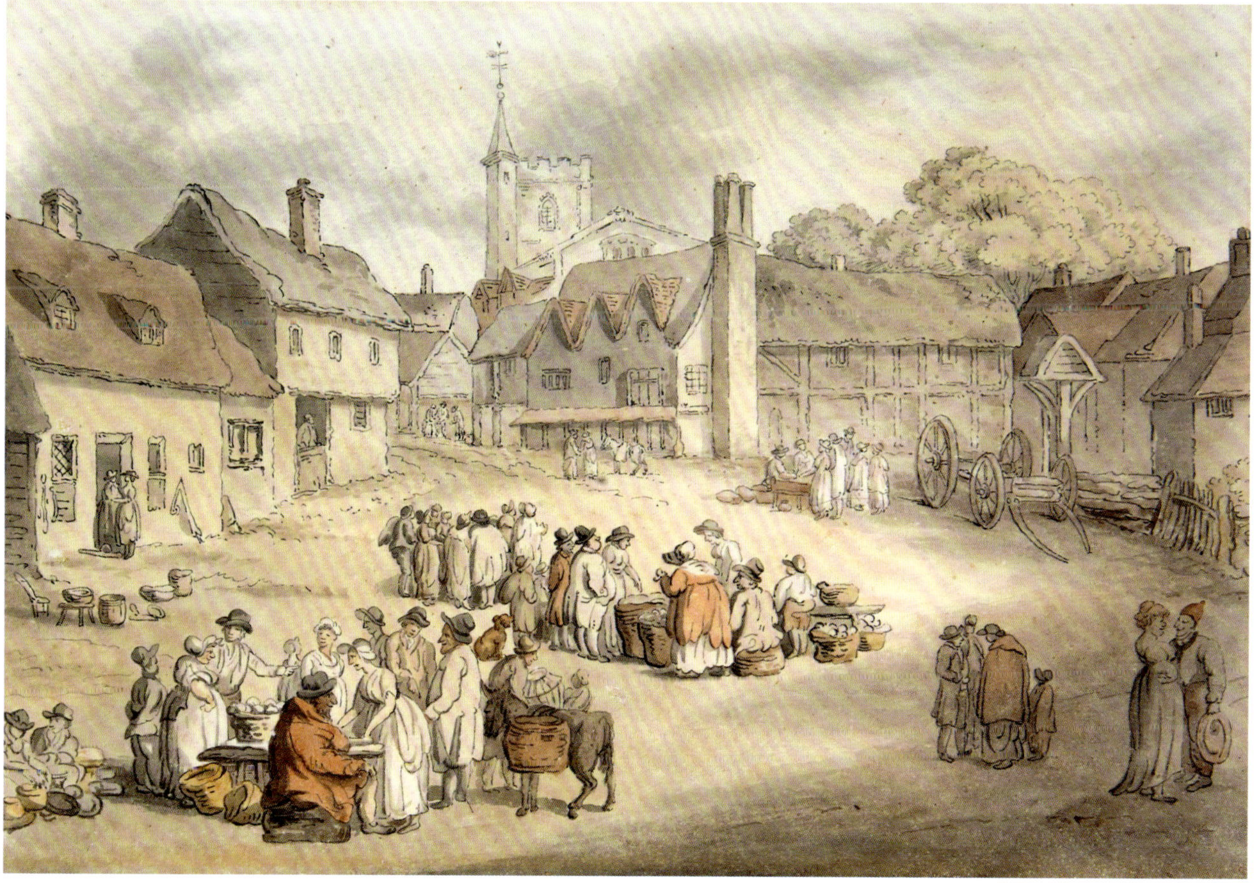

Ilfracombe and Looe

Between the 1790s and 1817, Thomas Rowlandson made frequent tours of the West Country. He usually based himself at Hengar House, St Tudy, six miles north of Bodmin, which was the Cornish estate of his close friend and most important patron, the banker, Matthew Michell (1751-1817). He produced many and varied drawings and watercolours of the region, significant groups of which were etched and published as *A Series of Views in Cornwall, Devon, Dorset, &c* (1805) and *Views of Cornwall* (1812), while others were included in more diverse topographical collections.

Looe is about 20 miles from St Tudy, on the south coast of Cornwall. As described by Britton and Brayley in the second volume of *The Beauties of England and Wales* (1801), 'East and West Looe are situated at the mouth of the river which bears the same name, and are connected by a long narrow, irregular bridge of fifteen arches' (page 397). This bridge – replaced in 1853 by the current seven-arched one – can clearly be seen in Rowlandson's watercolour, in a view downstream that takes in the confluence of the river's two tributaries. To the right stands the eighteenth-century house, Polvellan Manor, which, until his death in 1814, was the seat of Colonel John Lemon (and is now in a sad state of ruin). Rowlandson also etched a view of *West Loo, Cornwall*, possibly in 1822.

Ilfracombe is about 60 miles from St Tudy, on the north coast of Devon, so Rowlandson probably visited it *en route* to Hengar House, rather than as a day trip from it. Rowlandson's panoramic watercolour would have made a suitable illustration for Britton and Brayley's description of the place in the fourth volume of *The Beauties of England and Wales* (1803):

> the most northerly town in Devonshire … seated on the coast in the hundred of Braunton, and … a rich and populous sea-port. It derives considerable trade from the herring fishery in the Bristol Channel. The peculiar situation and safety of the harbour, occasions many vessels to put in here, when it is dangerous for them to enter the mouth of the Taw for Barnstaple. In consequence of this circumstance, many merchants of the latter place transact their business here. Nature and art seem to have jointly combined in forming the harbour, which appearing like a natural bason, is almost surrounded by craggy heights, overspread with foliage. On three sides the rocks rise in a semi-circular sweep; and on the fourth a bold mass of rock stretches nearly half way across the mouth of the recess; affording protection to the little cove from the northern tempests. This rock rises nearly to a point; and on the top is erected a light-house, which has the appearance of a place of worship. (page 267)

Other watercolours of Ilfracombe by Rowlandson include *Ilfracombe Beach, Devon*, (1791, National Gallery of Ireland), which shows a more close-focussed view of its harbour.

12 **Ilfracombe** (opposite above)
Watercolour with pen and ink on wove paper
5 ½ x 9 ¼ inches

13 **Cornwall, East and West Loo[e]** (opposite below)
Inscribed with title
Watercolour with pen and ink on wove paper
5 ½ x 9 inches

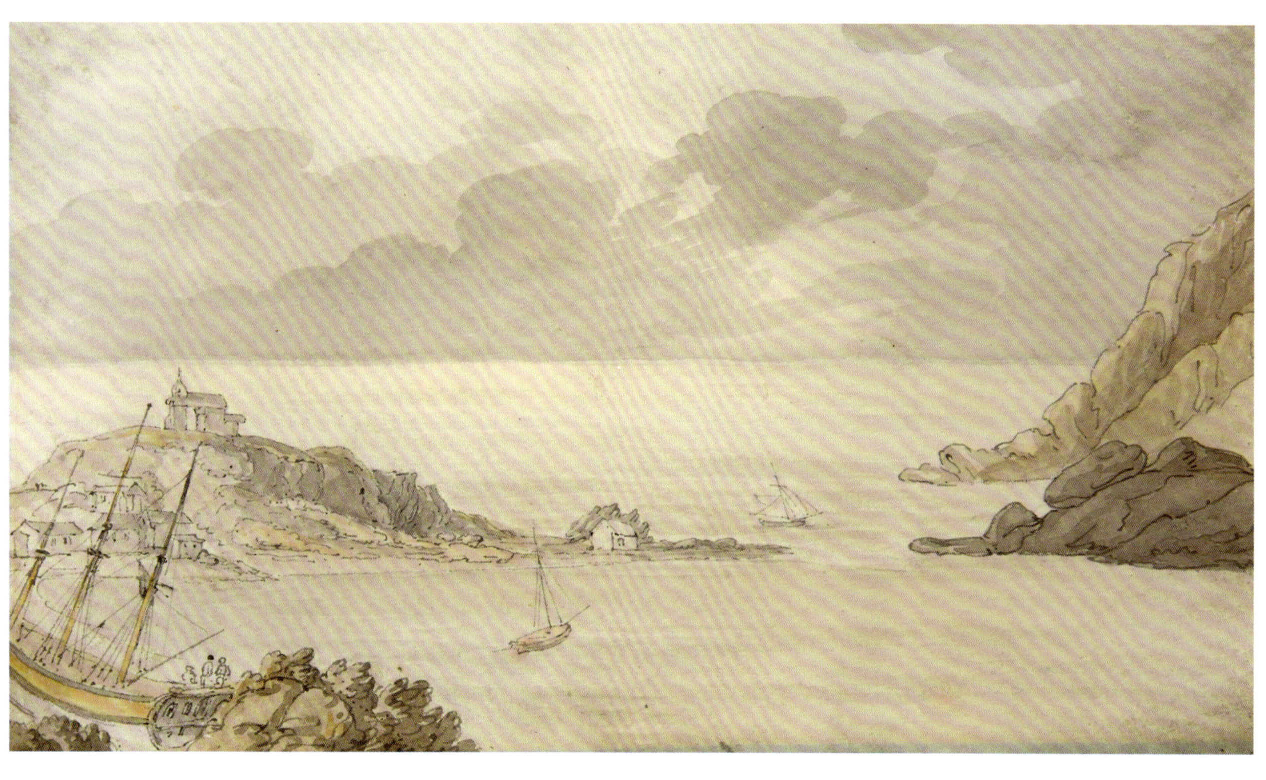

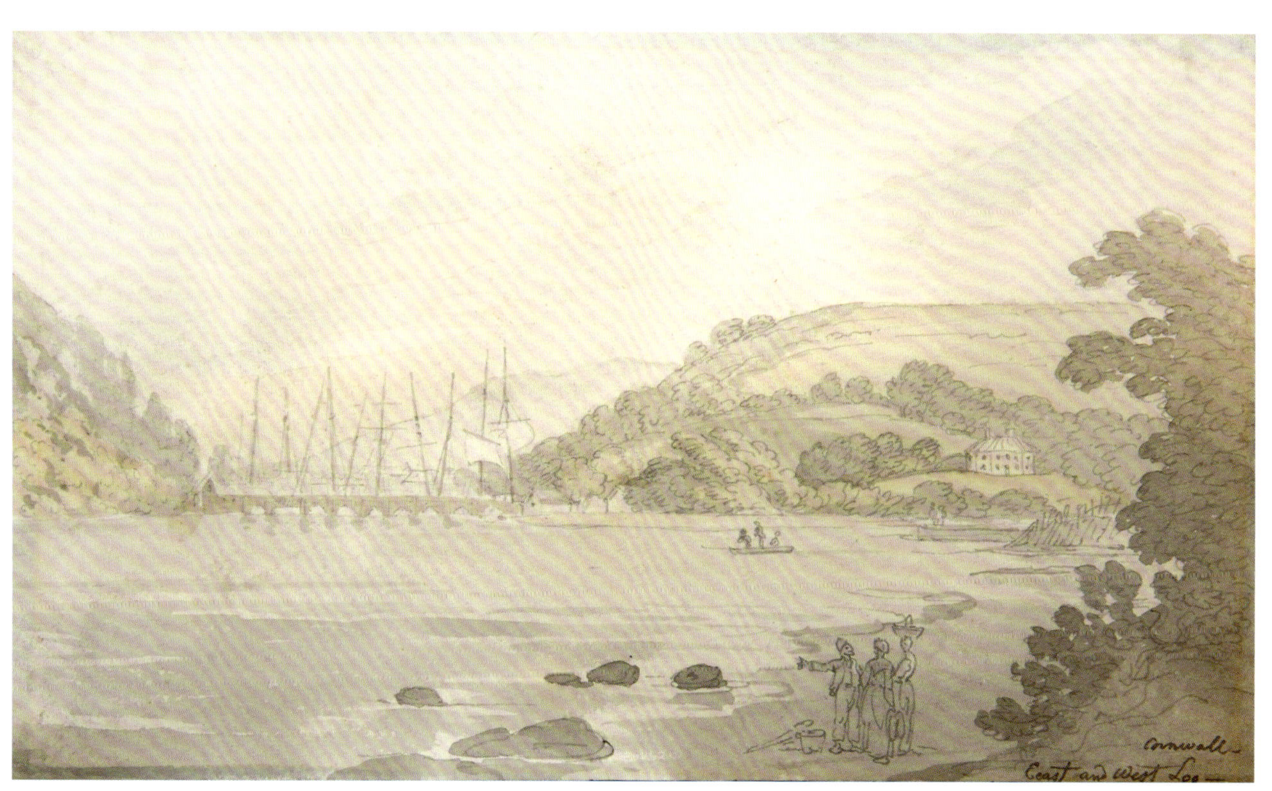
Cornwall
East and West Loo

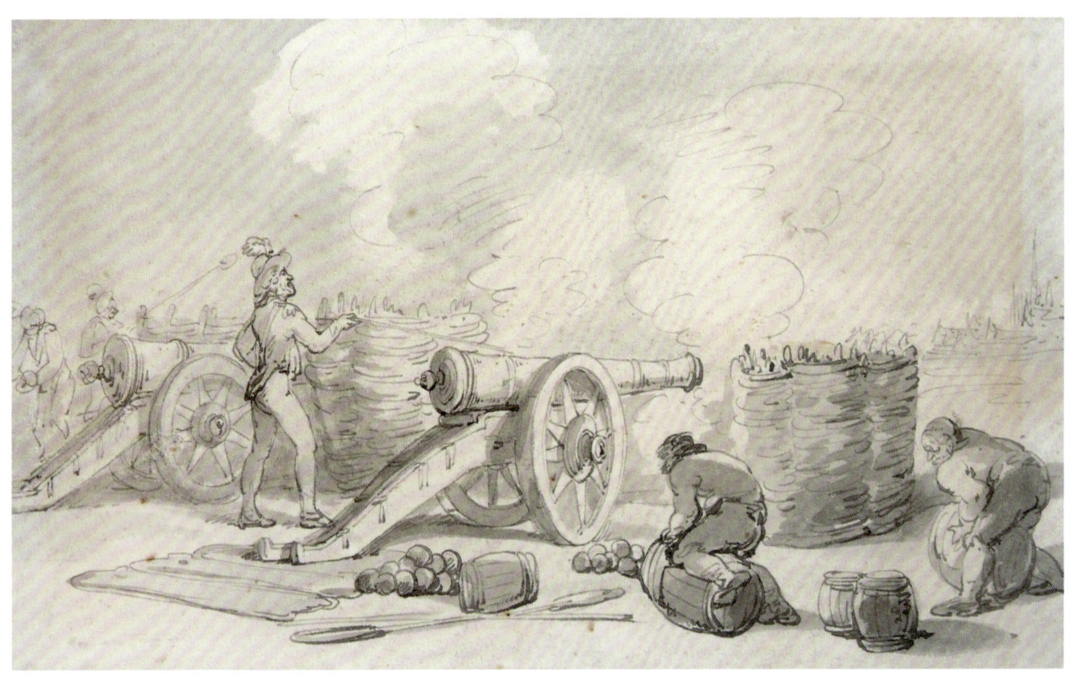

14 **A French Artillery Division in Action** (above)
Pen ink and watercolour
5 ¾ x 9 ½ inches

15 **Rustic Idleness** (below)
Pen ink and watercolour
8 x 12 inches

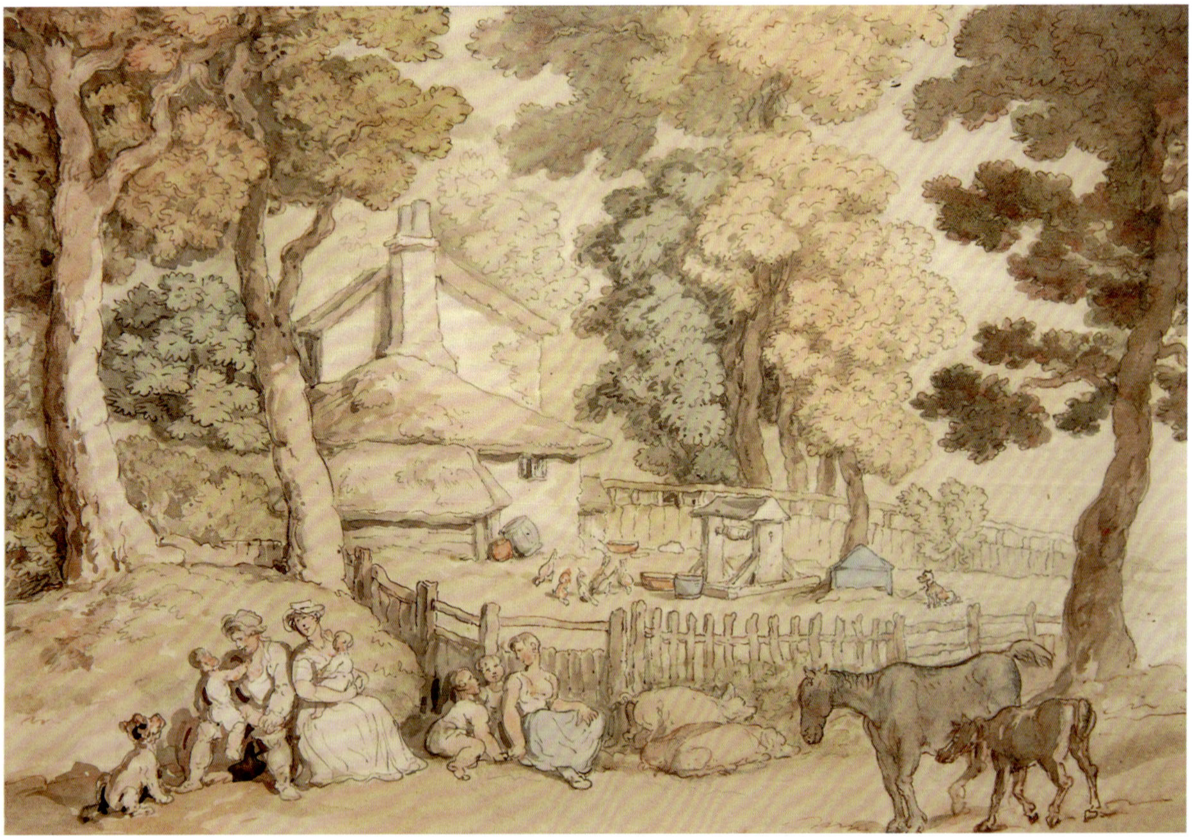

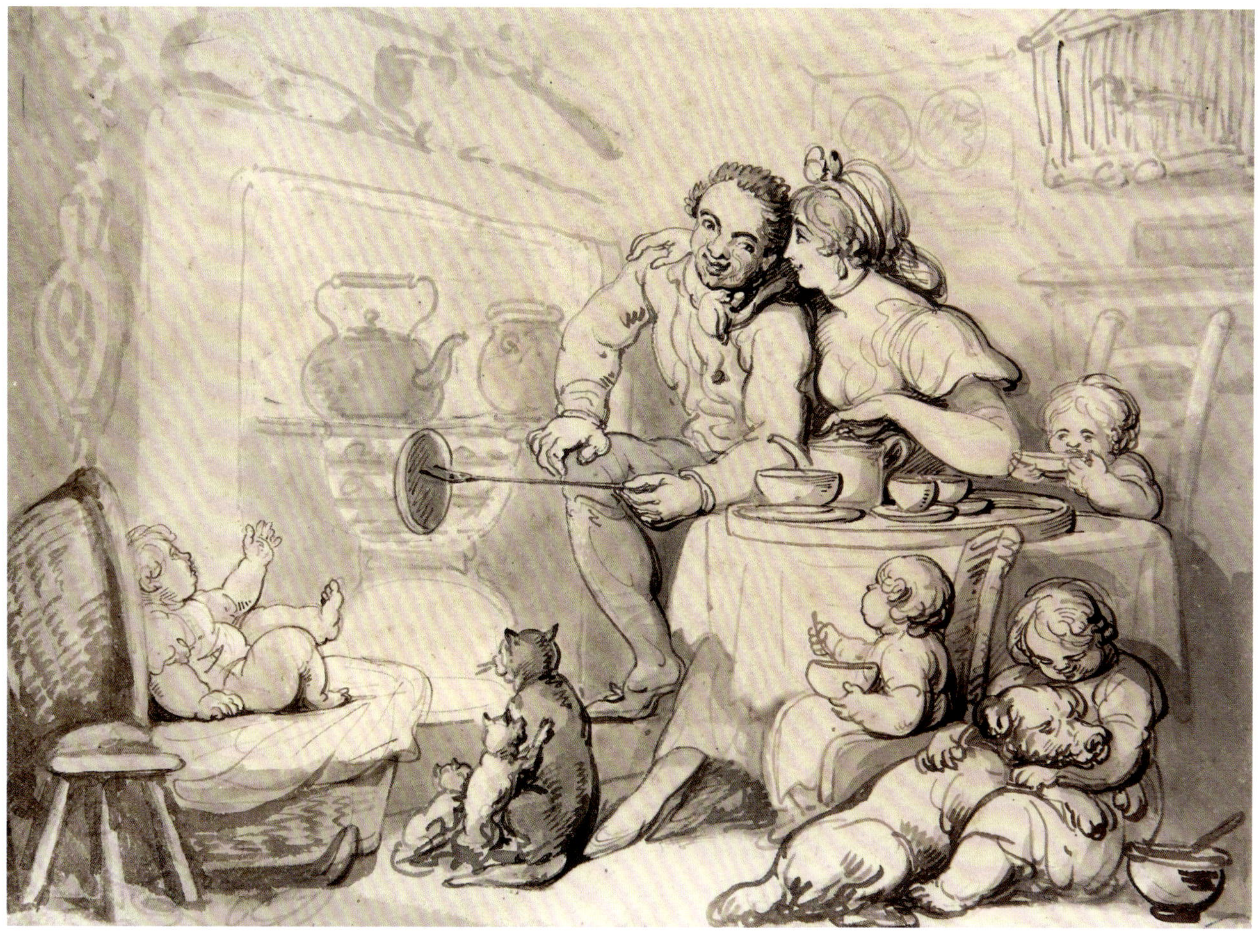

16 The Comforts of Matrimony: A Good Toast
Inscribed 'Matrimony' on reverse in a contemporary hand
Pen ink and watercolour
6 x 9 inches
Provenance: Christie's, London, 18 October 1966,
No 50, as 'A Family Tea'

The Comforts of Matrimony: A Good Toast

The present watercolour relates to the aquatint of the same title that was published by Reeve and Jones, 7 Vere Street, London, on 21 April 1809. It was issued as one of a pair of contrasting images, with *The Miseries of Wedlock: The Tables Turned*. The general composition of the present work is replicated in reverse in the printed aquatint. However, the print is not only coarser than this watercolour, but contains many small differences from it, which suggests that there was probably another, intermediary drawing on which it was directly based.

The essence of both the present watercolour and the aquatint has been described by Joseph Grego in the following way:

> The picture represents a scene of domestic felicity of the most touching completeness. The husband is browning a muffin for tea; his wife's arm is wound around his neck during this delicate operation; his children are enjoying their peaceful meal; an infant is tranquilly slumbering in the cradle; and a cat, surrounded by her family of kittens, carries out the unity of the subject. (*Rowlandson the Caricaturist*, London: Chatto and Windus, 1880, vol 2, page 134)

Yet, in the watercolour, the husband looks not at his wife but at the viewer, as if acknowledging and sharing his good fortune. Indeed, he and his pets are more fecund than his aquatinted counterpart, for he has four children (rather than three) and the cat has two kittens (rather that one), while all are far more alive and alert.

JOHN VARLEY

John Varley, OWS (1778-1842)

John Varley was a central figure for the watercolourists of the early nineteenth century. A founder member of the Society of Painters in Water Colours, and its most prolific exhibitor, he was also a highly significant teacher of both professionals and amateurs, and a writer of instruction manuals. He encouraged his students to paint in the open air, but also promoted the Picturesque theory of adapting nature to the requirements of composition.

For a biography of John Varley, please refer to *Chris Beetles Summer Show*, 2015, pages 5-6.

London Capriccio (opposite)
This fascinating image shows John Varley inserting three London landmarks into one of his characteristically luminous riverscapes. In the foreground, the ordinary life of a rural river proceeds undisturbed by a magisterial mirage. On the horizon stand St Paul's Cathedral, Westminster Abbey and – peaking above the trees to the right – the White Tower of the Tower of London. Varley has portrayed them with the accuracy of a seasoned topographer, but his placing of them disregards both their actual geographical relationship and their relative heights. In reality, St Paul's Cathedral is much the highest of the three buildings (at 364 feet) and is situated in the City of London, far to the east of Westminster Abbey and closer to the Tower of London.

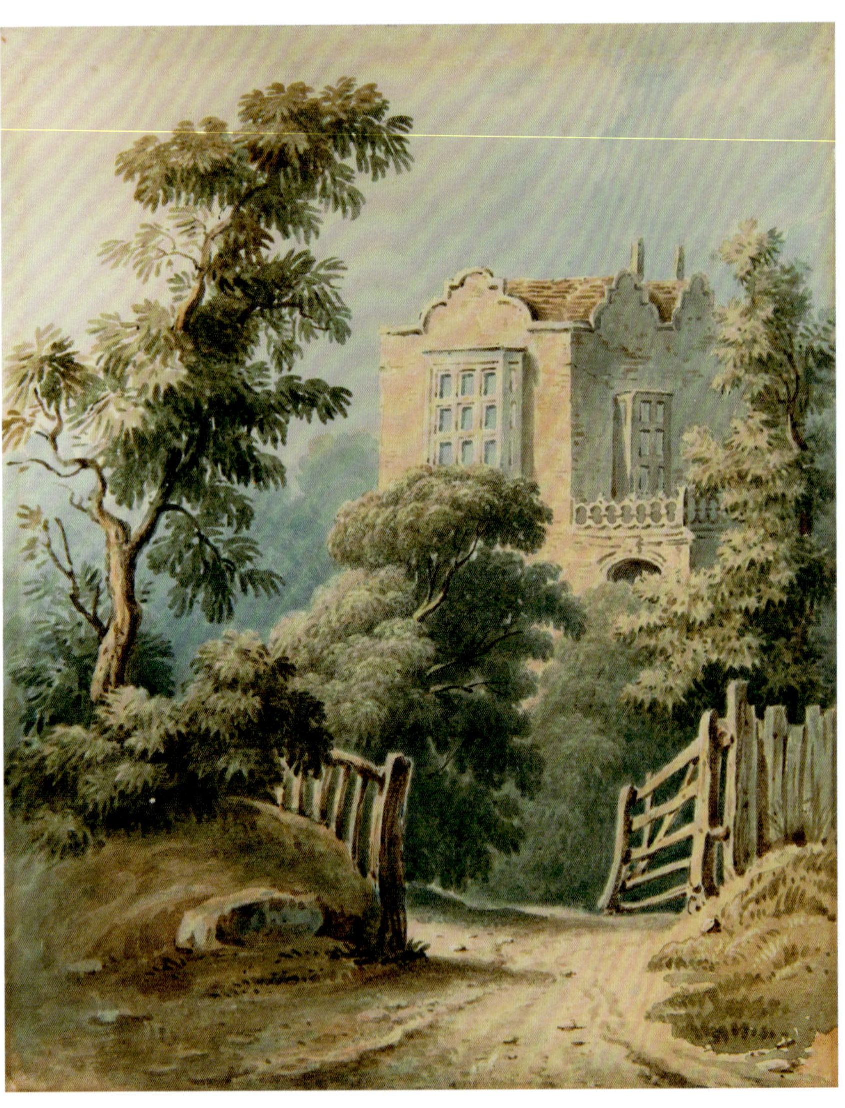

17 **Holland House, Kensington**
Watercolour
6 x 5 inches

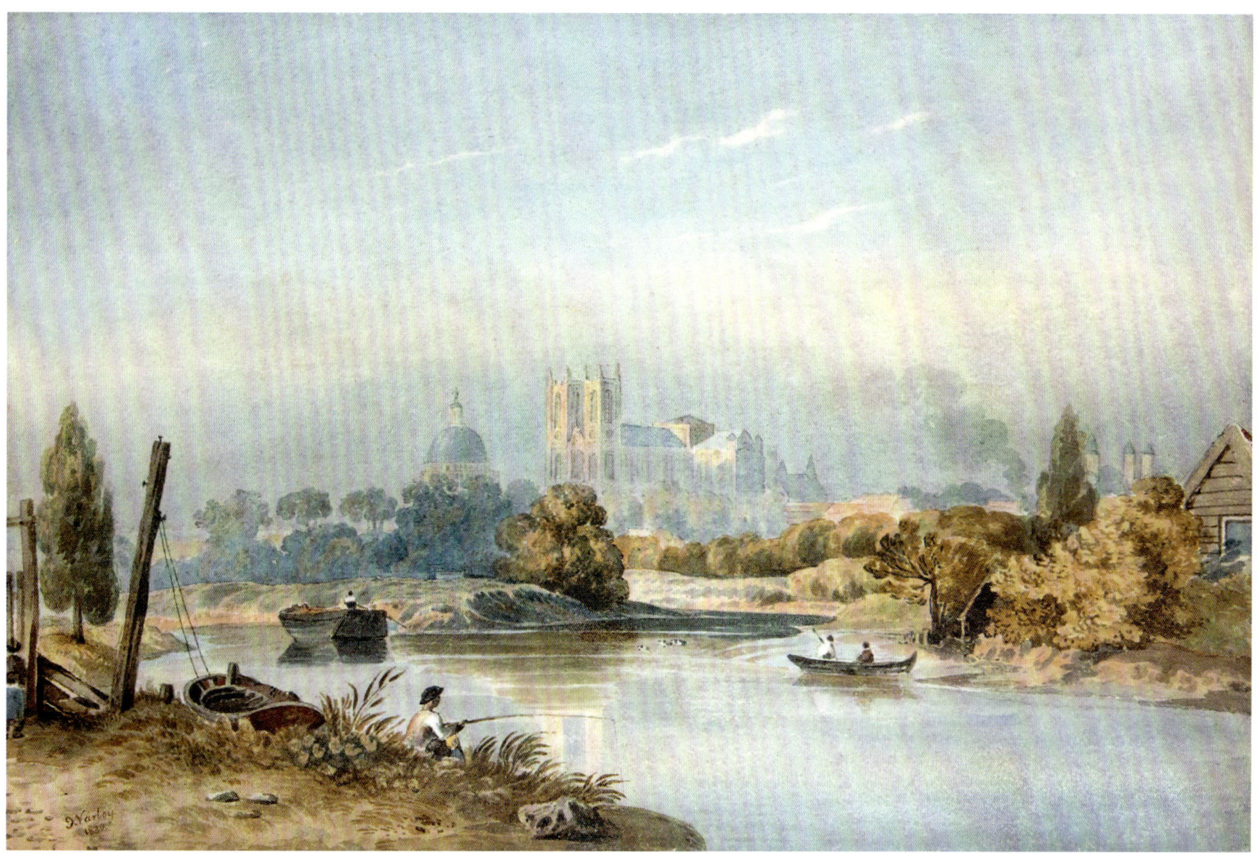

18 London Capriccio
Signed and dated 1830
Watercolour; 10 ¾ x 16 ¼ inches

Holland House, Kensington (opposite)

Holland House was a Jacobean mansion designed in 1605 by John Thorpe for the diplomat, Sir Walter Cope, and originally known as Cope Castle. It was built two miles to the west London, within a 500 acre country estate, the remains of which form the present Holland Park in Kensington. On Cope's death in 1614, the estate passed to his son-in-law, Henry Rich, who, a decade later, became 1st Earl of Holland, and set about extending the house and reshaping its gardens. From the Restoration to the Georgian period, it was mostly let on short leases to a variety of inhabitants, and was also the home of Joseph Addison (who married the widow of Edward Rich, and died in the house in 1719). In 1768, it was purchased by Henry Fox, and thus became the headquarters of the Whig party. The house remained a centre for literary, political and social life well into the nineteenth century, though much of the estate was turned over to residential development.

John Varley produced the present watercolour of the west corner of the south front of the house in the early nineteenth century. It focuses on the windows of the principal library, which ran the full length of the first floor of the west wing, and was famed for its decoration, its contents and its literary associations. Taking its cue from the antiquity of the architecture, the composition comprises a Picturesque vignette, with the fencing and foliage framing the building. Other views of the south front made at the time, such as those by John Buckler (in the British Museum and elsewhere), suggest that Varley has taken artistic licence, and that the grounds were well maintained.

Holland House remained relatively unchanged until the Blitz. On 27 September 1940, a German bombing raid destroyed almost all but the east wing and the ground floor surrounding the terrace. However, most of the contents of the library were undamaged. Given Grade I listed status in 1949, the remains of the building, with the 52 acres still surrounding it, was sold to London County Council, an eventually passed to the Royal Borough of Kensington and Chelsea. For some decades, the East Wing housed a youth hostel. The remains of the house now form the back drop to the open air Opera Holland Park, while the Orangery and Ice House provide spaces for exhibitions and the Ballroom contains a restaurant.

JOHN WILSON CARMICHAEL

John Wilson Carmichael (1799-1868)

The Newcastle artist, John Wilson Carmichael, has gained a particular reputation for his impressive marine subjects, which were informed by his own experience as a sailor and ship builder. However, he was a wide-ranging painter of landscapes and townscapes, especially early in his career, when he collaborated closely with leading local architect, John Dobson.

For a biography of John Wilson Carmichael, please refer to page 98.

19 **Boldon Rectory**
Signed with initials
Watercolour
9 ¾ x 13 ½ inches

Boldon Rectory

In the early 1830s, the Reverend Nathaniel John Hollingsworth, Rector of St Nicholas, West Boldon, County Durham, commissioned the leading Newcastle architect, John Dobson, to make some improvements to the ancient rectory. The previous incumbent, Henry George Liddell (grandfather of Lewis Carroll's Alice), had already added a wing to the rear of the building. The new improvements comprised 'a beautiful stone front, having two hexagonal projections' and 'new stables, coach-houses, and other out-offices, and much improved … garden and adjoining grounds' (Eneas Mackenzie and Metcalf Ross, *An Historical, Topographical and Descriptive View of the County Palatine of Durham*, Newcastle upon Tyne: Mackenzie and Dent, 1834, page 72).

John Wilson Carmichael worked closely with John Dobson, and his watercolour was probably intended to show Boldon Rectory before the architect began work on it. The rectory was demolished in 1970 to make way for a private housing development that stands on Rectory Green, and visual evidence of its appearance is scant, so the present work is of particular interest.

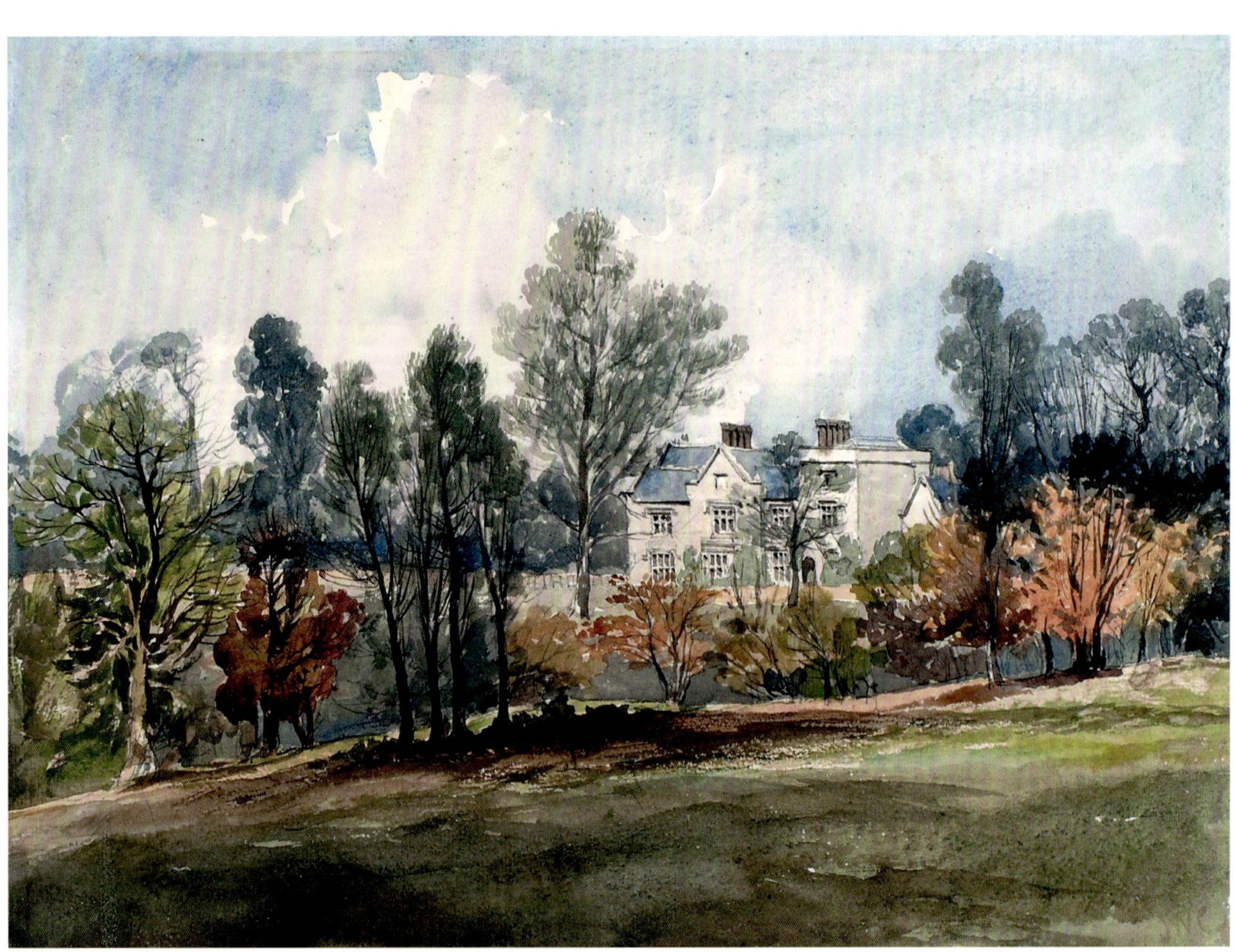

JAMES BAKER PYNE

James Baker Pyne, VPSBA (1800-1870)

Though he seems to have taught himself to paint, James Baker Pyne developed into a significant landscape painter, first as a member of the Bristol School, and then as a spirited follower of J M W Turner.

For a biography of James Baker Pyne, please refer to page 99.

Windsor Castle

Windsor Castle became one of James Baker Pyne's favourite motifs, and was the focus of *Windsor, with its Surrounding Scenery*, the first of his series of volumes of lithographed illustrations, which was published in 1839. The artist considered the royal residence from many angles and at many times of day, including the present view, looking in a southeastwardly direction early in the morning. The buildings that stand out on the horizon include the State Apartments, the Round Tower and St George's Chapel.

20 **Windsor Castle**
Oil on board
12 x 17 ¾ inches

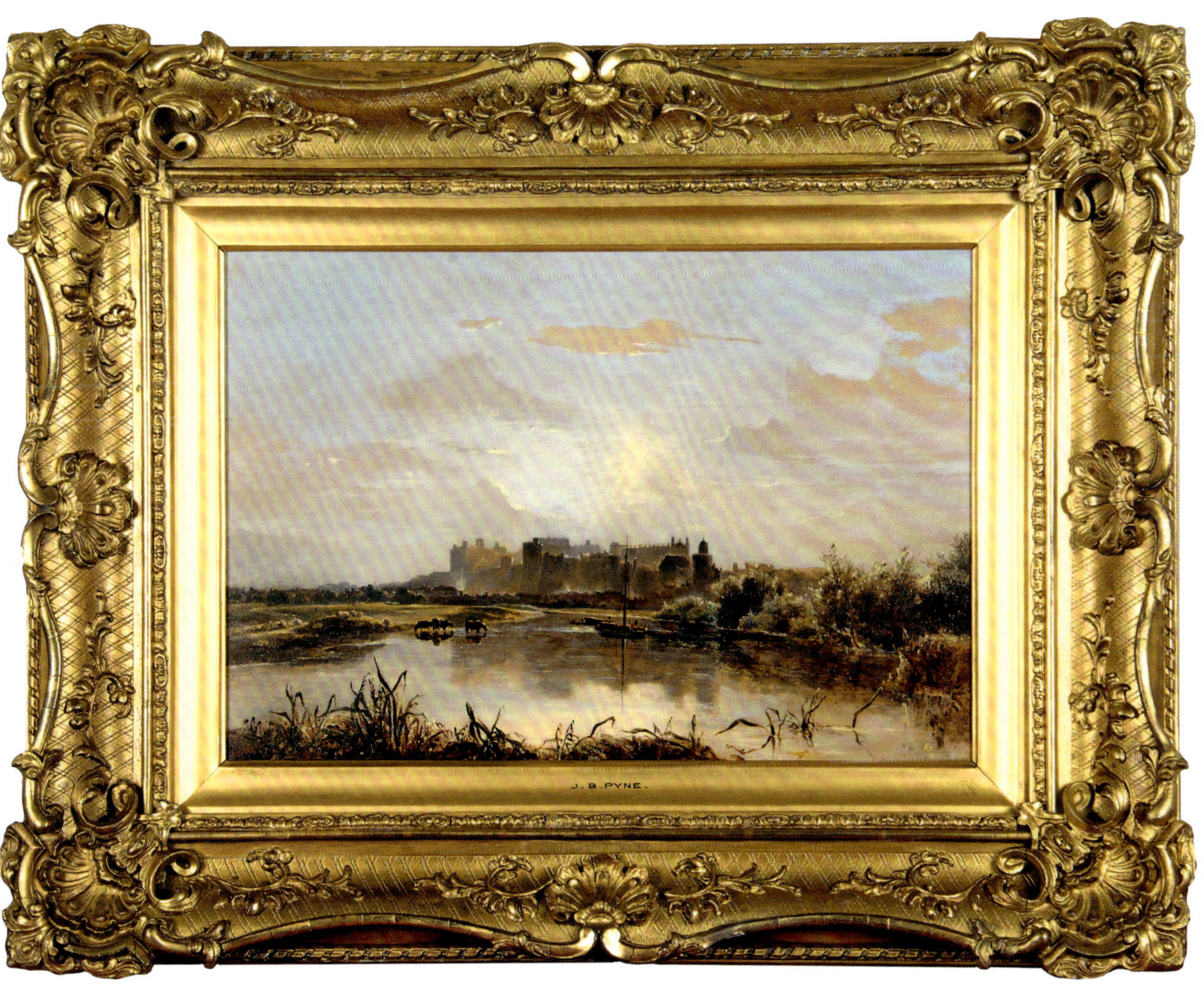

JOHN SKINNER PROUT

John Skinner Prout, NWS (1805-1876)

John Skinner Prout's talent as a landscape painter led him to develop a fascinating career. Having first established himself as a 'Picturesque Antiquarian' in emulation of his uncle, Samuel, he then migrated to Australia, where he gained a pioneering position as both a topographical artist and a teacher and lecturer. On his return to England, he capitalised on his antipodean experience by presenting entertaining and educative dioramas and panoramas, while also producing a substantial body of watercolours of British and European scenes, which he exhibited as a leading member of the New Society of Painters in Water Colours.

For a biography of John Skinner Prout, please refer to page 100.

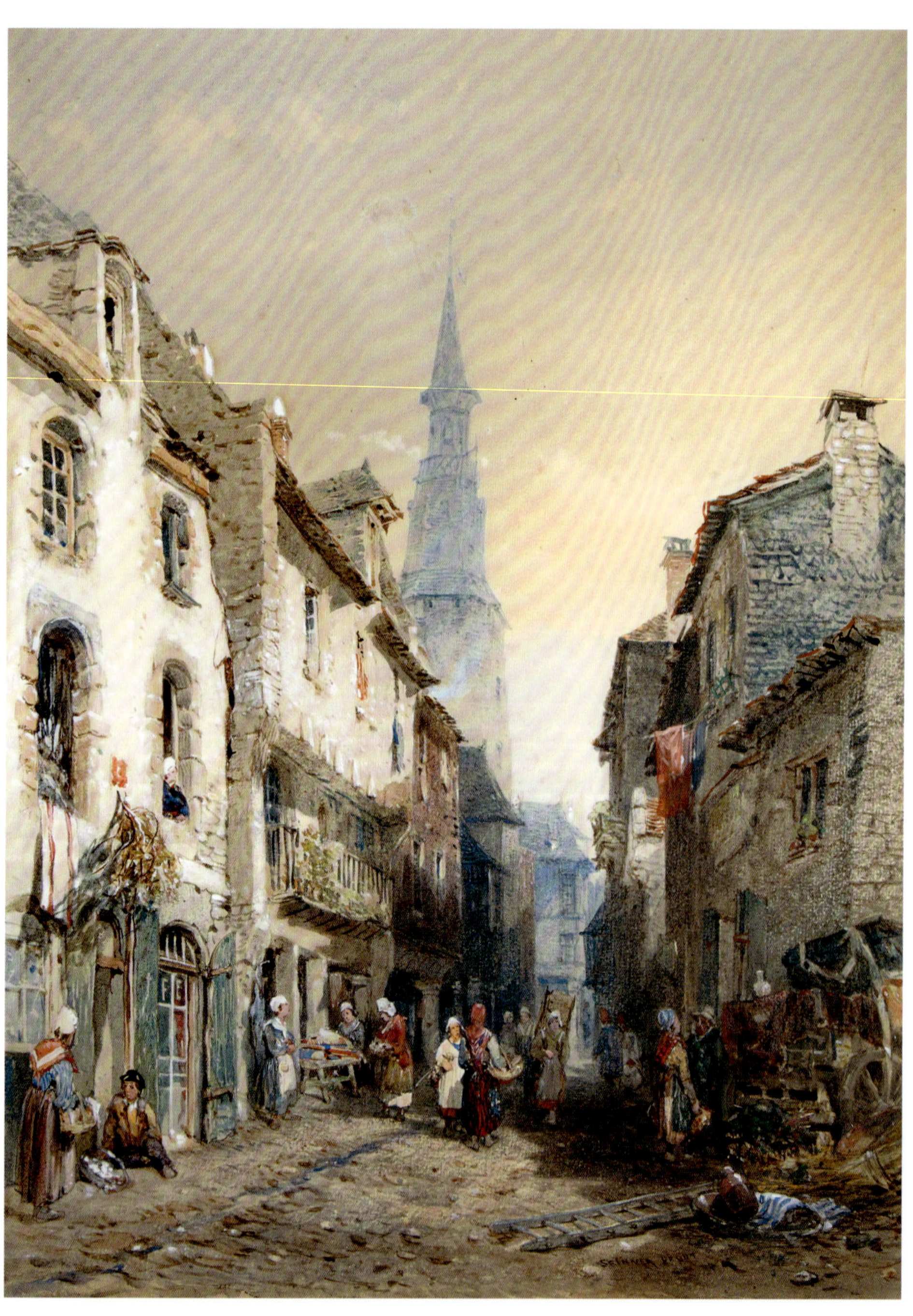

21 A Continental Town
Signed
Watercolour
18 ½ x 13 inches

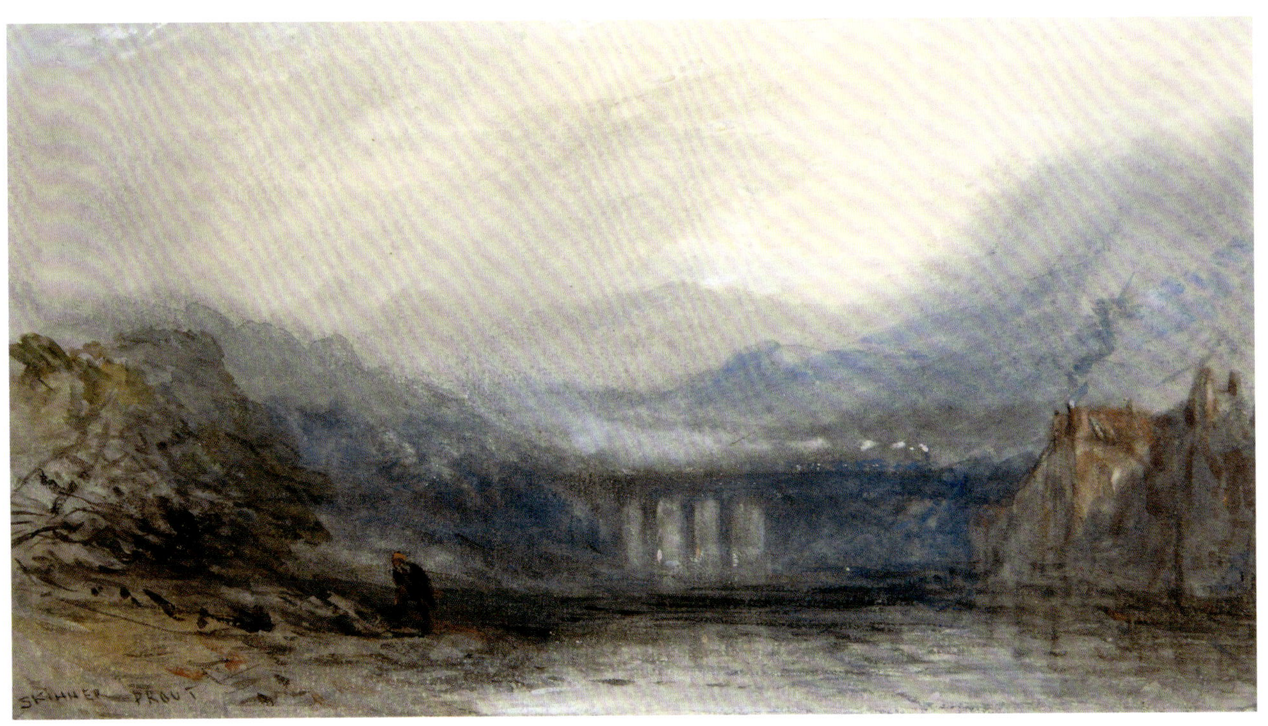

22 **Rain, Steam, and Speed; The Railway Viaduct** (above)
Signed
Watercolour with bodycolour
6 x 10 inches

23 **On the River's Edge** (below)
Signed
Watercolour with bodycolour and pencil
8 ¾ x 13 inches

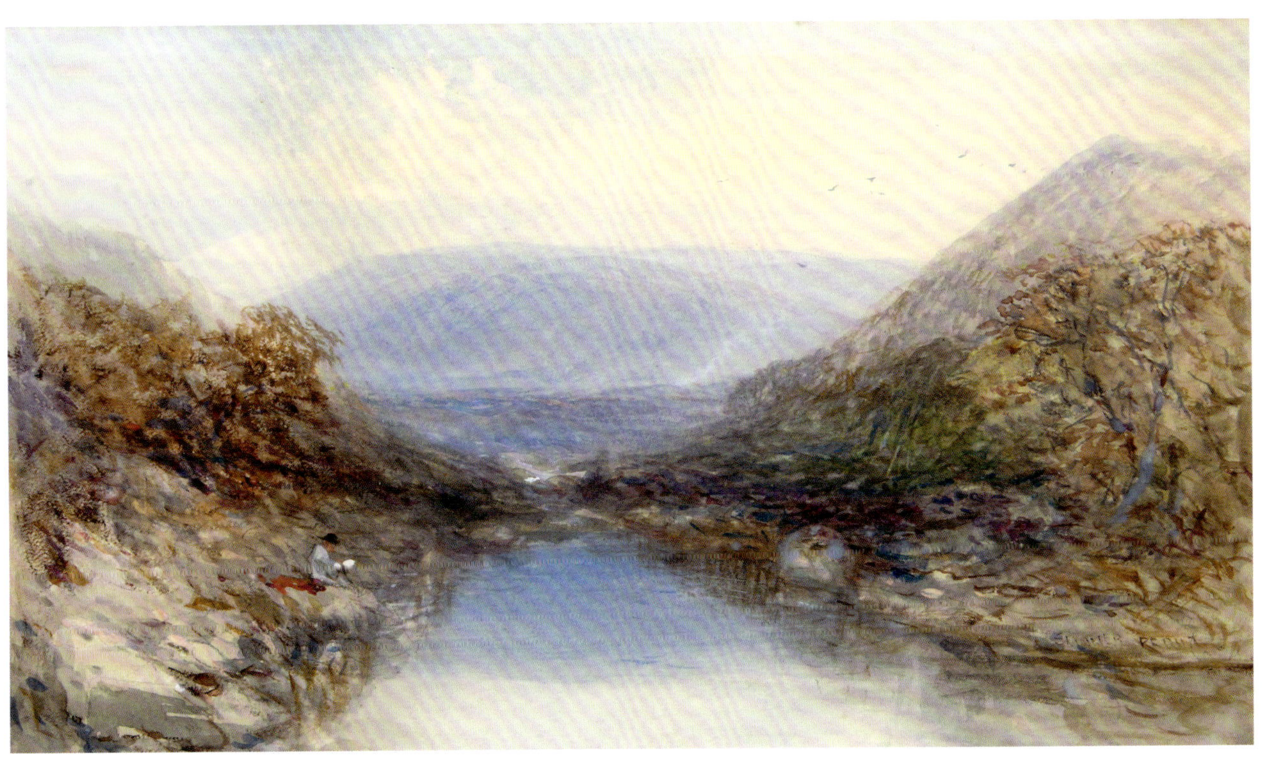

EDWARD LEAR

Edward Lear (1812-1888)

Though now best known for his nonsense poems and drawings for children, Edward Lear made his initial reputation as an ornithological illustrator, and then earned his living as a landscape painter. During extensive travels in Europe, the Middle East and Asia, he made frequent, evocative sketches that acted as the basis for astonishing oils and watercolours.

For a biography of Edward Lear, please refer to *Chris Beetles Summer Show*, 2014, page 5.

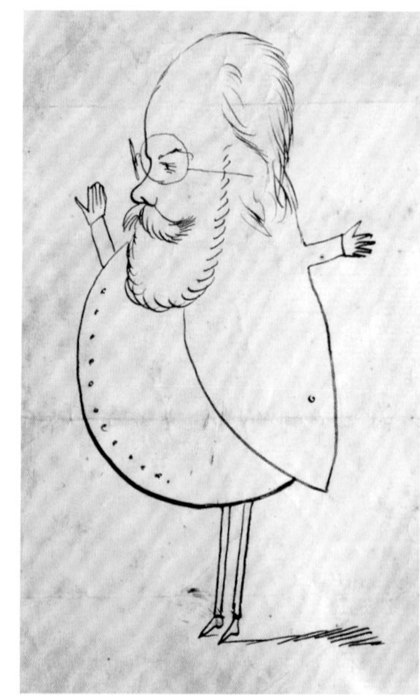

Edward Lear by Himself, Pen and ink
(Private Collection)

Edward Lear in Italy in 1838

Early in 1837, a group of subscribers, led by the Earl of Derby and his cousin, Robert Hornby, commissioned Edward Lear to go to Rome to produce drawings (and, at the same time, to improve the state of his health). It would be his third trip to the Continent, but his first to Italy. He left England in July that year, and arrived in Rome in the December. Apart from two visits to England in 1841 and 1845-46, he then remained in Italy for a decade.

Each summer of that decade, Lear would travel to a different part of the country. In May 1838, he made a slow journey to Naples in the company of fellow artist, James Uwins. On their arrival, they found that they were staying in the same hotel – the Hotel de La Ville de Rome – as Samuel Palmer and his wife, Hannah, who were in the middle of their Italian honeymoon. However, Lear found Naples 'all noise, horror – dirt, heat – & abomination' (as he expressed in a letter to John Gould in the following year, on 17 October 1839). So, after a few days, he and Uwins moved on.

Travelling in a south-easterly direction, they settled at Corpo di Cava, a village situated at the head of a high wooded valley looking down to the Bay of Salerno. It had been the haunt of artists since the time of Poussin and Rosa, and James Uwins' uncle, Thomas Uwins RA, had painted there 10 years before, which may have prompted his and Lear's visit. There they established a daily pattern of walking and sketching, punctuated by some longer expeditions, including that, in the middle of June, to the classical ruins of Paestum, which dominate the coastline about 30 miles south of Salerno.

Late in June, Lear and Uwins moved from Corpo di Cava to Amalfi, on the coast west of Salerno, and stayed for three weeks at the Albergo Cappucini, until 18 July. The visitors' book reveals that they overlapped with Achille Vianelli and Ercole Gigante, two landscape painters of the School of Posillipo. The rustic still life produced in Amalfi on 11 July [25] and the undated study of ferns [24] show Lear experimenting with oil – on paper – for the first time, sometimes purely, and sometimes in conjunction with other, water-based media. His decade in Italy is defined in part by his decision to take seriously to oils. He and Uwins returned to Corpo di Cava in late July and moved on to Sorrento at the beginning of August. At the end of that month, they began their slow return to Rome.

24 **Ferns** (opposite above)
Watercolour with oil and pencil
5 x 7 ¾ inches

25 **Rustic Still Life** (opposite middle)
Inscribed 'Amalfi' and dated 'July.11.1838'
Watercolour with oil and pencil
5 ¼ x 7 ½ inches

26 **Foliage** (opposite below)
Watercolour with pencil
2 ¾ x 6 ¾ inches

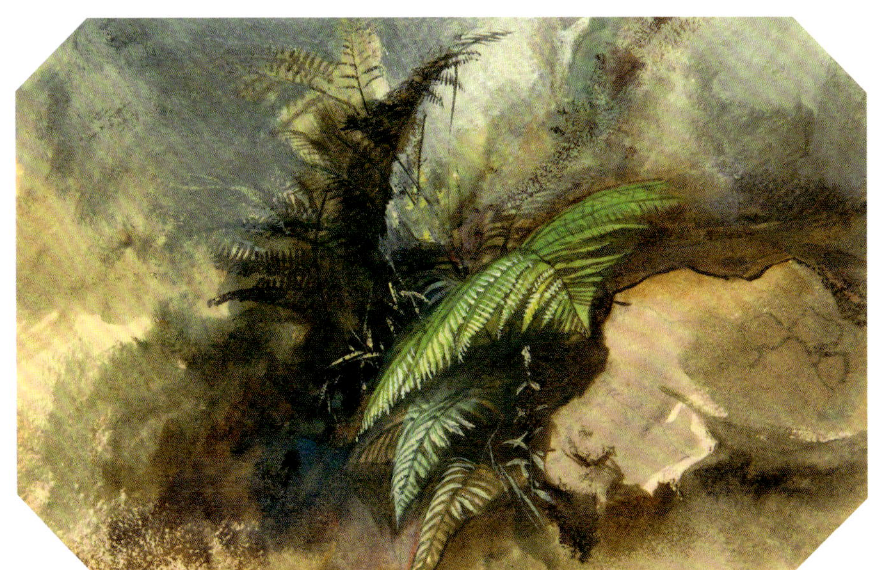

24

25

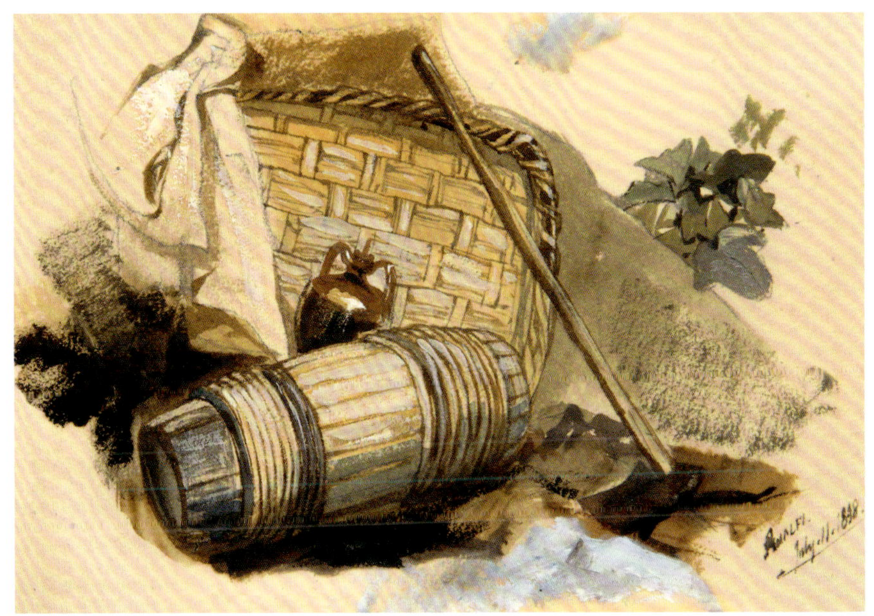

26

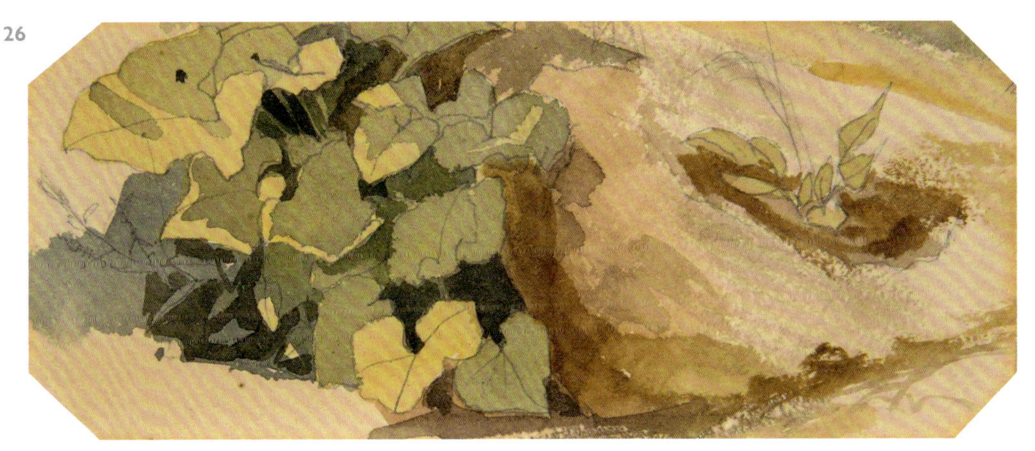

EDWARD LEAR AND FRANKLIN LUSHINGTON

FRANKLIN LUSHINGTON

Sir Franklin Lushington, JP (1823-1901)

Franklin Lushington has gained lasting fame as a close friend of Edward Lear, so close that they produced collaborative drawings, Lushington being a talented amateur artist, like many cultivated men and women of his time. He had a distinguished legal career, initially as a judge to the Supreme Court of Justice in the Ionian Islands and later as a magistrate in London.

No 28 is by Edward Lear and Franklin Lushington.

Lear and Lushington in Greece in 1849

In 1848, Edward Lear left Italy, after a decade of living in that country. He did so partly to escape its increasingly unsettled political climate – despite his support of those driving reform – and partly to explore and record the eastern Mediterranean.

Lear was particularly excited at the prospect of visiting Greece, which had long impressed itself upon his imagination, whether in the form of classical myth or in Lord Byron's involvement in the Greek struggle for liberation from Turkish domination. Between Spring 1848 and Summer 1849, he undertook extensive travels in mainland Greece, including two trips, each shared with a younger friend. In June and July 1848, he travelled in the company of Charles Church, while, in March and April 1849, he travelled with Franklin Lushington.

Having left Malta on Saturday 3 March 1849, Lear and Lushington arrived in Patrás on Wednesday 7, and two days later they began their exploration of the Peloponnese on horseback in the company of a dragoman, travelling eastwards. During the following three weeks, they took in much of the peninsula, including Andritzena (16-17 March), Bassae (18-19), Sparta (23-24) and Corinth (31).

From Corinth, Lear and his companions left the Peloponnese to travel east into Attica and onto Athens. Their time in Athens included a visit to Cape Colonna (Sounion) on Friday 6 April, to see the Temple of Minerva; and another to Colonus on 8 April (see separate note).

On Tuesday 10 April, Lear's party headed northwest to Thebes, in Boeotia. From Thebes, it went, via Livadeia (13 April), to Mount Parnassus, the home of the gods (14 April). Continuing west, it stayed at Arachova, on the night of Saturday 14 April, *en route* to Delphi, where it spent four days.

On the last days of their tour together, Lear, Lushington and their dragoman journeyed along the coast of Locris towards Antirrio, so that they could cross the Gulf of Corinth at its narrowest point and thus return to Patrás. From there, Lushington went back to Malta, while Lear took the steamer north, to embark on the next stage of his travels, alone.

For a longer essay on 'Edward Lear and Franklin Lushington in Greece in 1849', please refer to *Chris Beetles Summer Show*, 2020, pages 32-34.

EDWARD LEAR

Nice (opposite above)

Edward Lear spent the winter of 1864-65 in Nice, on the French Riviera, staying with his Souliote servant, Giorgio Kokali, in rooms at 61 Promenade des Anglais. He worked hard and produced a large number of drawings both of Nice and – during December – of the coast between Nice and Genoa.

The present view looks in a south-westerly direction over the roofs of Villefranche-sur-Mer to Mont Boron, and then across the bay towards Antibes.

Colonus (opposite below)

Colonus (or Kolonos) was once an aristocratic municipality of ancient Attica, and is now a working-class suburb in north-west Athens. It was dedicated to the Equestrian Poseidon, and so is sometimes known as Hippeios Kolonos. The birthplace of the tragedian, Sophocles, in 496 BC, the area was also the setting of the third and last of his famous Theban plays, *Oedipus at Colonus* (which premiered in Athens in 401 BC, five years after Sophocles' death). According to the play, and the mythology on which it was based, Oedipus was buried there. In the early nineteenth century, the leading German Classicist, Karl Otfried Müller (1797-1840), was similarly interred, while, almost 20 years later, his body was joined by the heart of the French archaeologist, Charles Lenormant (1802-1859). Monuments to both men still stand in what is now a local park.

The present drawing, by Edward Lear and Franklin Lushington, takes in the view southwest from Colonus, across the Saronic Gulf to Aegina and the coast of Argolis on the Peloponnese.

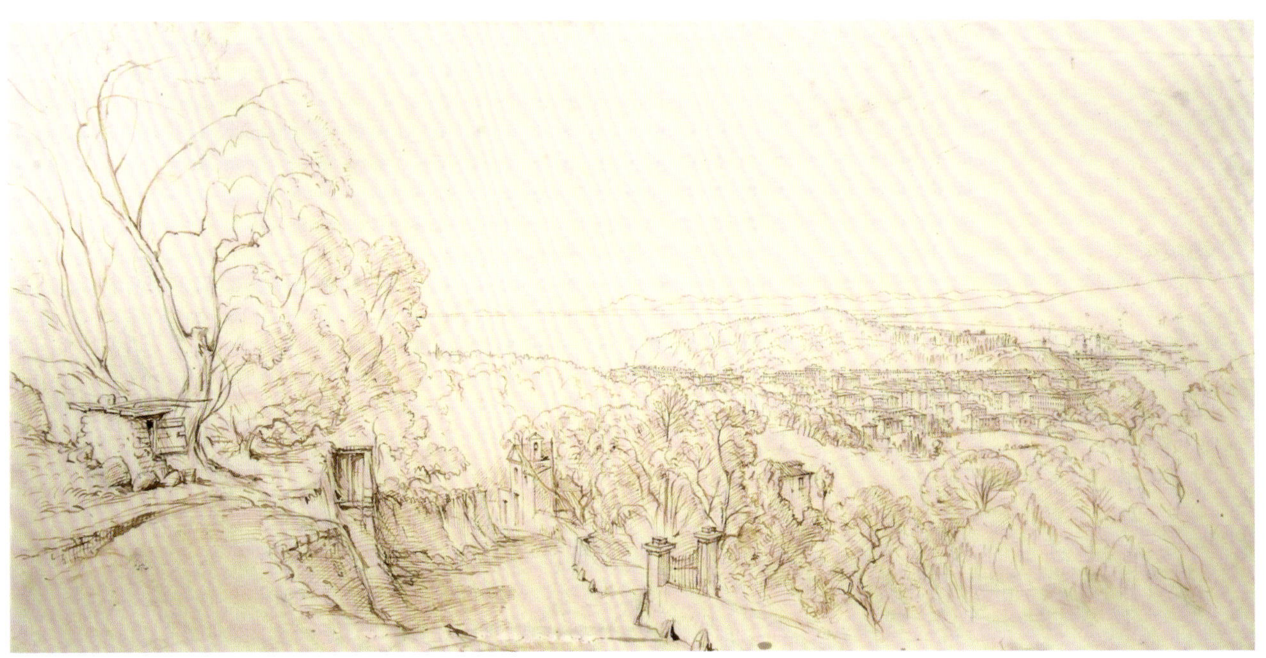

27 Nice (above)
Pen and ink with pencil
9 ½ x 18 inches

28 Colonus (below)
Signed, inscribed with title and dated 'April 8/49'
Pen ink and watercolour on tinted paper
8 ¾ x 13 ½ inches

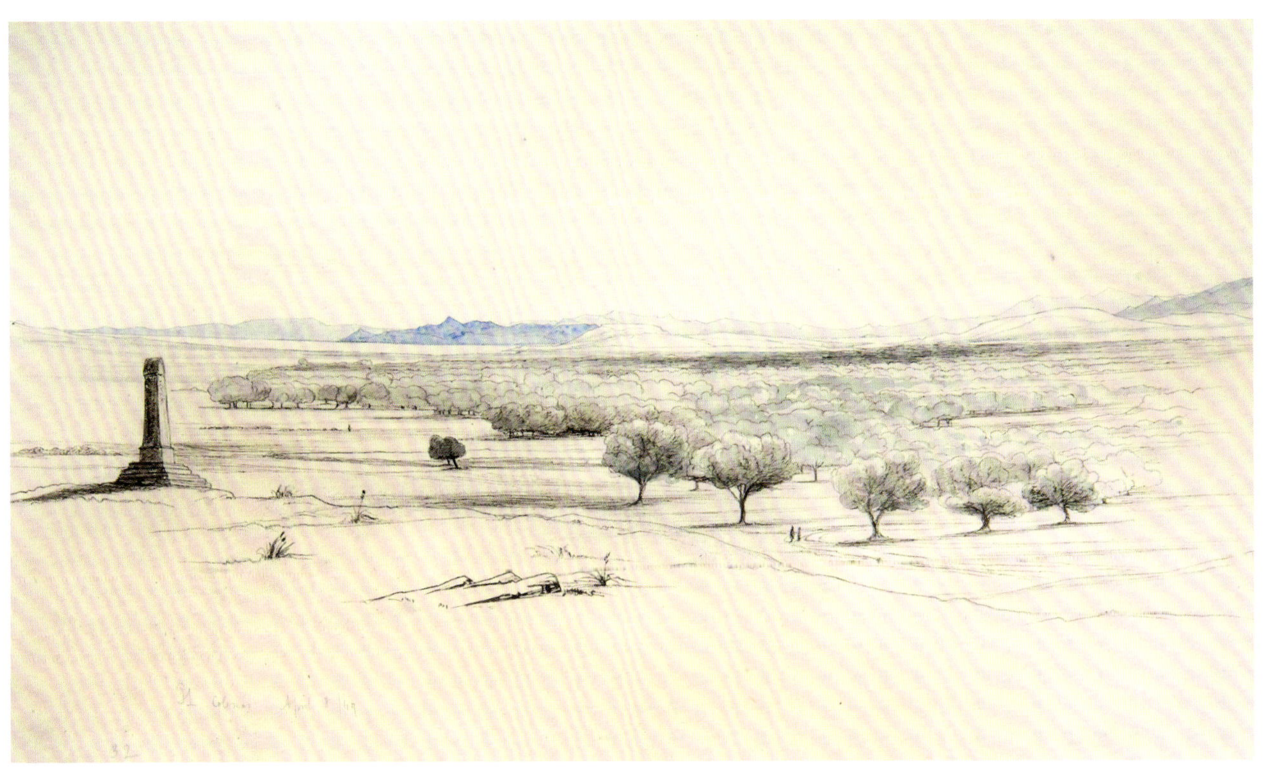

Letter to 'My dear Montgomery'

The recipient of the present letter, written by Edward Lear, was Hugh de Fellenberg Montgomery (1844-1924). Montgomery was the owner of the Blessingbourne estate, Fivemiletown, County Tyrone, Northern Ireland. A Justice of the Peace and Deputy Lieutenant of Tyrone, he also held the positions of High Sheriff of Fermanagh (1871), High Sheriff of Tyrone (1888) and later Ulster Unionist Party member of the Senate of Northern Ireland (1922-24).

Montgomery and his wife, Mary, spent some time in San Remo in the late 1870s, and there befriended Lear. He commissioned works from the artist, including a pair of extensive views of the Acropolis, Athens, from the north and south, that are mentioned in the present letter (and which were auctioned at Sotheby's, London, in 1971). A Grecian subject by Lear still hangs on the walls of Blessingbourne House, which was designed for Montgomery by Frederick Pepys Cockerell in the early 1870s.

Villa Emily. Sanremo.
16. April. 1881.

My dear Montgomery,
I am just about to pack
& send off your 2 drawgs of
Athens – after all without any
'howls' – large or small.
But I have to thank you for
your criticism about the Parthenon,
& it is bestonishing how much
the drawing has improved since
I have done away with the
dark shadow, & the thunder-
-cloud. I could not have
fancied so great a change

for the better, but the fact has
been that I am often so
blinded by the glare of
Jenny Sneak's Hotel, that
I do not well see what color
I do or do not use.
I hope you will like the
drawing now much better than
you did, though I acknowledge
it has many imperfections, –
& when I have completed one more
Athenian drawing (for H F Tozer,)
I never intend to do any
architectural subjects any more,
but to stick to pure Landscape,

29 Letter to 'My dear Montgomery'
Signed, inscribed 'Villa Emily Sanremo'
and dated '16. April. 1881'
Pen and ink on two sheets of paper
8 x 5 ¼ inches

[1] 'Villa Emily, Sanremo,
16. April. 1881.
My dear Montgomery,
I am just about to pack & send off your 2 drawings of Athens – after all without any "howls" – large or small.
But I have to thank you for your criticism about the Parthenon, and it is bestonishing how much the drawing has improved since I have done away with the dark shadow, & the thunder-cloud. I could not have fancied so great a change

[2] for the better, but the fact has been that I am often so blinded by the glare of Jenny Sneak's Hotel, that I do not well see what colour I do or do not use.
I hope you will like the drawing now much better than you did, though I acknowledge it has many imperfections, – and when I have completed one more Athenian drawing (for H F Tozer,) I never intend to do any architectural subjects anymore, but to stick to pure landscape,

In this letter, Lear complains at the difficulty of drawing architecture, and states his determination 'to stick to pure landscape' once he has 'completed one more Athenian drawing (for H F Tozer)'. 'H F Tozer' was Henry Fanshawe Tozer (1829-1916), a tutor at Exeter College, Oxford, and curator of the Taylorian Institution. He had a particular interest in historical geography and, like Lear, travelled widely in Greece and Turkey. Of his books, Lear greatly admired his *Researches in the Highlands of Turkey* (1869). In later years, Tozer joined his wife, Augusta, in San Remo, where she wintered for her health, and there socialised with Lear. He purchased a number of the artist's drawings, which he bequeathed to the Ashmolean Museum, including the watercolour and bodycolour, *View of Athens* (1881), which is probably the work mentioned in the present letter.

[3] – trees – plains, – hills, – rivers – toads etc – but no prominent building henceforth & forever, my sight having been so injured by this Cursed Hotel that I cannot trust my one remaining eye for lines, diameters, hexameters, or thermometers.
The 2 drawings are to be left in charge of {frames as you know are <u>included</u> in the price} Messrs Foord & Dickenson, 129 Wardour Street Oxford Street W London until you direct when & where they are to be sent. And you

[4] can now at your pleasure & leisure, pay me the 70£ in a <u>crossed</u> cheque sent me here by post – the easiest way; – or by paying the same into my account at Drummond's, Charing Cross.
The box of drawings – (yours, Earl Derbys, Ld Wenlock's & others –) will go off next week; & will be, I hope, in London, quite early in May.
I am so glad that you are so much better.
Yours sincerely, Edward Lear
I send you a Grotograph of myself, lately taken, & thought to be good.'

HERCULES BRABAZON BRABAZON

Hercules Brabazon Brabazon, NEAC PS (1821-1906)

For much of his life, Hercules Brabazon Brabazon pleased himself as a gentleman traveller, producing luminous, loosely-handled watercolours of favourite paintings and places (including India, which he visited in 1870, 1875 and 1876). Admired by John Ruskin as an heir to J M W Turner, he joined the eminent critic on a sketching tour of Northern France in 1880. Yet his startling modernity was probably recognised only in the 1890s, by a younger generation of artists, which included John Singer Sargent, Walter Sickert and Philip Wilson Steer. Through their enthusiasm, he was elected a member of the New English Art Club in 1891, and held the first of a series of solo shows at the Goupil Gallery in the following year.

For a biography of Hercules Brabazon Brabazon, please refer to *Chris Beetles Summer Show*, 2016, page 36.

Moroccan Market, Outside the Gates

Hercules Brabazon Brabazon travelled to various countries of North Africa, including Morocco. On trips between 1868 and 1884, he visited and painted in several places on or accessible from the Moroccan coast, including Marrakesh, Casablanca, Tangiers and Oujda [31]. Though the location of the present watercolour has not been positively identified, it shows a characteristic market square before a walled city, such as Place el-Hedim before the Kasbah of the imperial city of Meknes.

A favourite painter of Brabazon, Eugène Delacroix, had visited Meknes in 1832, as a member of a French diplomatic mission. While there, he made studies for what became one of his masterpieces, *Le Sultan du Maroc* (1845, Musée des Augustins, Toulouse). Its depiction of Moulay Abd-Er-Rhaman surrounded by his guards and principal officers may have inspired Brabazon to produce the present exotic scene, with its swirling crowd of turbaned figures surrounding two others raised loftily on horseback.

30 **Moroccan Market, Outside the Gates** (opposite above)
Signed with initials
Watercolour and bodycolour
7 ½ x 12 ¾ inches

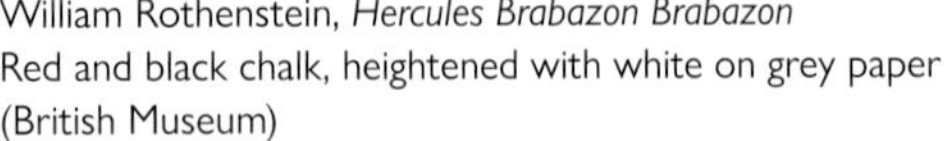

William Rothenstein, *Hercules Brabazon Brabazon*
Red and black chalk, heightened with white on grey paper
(British Museum)

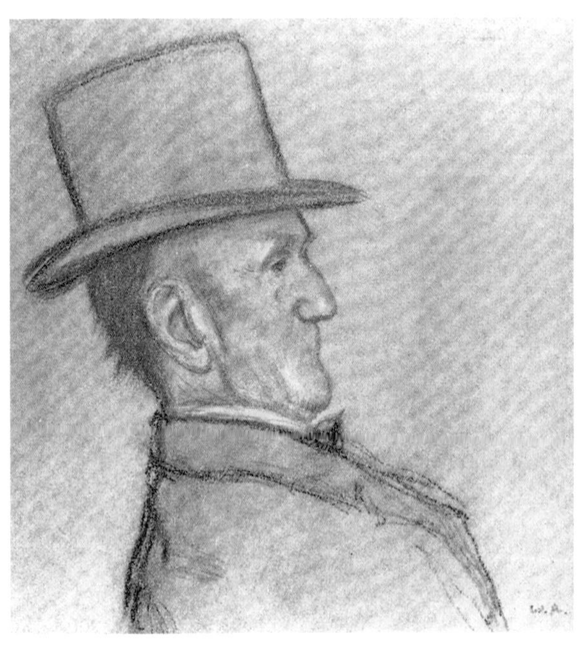

The Walls of Oujda, Morocco

Morocco's easternmost town, Oujda was founded in 994 by Ziri ibn Atiyya, Berber chief of the Zenata Maghrawa tribe. Through subsequent centuries, it held a strategic position for the various political forces that controlled it, notably the Almoravids (in the eleventh century), the Almohads (twelfth century) and the Marinids (thirteenth century). The Marinid sultan, Abu Yussuf Yaqub rebuilt it in 1297, constructing a kasbah, a mosque and a palace – and new walls. However, it continued to be contested, and the powers that occupied it ranged from the Kingdom of Tlemcen (fourteenth century) to France (1844, 1859).

31 **The Walls of Oujda, Morocco** (opposite below)
Signed with initials
Watercolour with bodycolour
7 ¾ x 11 ½ inches

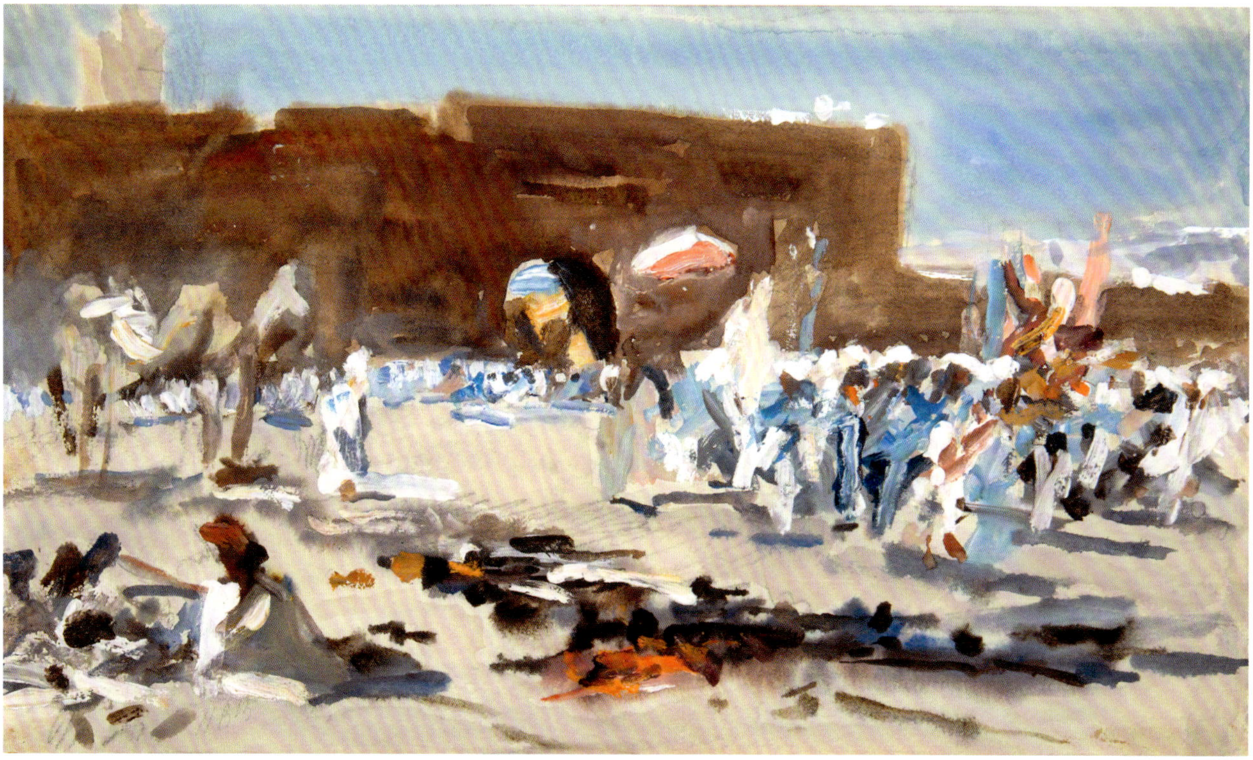

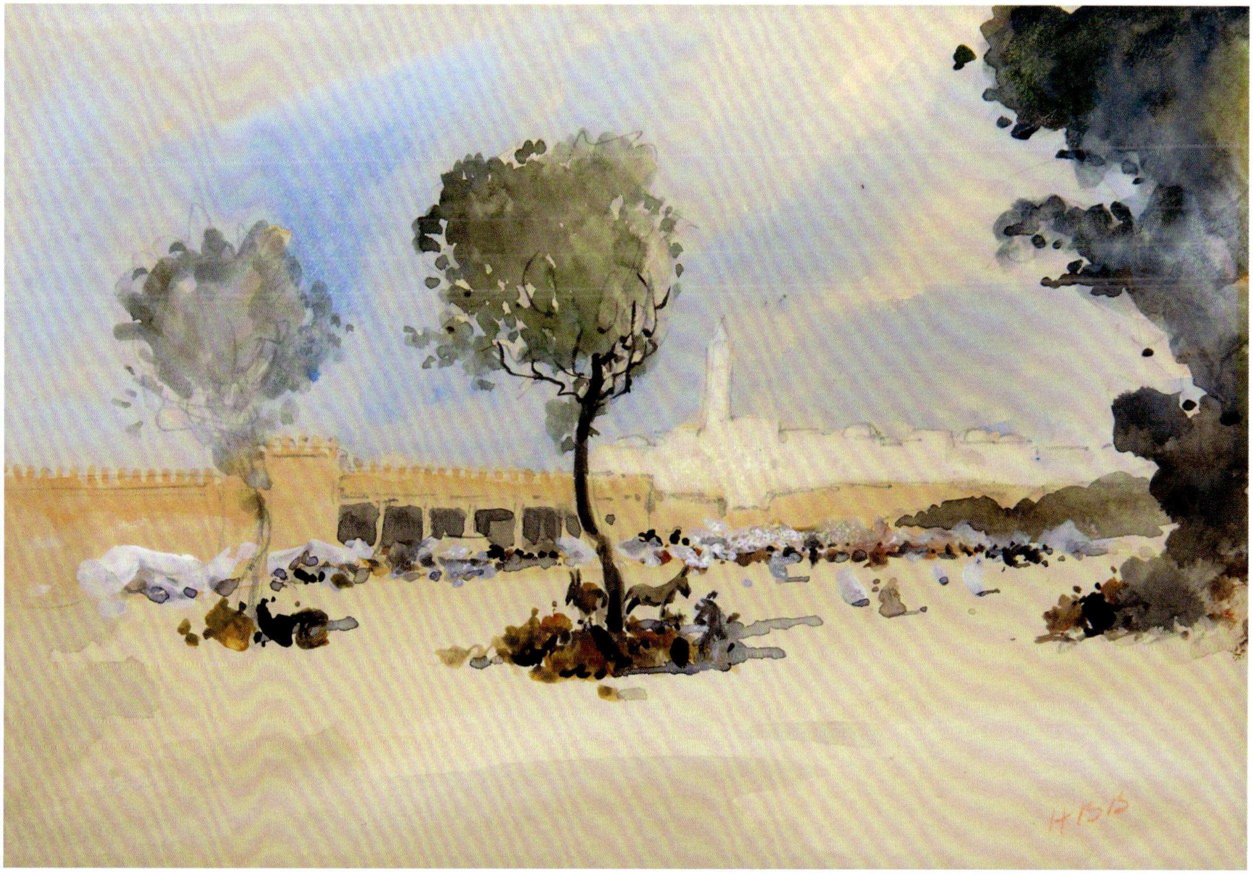

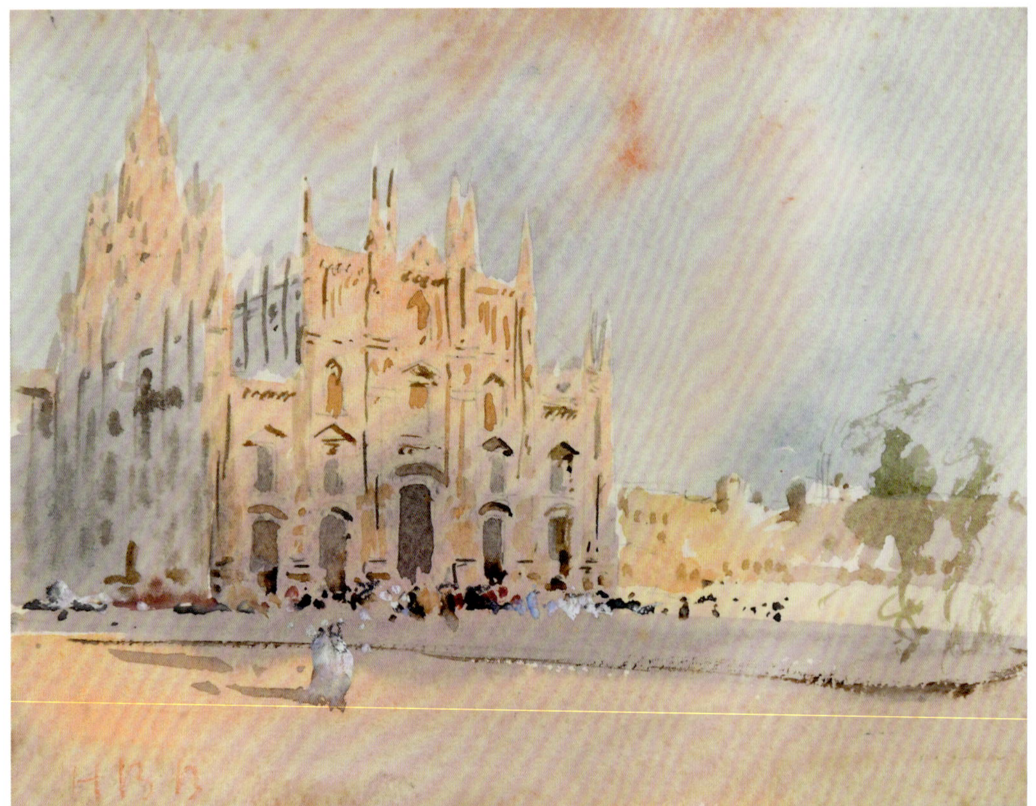

32 Milan Cathedral
Signed with initials
Watercolour
with bodycolour
6 x 7 ½ inches
Exhibited: 'The Long Nineteenth Century: Treasures and Pleasures', Chris Beetles Gallery, March-April 2014, No 45

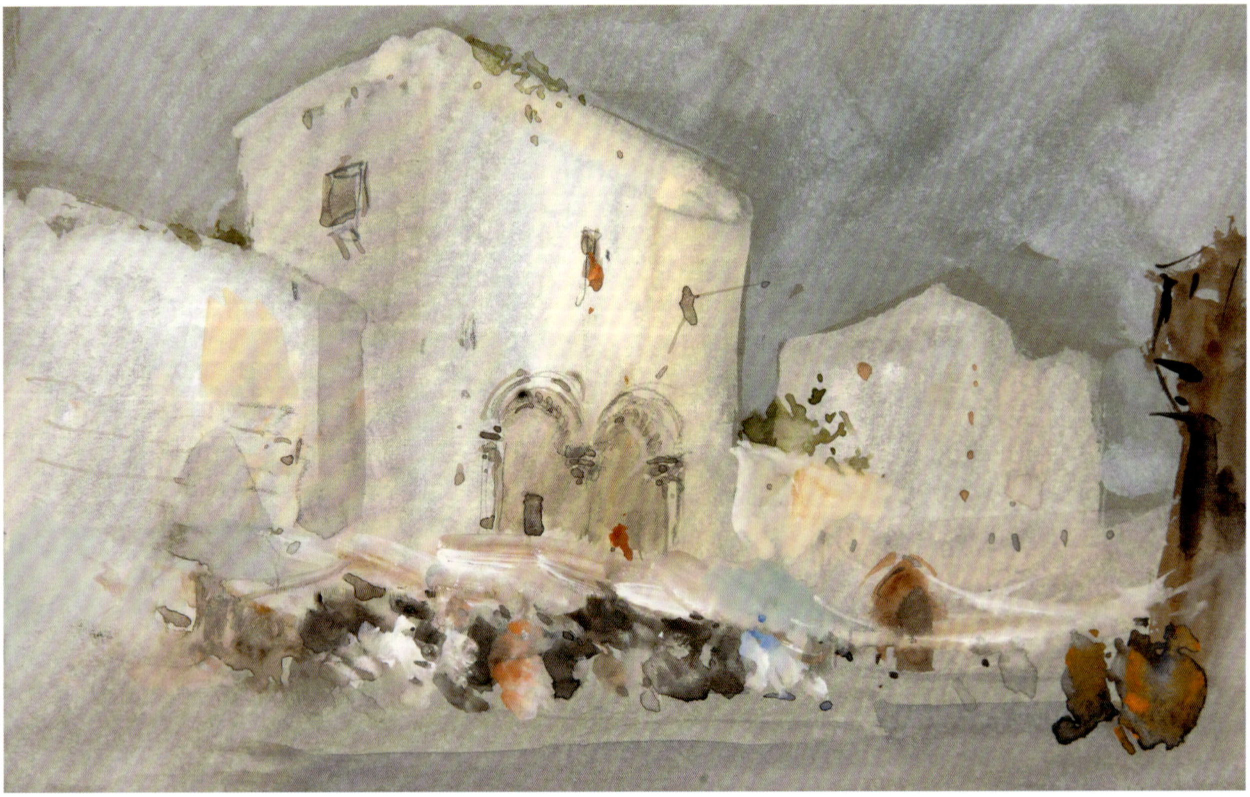

Jerusalem

Hercules Brabazon Brabazon visited Jerusalem in 1860, on a journey that also took in Cairo, Baalbek and Istanbul, and other places in Palestine. Though the subject of the present watercolour has not been positively identified, the central structure may be based on the Golden Gate, or Gate of Mercy, the Eastern gate of the Temple Mount, which was built by the Romans in the 520s, and has been almost permanently sealed since 1541. If so, then Brabazon has taken the artistic licence to use its external façade as the backdrop for an atmospheric market scene. In reality, an Islamic cemetery lies in front of it.

33 **Jerusalem** (opposite below)
Watercolour and bodycolour
6 ¼ x 9 ¼ inches
Exhibited: 'Watercolours by H B Brabazon', J Leger & Son, London, December 1949, No 61

Shri Kunj Bihari Temple, Jodhpur, Rajasthan

This watercolour shows the west façade of the Shri Kunj Bihari Temple, overlooking a square in central Jodhpur (a square that has since been converted into Katla Bazaar). It belongs to the Rama Nandi Vaishnava Sect of Hindus and is dedicated to Kunj Bihari (better known as Krishna). The temple and its accompanying monastery were built in about 1790 by Gulab Rai, one of the wives of Maharaja Vijay Singh (1729-1793), in memory of their son, Sher Singh, who died young. It is known for the excellence of its carvings.

34 **Shri Kunj Bihari Temple, Jodhpur, Rajasthan** (below)
Signed with initials
Watercolour with bodycolour
5 ¾ x 8 ½ inches

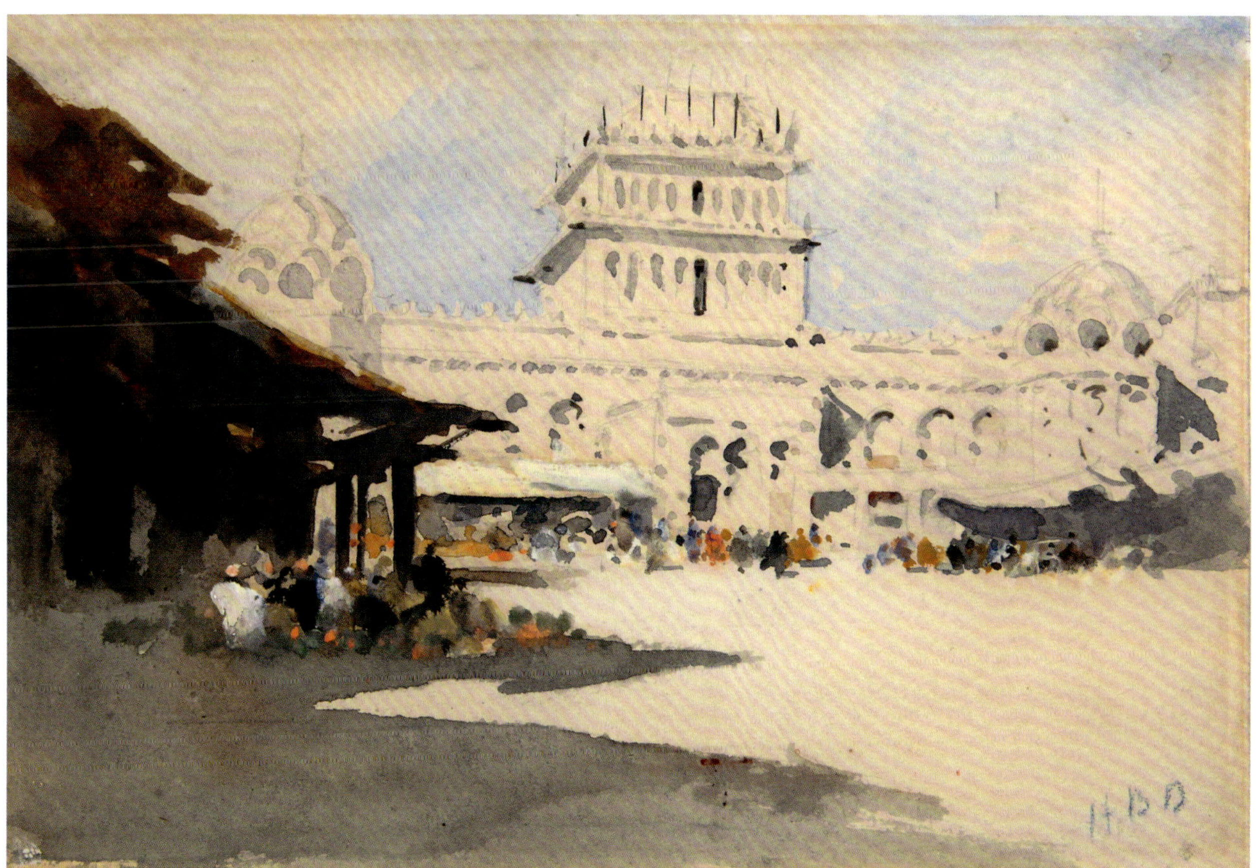

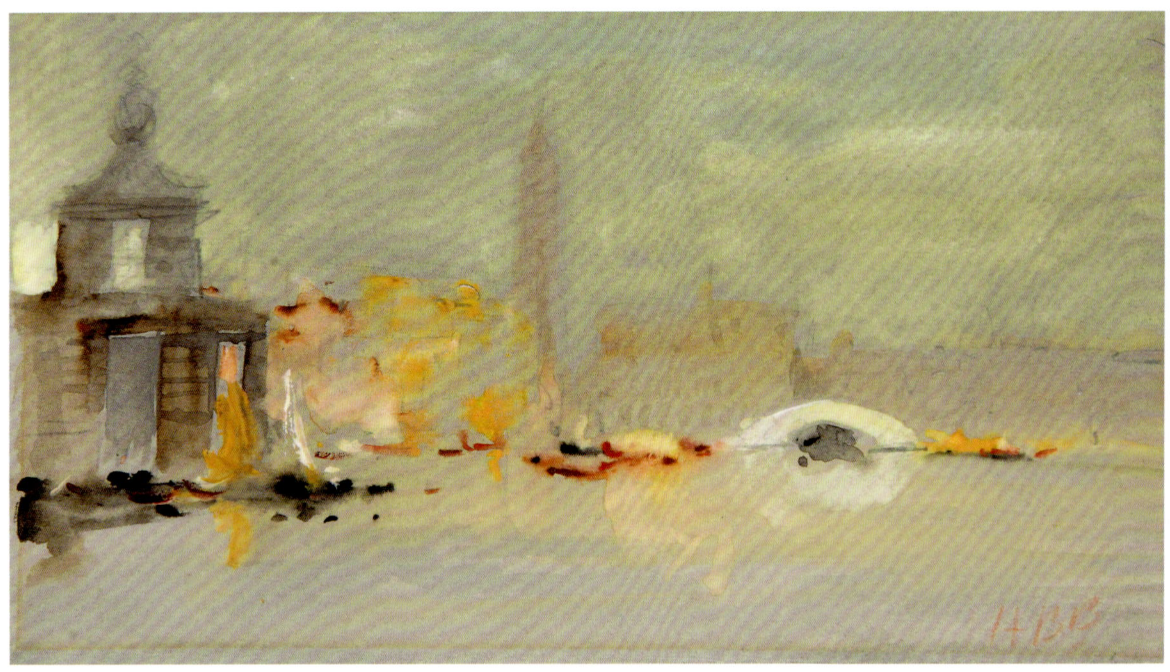

35 Bacino San Marco, Venice (above)
Signed with initials
Watercolour with bodycolour;
5 ¼ x 9 inches

36 Venice Skyline (below)
Signed with initials
Pastel; 5 x 7 ½ inches
Exhibited: 'The Long Nineteenth Century: Treasures and Pleasures', Chris Beetles Gallery, March-April 2014, No 42

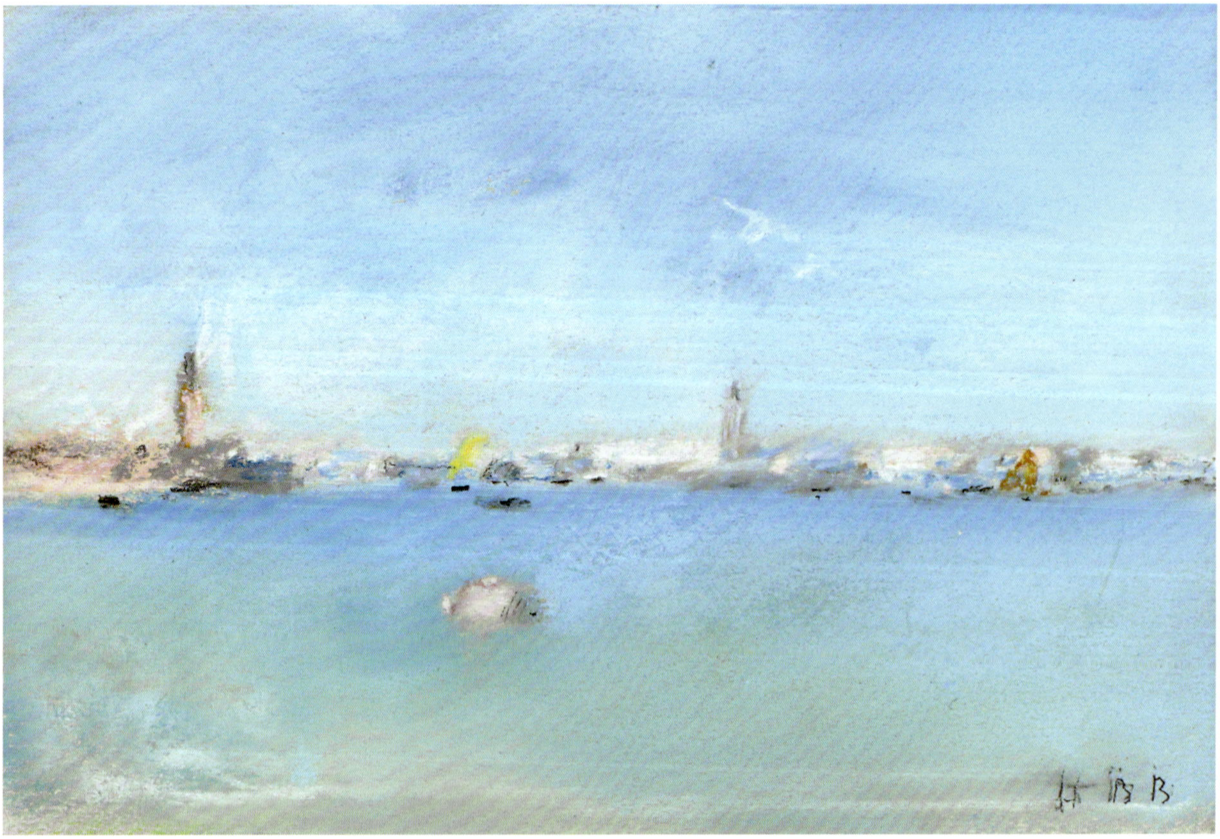

EDWARD ANGELO GOODALL

Edward Angelo Goodall, RWS (1819-1908)

A member of a well-known family of artists, Edward Angelo Goodall established his individuality by recording the places and people that he encountered on wide-ranging travels. These included an early expedition to British Guiana (1841-44) and a commission from *The Illustrated London News* to cover the Crimean War (1854-55). Increasingly, he became associated with scenes of the Mediterranean, from Gibraltar to Constantinople, and especially Venice, which he visited on 15 occasions. His work is restrained, meticulous yet often luminous.

For a biography of Edward Angelo Goodall, please refer to page 101.

37 **St Georgio by Moonlight, Venice**
Signed and indistinctly dated
Watercolour
7 ½ x 12 inches

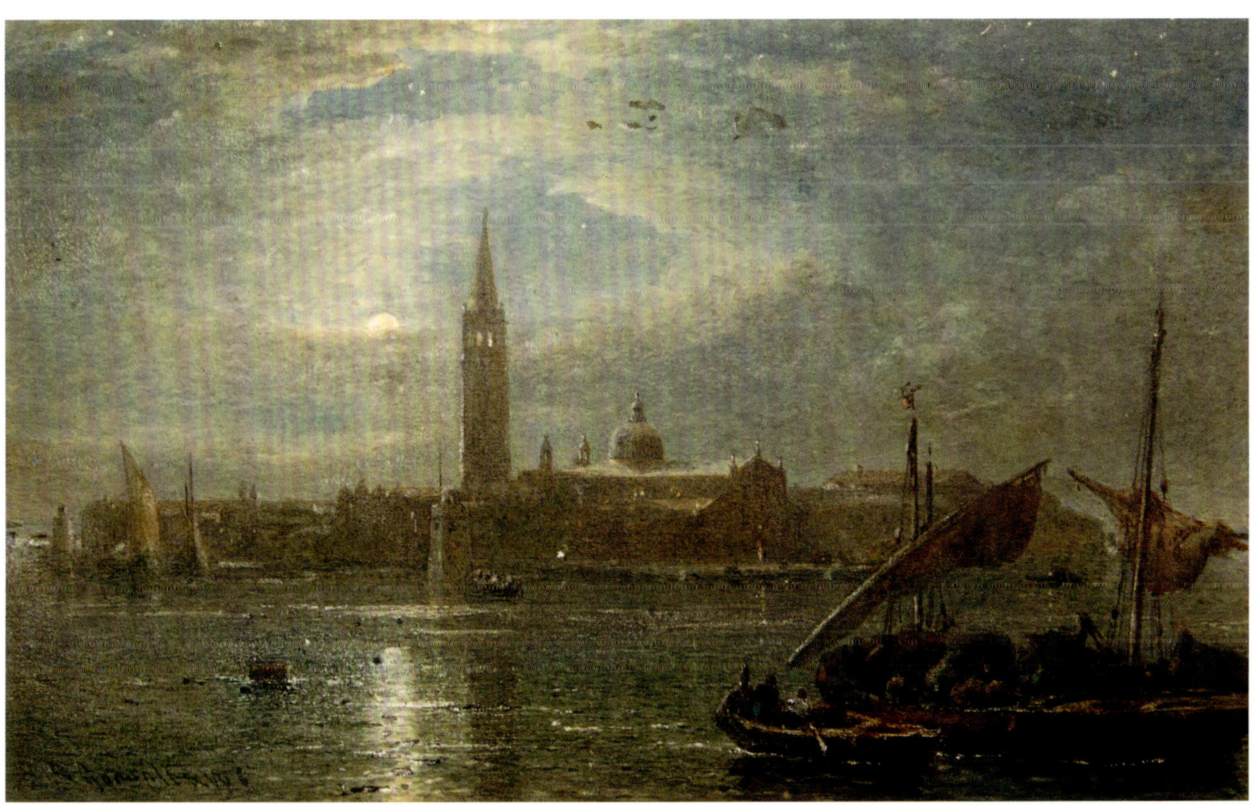

ALFRED WATERHOUSE

Alfred Waterhouse, PRIBA RA (1830-1905)

Alfred Waterhouse was one of the most important and successful of Victorian architects and designers. He was also admired for his architectural perspectives and landscape watercolours.

For a biography of Alfred Waterhouse, please refer to page 102.

38 **Pont Aven**
Signed with monogram
Inscribed with title and dated '21 Aug 85'
Watercolour
13 ¾ x 10 inches

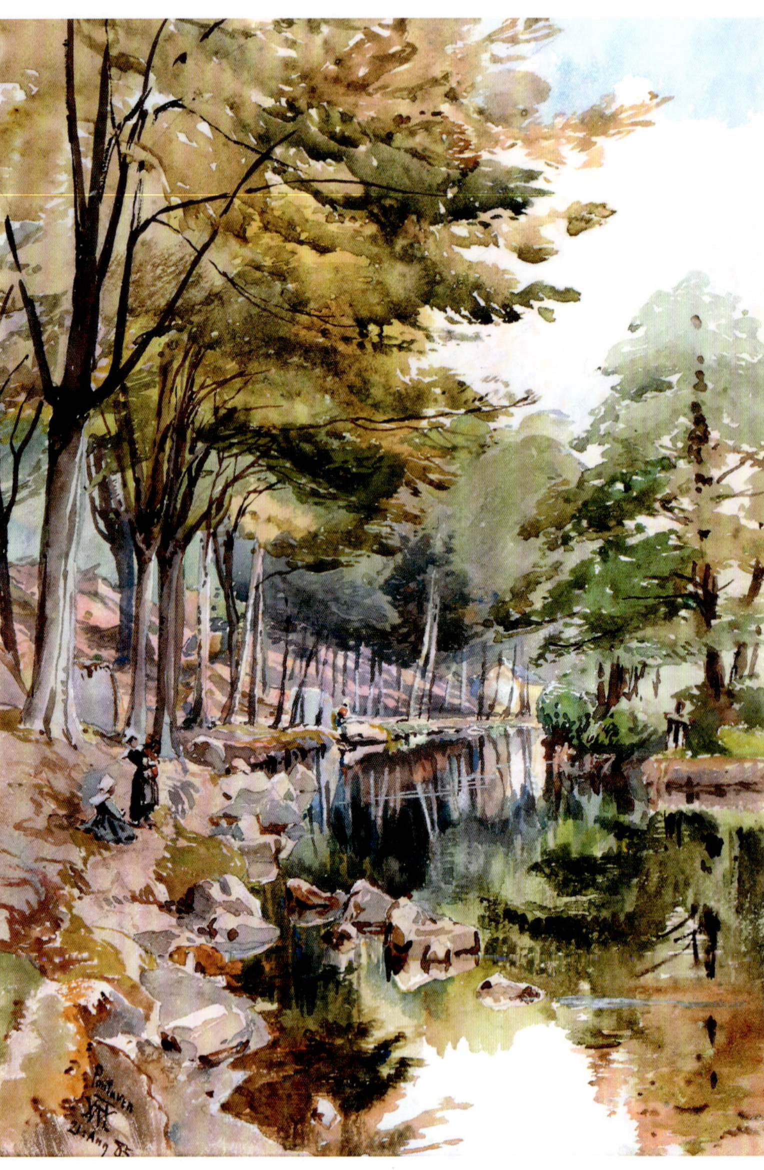

Pont Aven

The architect, Alfred Waterhouse, had originally wanted to be an artist, and is known to have studied the drawing manuals of James Duffield Harding and Samuel Prout. He put his skills as a watercolourist to good use in recording buildings and landscapes on tours of Britain and the Continent, and in creating exciting picturesque perspectives of his own building projects. From the late 1880s, he exhibited landscapes as well as his own architectural designs at the Royal Academy of Arts.

In 1886, Waterhouse exhibited a watercolour view of Chartres Cathedral at the Royal Academy, so marking a tour of Northern France that he had taken in the previous year. On that tour he had visited the Breton village of Pont-Aven, which since the 1860s had regularly attracted artists. However, his visit took place almost exactly a year before the arrival of Paul Gauguin, who attracted the colony of Post-Impressionist artists now most associated with Pont-Aven. Moreover, he recorded the exact view of the Bois d'Amour on the River Aven that, in 1888, would inspire Paul Sérusier to paint under Gauguin's influence the famous landscape now known as *The Talisman* (Musée d'Orsay, Paris). As Maurice Denis later recorded, Gauguin gave Sérusier one lesson:

> How do you see this tree…is it really green? Use green then, the most beautiful green on your palette. And that shadow, rather blue? Don't be afraid to paint it as blue as possible. (see Hirschel B Chipp, *Theories of Modern Art*, Berkeley, CA: University of California Press, 1968, page 101)

The resulting combination of anti-naturalistic colour and simplified form proved highly influential, especially among the Nabis, the group founded in 1889 by Pierre Bonnard and Edouard Vuillard with Denis and Sérusier. The fresh, naturalistic observations of Waterhouse represent the established tradition that Gauguin and his disciples intended to counter.

ETTORE ROESLER FRANZ

Ettore Roesler Franz (1845-1907)

Ettore Roesler Franz was an Italian painter in oil and watercolour, of landscapes and genre scenes, who exhibited regularly in London during the late nineteenth century. He remains best known for his immediate and atmospheric views of Rome and its environs, including places and practices that have since been lost to redevelopment and social change. In recent years, his pioneering work as a photographer has also attracted attention.

For a biography of Ettore Roesler Franz, please refer to page 103.

39 **Country Commissariat at Tivoli**
Signed and inscribed 'Roma'
Inscribed with title on a label on the original backboard in a contemporary hand
Watercolour
19 ¼ x 29 inches

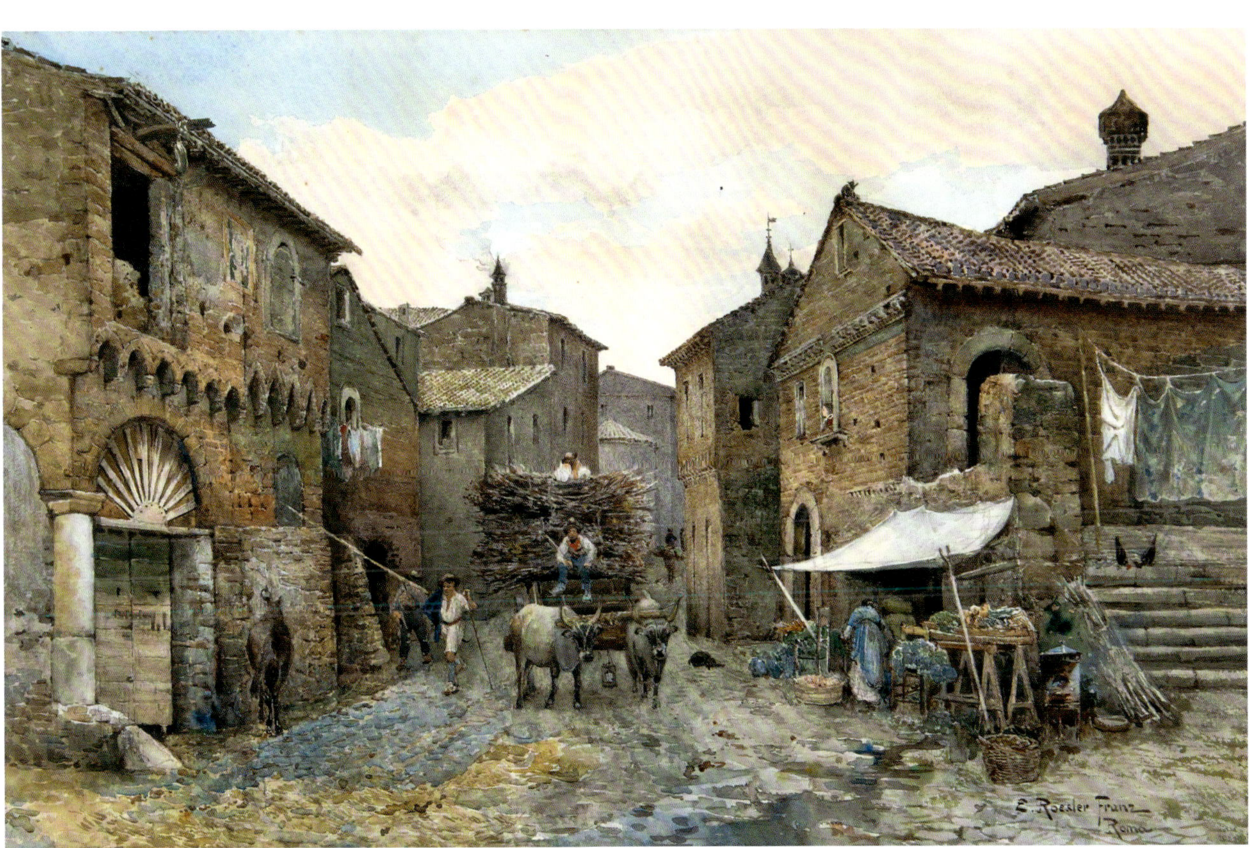

Country Commissariat at Tivoli

The present composition brilliantly conflates two views of the steep, narrow Via del Colle in Tivoli, the historic town in the Sabine foothills to the east of Rome. The left hand side is a fairly accurate view looking up the street, towards the apse of the early mediaeval church of San Silvestro. However, the right-hand side comprises a view from the other direction of the two picturesque houses in the left foreground. Note especially the narrow, arched windows on the first floor of the second building on the left and first building on the right, for these are actually one and the same. This evocation of turn-of-the-century Tivoli has been brought to life through the presence of locals going about such business as transporting wood by bullock cart and selling flowers, vegetables and fruit – characteristic features of the art of Ettore Roesler Franz.

CONSTANCE FREDERICA GORDON-CUMMING

Constance Frederica Gordon-Cumming (1837-1924)

Constance Frederica Gordon-Cumming was one of the most intrepid and enterprising women travellers of the Victorian period, who also had the skill and industry to record her journeys in word and image. Encouraged by her many distinguished connections, during the height of the British Empire, she visited India, Ceylon and many of the countries of the Pacific Rim, between 1868 and 1880. The extent of her achievement is still in the process of evaluation.

For a biography of Constance Frederica Gordon-Cumming, please refer to *Chris Beetles Summer Show*, 2014, pages 13-14.

Constance Frederica Gordon-Cumming's Third Tour Abroad, 1875-80

During the winter of 1874-75, Constance Frederica Gordon-Cumming received an invitation from Arthur Hamilton-Gordon, to join him and his wife on their journey to Fiji, where he was to become its governor. Leaving England in March 1875, they travelled via Singapore and Sydney. While Hamilton-Gordon was keen to move on to Fiji, Gordon-Cumming spent over three months in **Australia**, and took the opportunity to visit the Blue Mountains and the sheep station of Duntroon.

Between September 1875 and March 1878, Gordon-Cumming explored **Fiji**, New Zealand and the South Seas – partly in the company of the Bishop of Samoa – before leaving for California. *At Home in Fiji* (1881) and *A Lady's Cruise in a French Man-of-War* (1882) record this period; *Granite Crags* (1884) covers the months that she spent painting in California's Yosemite Valley. She showed the results in what comprised the Yosemite's first ever art exhibition.

From California, Gordon-Cumming set out for **Japan**, arriving in Nagasaki on 6 September 1878 and departing from Yokohama for China in mid-December. Her exploration of China, between December 1878 and June 1879, would be recorded in *Wanderings in China* (1886).

Gordon-Cumming returned to the United States via Japan, arriving in San Francisco in late September 1879. However, just a week later, on 1 October, she embarked for Hawaii, and spent two months touring the islands, and studying its volcanoes. These she described in *Fire Fountains: The Kingdom of Hawaii* (1883). Crossing the United States from 2 December 1879 to 2 March 1880, she arrived in Liverpool on 13 March.

40 **The Weatherboard, Blue Mountains, New South Wales, Australia** (opposite)
Signed, inscribed with title and 'Alfred P Maudslay', and dated 'August 18th 1875'
Watercolour with pencil and bodycolour
19 ¼ x 29 ½ inches

Detail of *Fujiyama From Otomi Toge (Otome-Toge) Pass, Japan* [42]

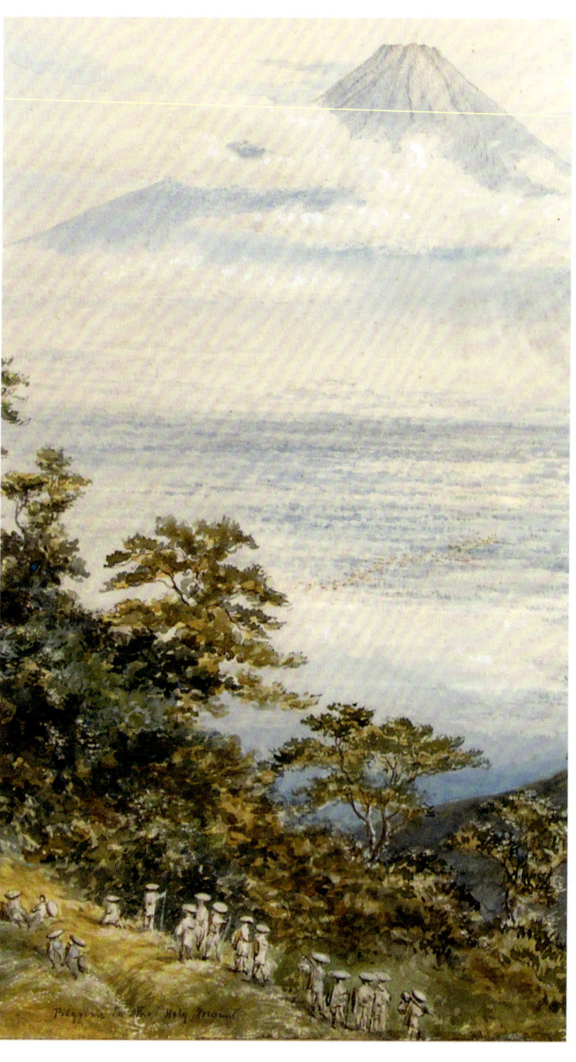

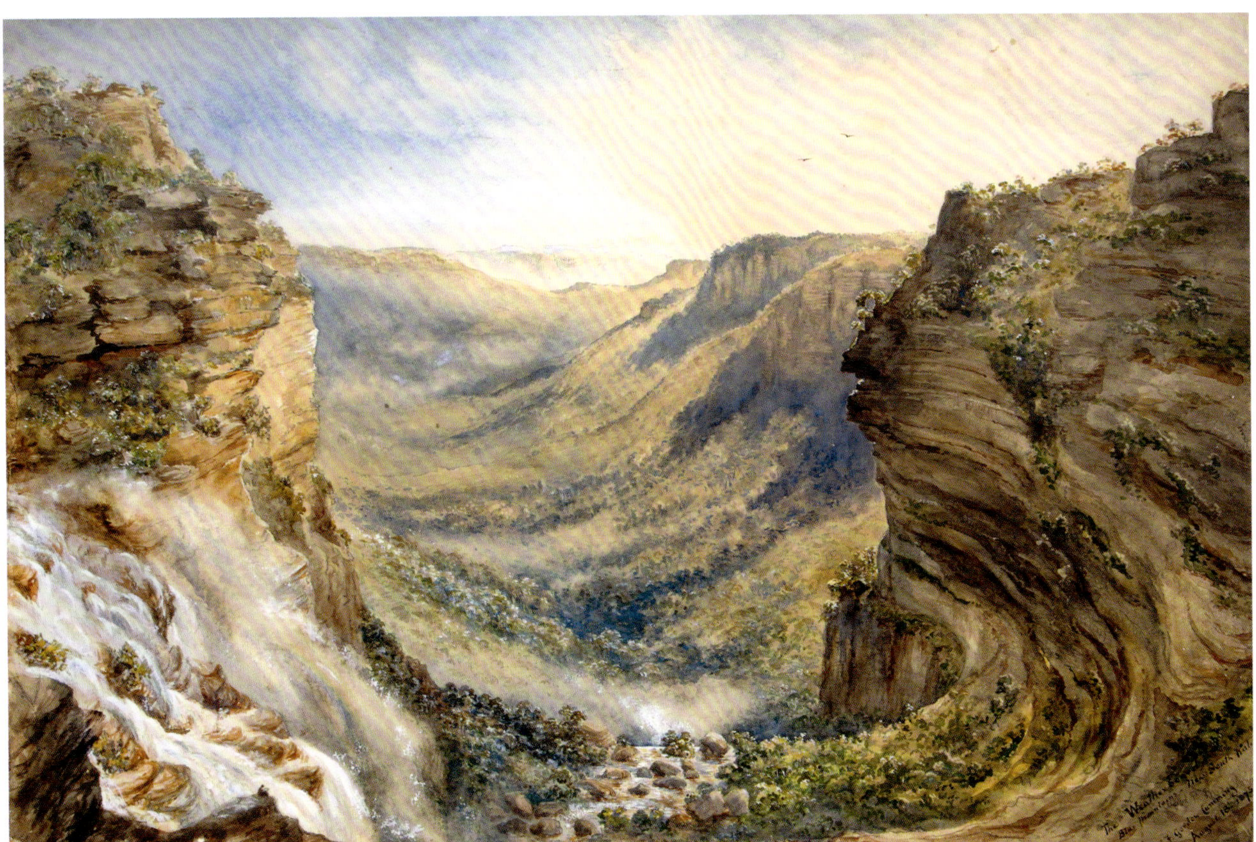

The Weatherboard, Blue Mountains, New South Wales, Australia

Constance Frederica Gordon-Cumming gave an account of her 'life in the Blue Mountains' in a letter published in *At Home in Fiji* (1881). She headed that letter, 'From a tiny Cottage at the Weatherboard in the Blue Mountains, New South Wales, Begun Aug 19, 1875', which was the day after she produced the present watercolour. The account is as follows:

> Mr [Alfred P] Maudslay [secretary to Arthur Hamilton-Gordon] and another gentleman escorted me to the Blue Mountains last week, where we put up at a very cosy inn and expeditioned. The gorges with great cliffs are very fine, and the valleys densely wooded. Sometimes we went down into deep gullies with tree-ferns far above our heads – very beautiful. When my two companions had to return to Sydney, I went to the tiny cottage where I began this letter. My host was a wood-cutter, with a clean, tidy wife, and a number of very neat children … It does seem odd to think of my being so at home, alone in these wild mountains, sitting all day by myself, miles from any human habitation, only seeing a pair of great eagles soaring overhead – no other living thing. (pages 21-22)

The 'cosy inn' in which Gordon-Cumming and her companions stayed is undoubtedly the Weatherboard Inn. This was initially constructed in 1827, and took its name from a weatherboard hut, built by convicts in 1814 as a road building depot. Around this hut grew up a township that was officially called Jamison Valley but popularly known as the Weatherboard. In 1879 – the year of Gordon-Cumming's visit – it was renamed Wentworth Falls. Her watercolour shows an interesting viewpoint from above the waterfall looking in a southwesterly direction down Jamison Valley. A solitary figure with a drawing board, sitting by the side of the waterfall, may be intended as a self-portrait.

'My dear George, – We are settling down into the quietest of lives, and I have no special news to give you; but the day is so lovely that I could not stay in the house, so I wandered up the hill to a huge boulder of grey rock, fringed with the loveliest of ferns, on which I am now sitting, looking across the bluest of seas to the great isle of Viti Levu, whose mountains lie dreamily on the horizon. I must tell you that Viti Levu simply means great Viti, which is the name by which these islands are always called by their own inhabitants, the name of Fiji, which we have adopted, being simply the Tongan mispronunciation of the word. If you look at a map of the group, you will see that this isle of Ovalu, though important by reason of its being the site of Levuka, the white men's capital, is only a small isle lying off Viti Levu, as does also the tiny isle of Bau, on which is King Thakombau's own particular capital.'

(*At Home in Fiji*, pages 53-54)

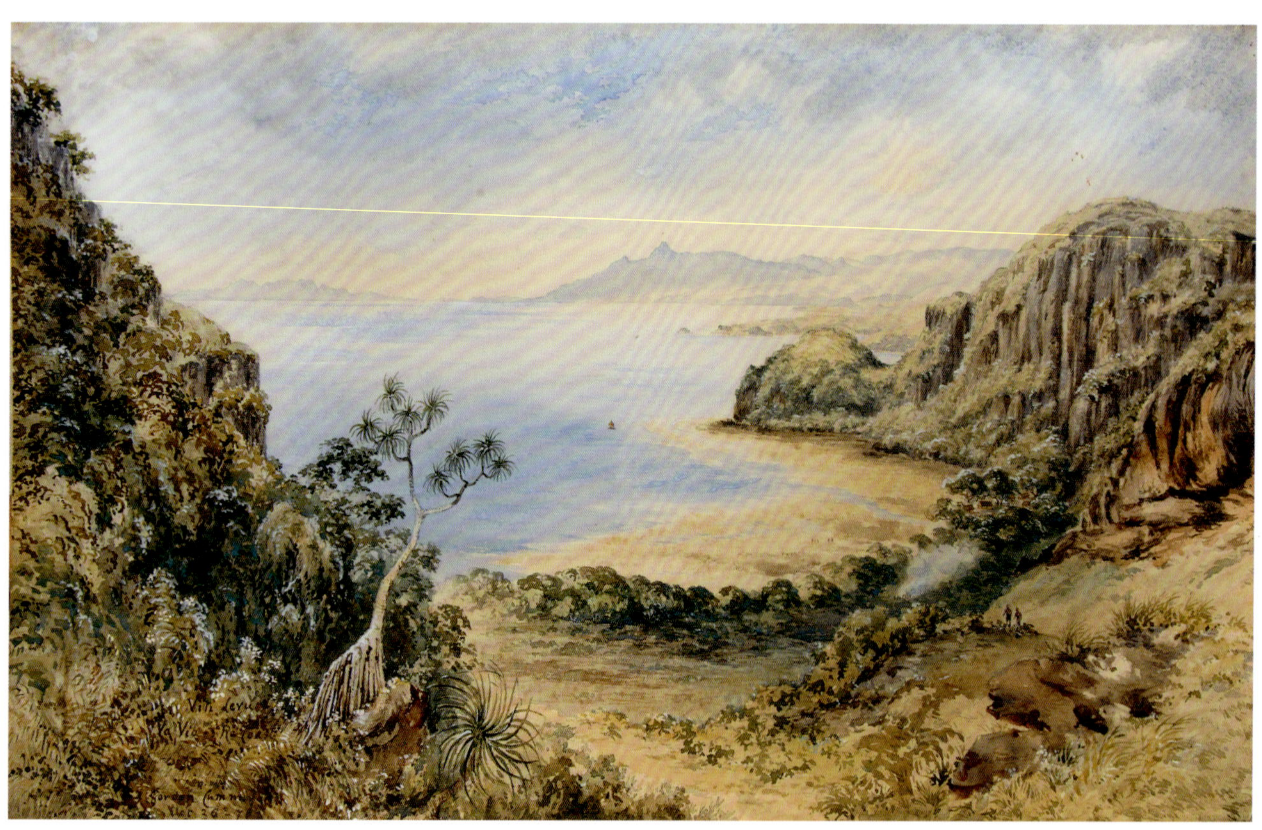

41 **Viti Levu, Va Via Ra Coast, Fiji**
Signed and dated 'Oct 26th 76'
Watercolour with pencil and bodycolour
15 ¼ x 26 inches

Fujiyama From Otomi Toge (Otome-Toge) Pass, Japan

In August 1879, Constance Frederica Gordon-Cumming climbed Mount Fuji in the company of 'a lady as anxious as myself to make the ascent, and a gentleman who had already accomplished it four times' ('The Ascent of Fujiyama', *Harper's New Monthly Magazine*, October 1880, page 649). These were probably Emily Jane Forster and William F H Garratt, the names of whom are inscribed on the present watercolour.

Their route from Yokoyama to Fujiyama took in the Otome-Toge, or Maiden Pass, which is considered one the best spots from which to view the mountain. However, on their outward journey, the vision of Gordon-Cumming and her companions was obscured by 'close gray mist which clung around us as a pall' (page 650); so it was only on the return journey that she was able to produce this watercolour, and demonstrate quite how magnificent the view is.

Gordon-Cumming's account of her ascent, published in *Harper's New Monthly Magazine* in 1880, is informative about the geography of Fujiyama and sensitive to the practice of the Shinto pilgrims who reverenced it.

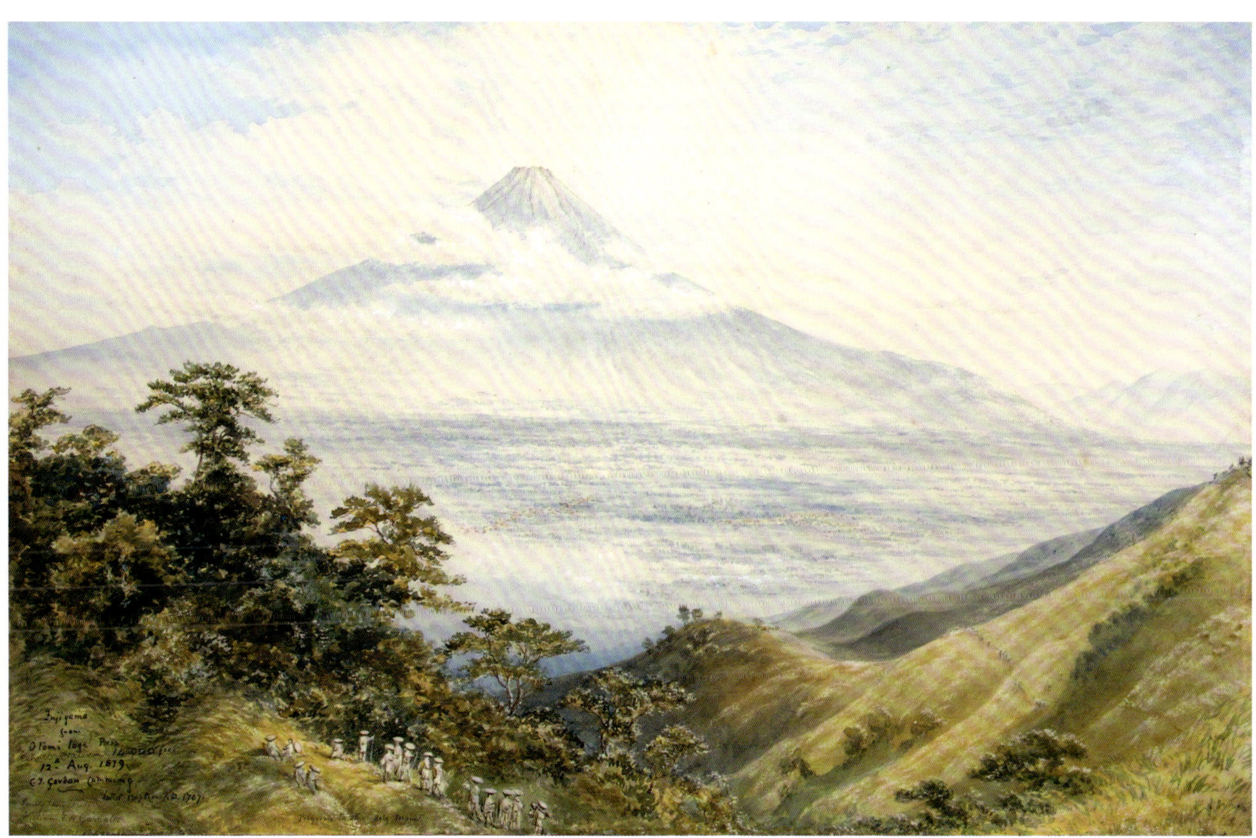

42 **Fujiyama From Otomi Toge (Otome-Toge) Pass, Japan**
Signed, inscribed with 'Fujiyama from Otomi Toge Pass', 'Extinct Crater 14000 feet', 'Latest Eruption AD 1707', 'Emily Jane Forster', 'William F H Garratt' and 'Pilgrims to the Holy Mount', and dated '12th Aug 1879'
Watercolour with pencil and bodycolour
15 x 24 inches

CONSTANCE FREDERICA GORDON-CUMMING

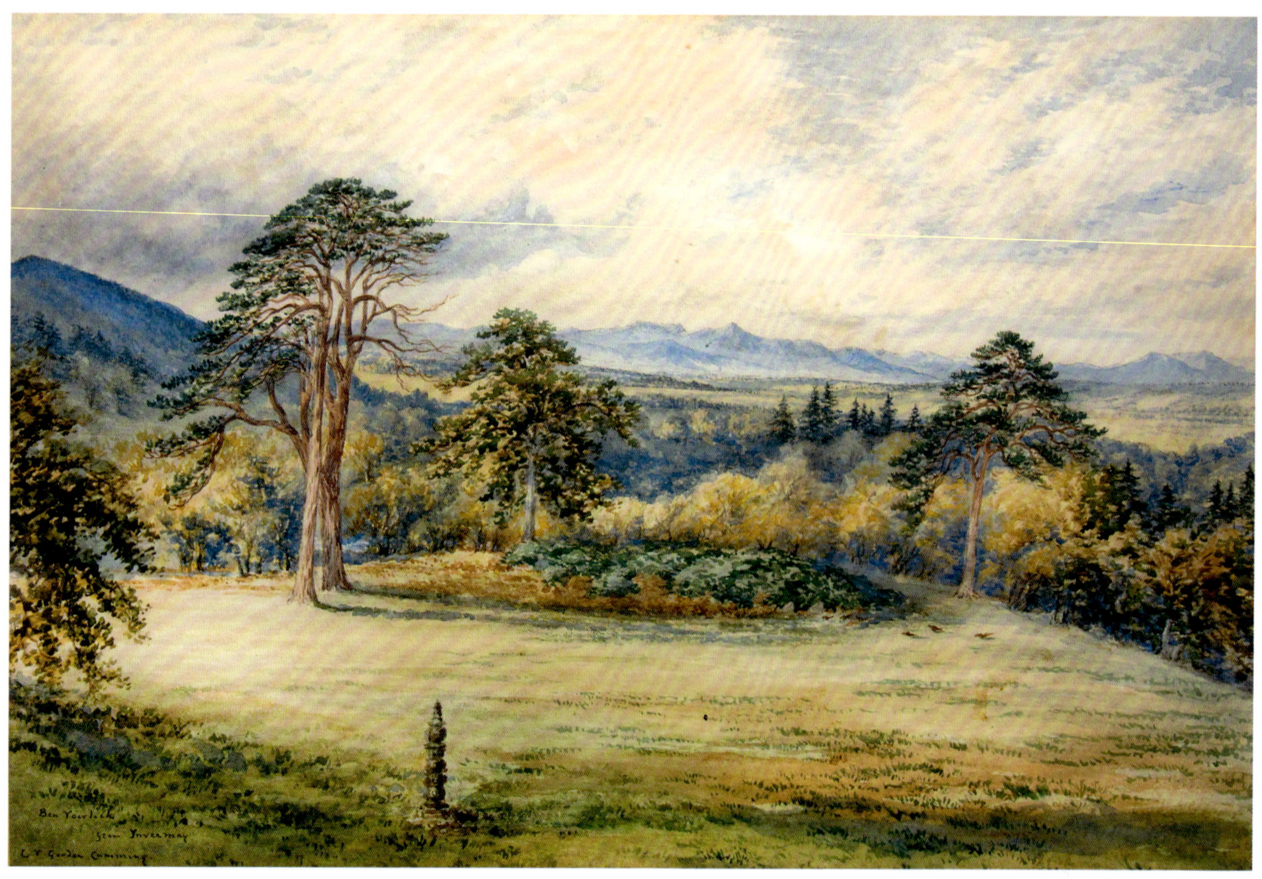

43 Ben Vorlich from Inveraray
Signed and inscribed with title
Watercolour with pencil and bodycolour
14 x 20 inches

Ben Vorlich from Inveraray

Inveraray is on the north shore of Loch Fyne, in the historic Scots shire of Argyll. It was the birthplace of Eliza Maria Campbell, the mother of Constance Frederica Gordon-Cumming and granddaughter of the 5th Duke of Argyll, whose seat was Inveraray Castle. The present watercolour shows the view from the castle's grounds looking towards Ben Vorlich, which stands 30 miles to the east.

EDWARD THEODORE COMPTON

Edward Theodore Compton (1849-1921)

An active member of the British Alpine Club, as well as that of Germany and Austria, E T Compton based himself in Bavaria, and became one of the first artists to devote himself to depicting the remote and inaccessible heights of the Alps. Nevertheless, he travelled widely, from Scandinavia to North Africa, in search of subject matter for his brush.

For a biography of Edward Theodore Compton, please refer to page 104.

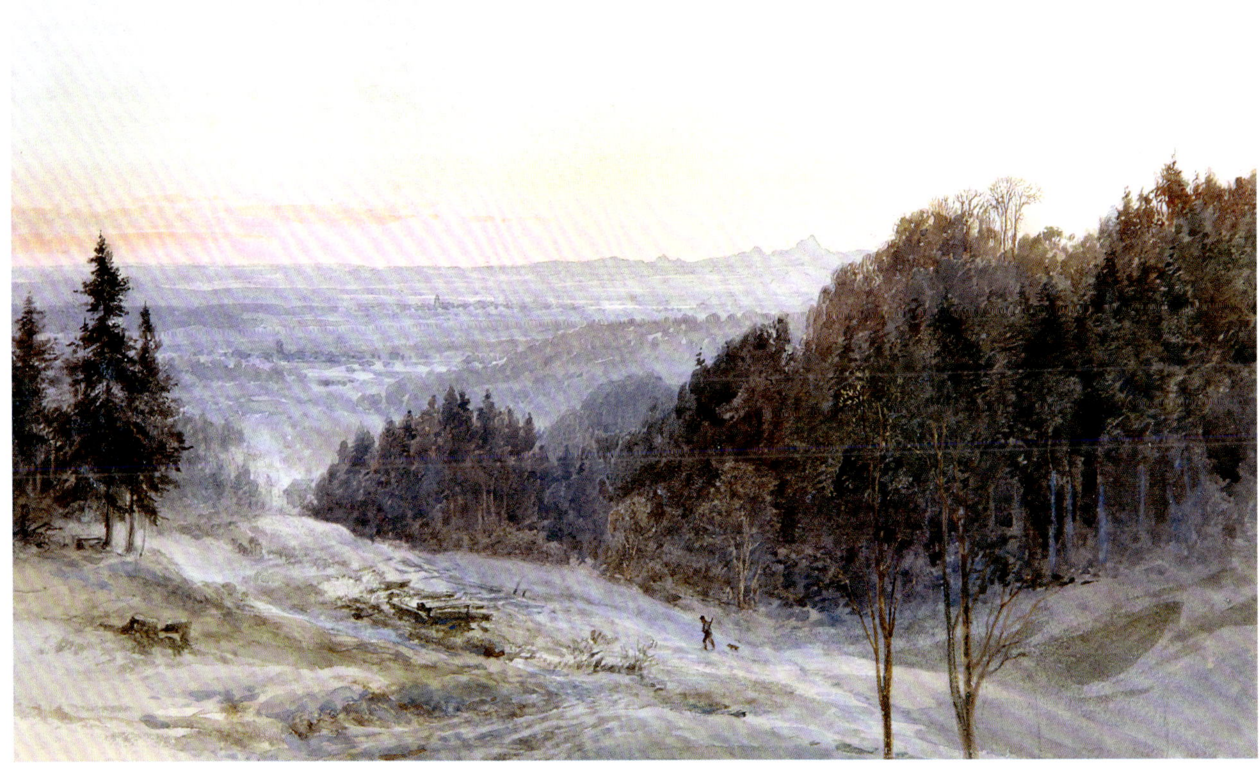

44 **Winter Landscape**
Signed and dated 1878
Watercolour
10 ¼ x 14 ½ inches

GEORGE SAMUEL ELGOOD

George Samuel Elgood, RI ROI (1851-1943)

George Samuel Elgood is best known for his watercolours of gardens, which were informed by a combination of observation and knowledge, and epitomise a classic genre of the Edwardian age. However, his range encompassed landscapes and interiors, as suggested by the works included here.

For a biography of George Samuel Elgood, please refer to page 105.

The Screen, Le Folgoët, Brittany (opposite)
George Samuel Elgood made visits to France from 1882, and initially focussed on architectural subjects. These visits included some summer months spent in Brittany, at the same time as Paul Gauguin and his followers – and possibly at the same time that Alfred Waterhouse was painting *Pont Aven* [38] – though it is not known whether their paths crossed. The works that resulted include *Calvary, Brittany* as well as the present watercolour, which shows the interior of the church of Le Folgoët, situated in the far west of Brittany.

The Basilique Notre-Dame du Folgoët is an example of Breton Decorated Gothic of the period 1350-1410, 'while Perpendicular was establishing itself in England, and while in France proper but little was being built' (Camille Enlart, 'Origine Anglaise du Style Flamboyant', *The Architectural Review*, April 1907, page 209). Elgood's watercolour focusses on the particularly fine rood screen of Kersanton stone that separates the nave from the chancel, and contains two small altars, either side of the portal.

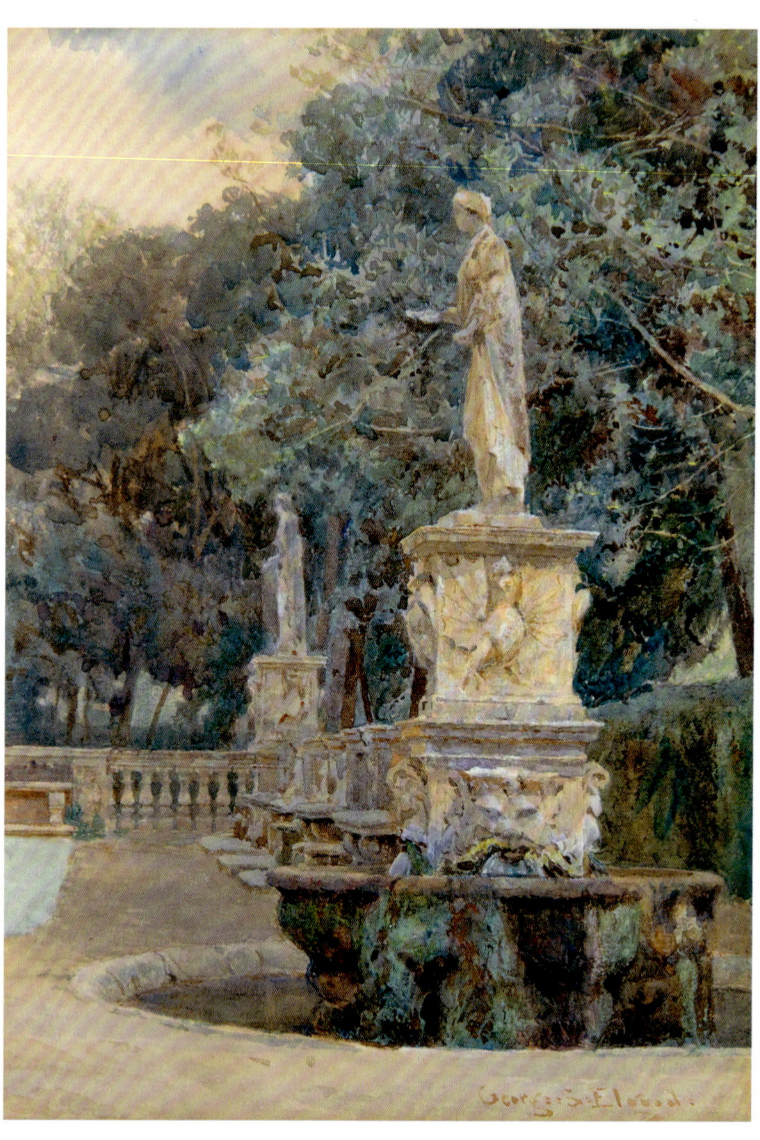

45 **Fountains in the Borghese Gardens, Rome**
Signed
Watercolour with bodycolour
9 ½ x 6 ¾ inches

46 The Screen, Le Folgoët, Brittany

Signed; Watercolour; 14 x 11 ¾ inches

Literature: Charles Holme (ed), *The Royal Institute of Painters in Water-Colours, The Studio,* Special Number, Spring 1906, Plate XVII, as 'Le Folgoet'

Exhibited: Royal Institute of Painters in Water Colours, 1889, as 'Church of Le Folgoet, Brittany';
'The Long Nineteenth Century: Treasures and Pleasures', Chris Beetles Gallery, March-April 2014, No 118

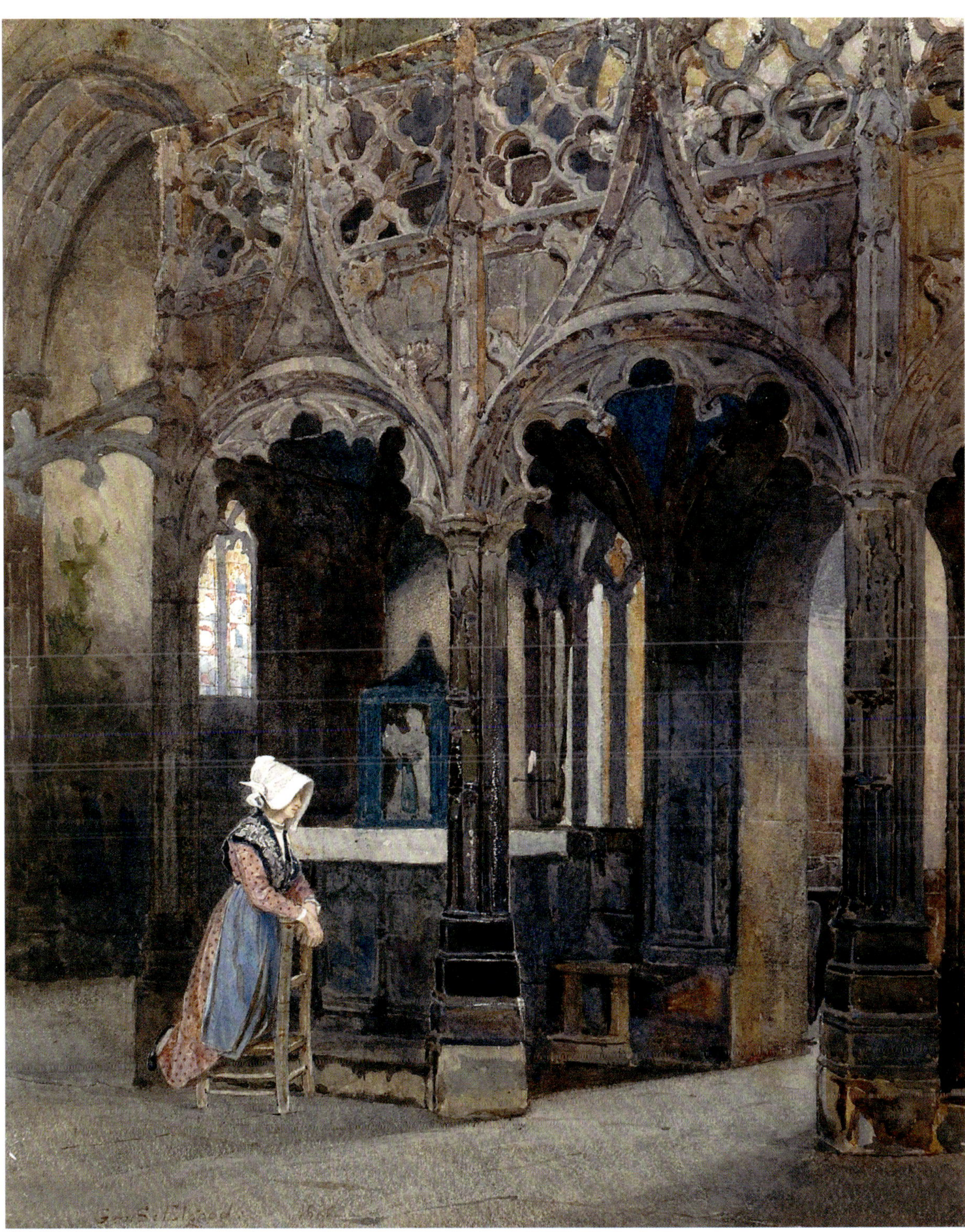

JOHN FULLEYLOVE

John Fulleylove, RI (1844-1908)

Working mainly in watercolour, John Fulleylove was a painter and illustrator who specialised in landscapes, and particularly gardens, as settings for impressive architecture, from Hampton Court to Athens.

For a biography of John Fulleylove, please refer to *Chris Beetles Summer Show*, 2019, pages 56-57.

47 **6 The Terrace. Kensington. Garden Front. John Leech's House**
Signed, inscribed with title and dated 1892
Watercolour with pencil
7 x 9 inches
Similar to the illustration in *The Magazine of Art*, 1893, Page 164, 'The Home Life of John Leech' by Henry Silver

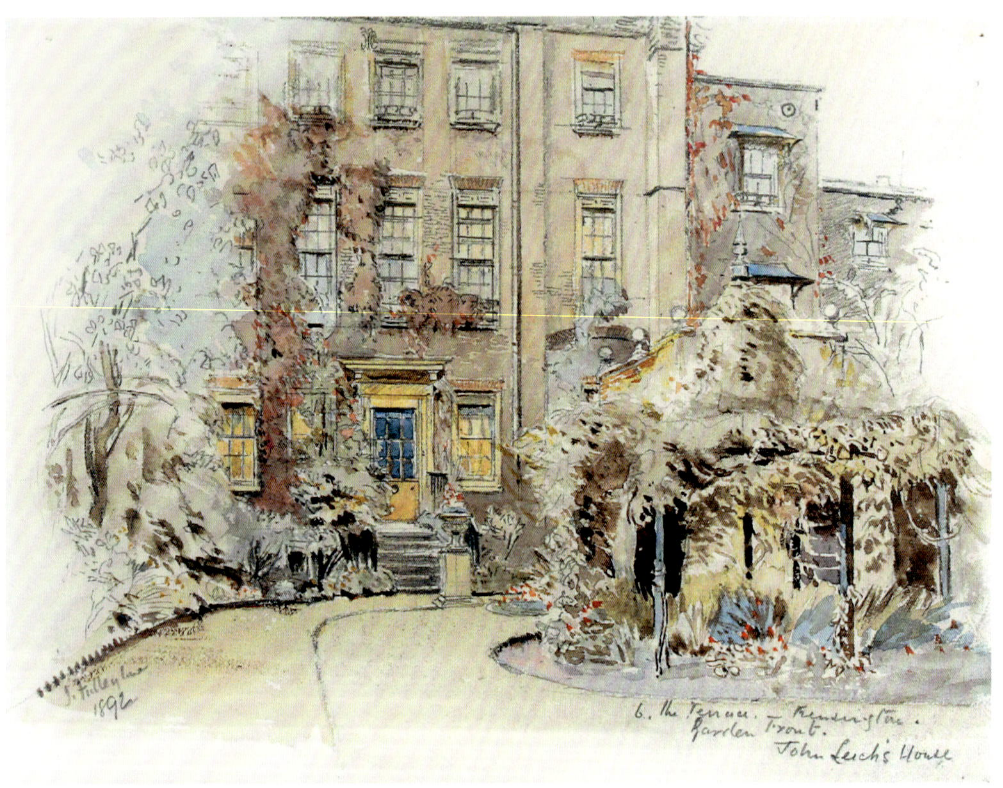

'Here [the Punch *cartoonist, John Leech (1817-1864),] often gave a garden party, which was far more pleasant than is usual for such merry-makings. A plateful of good soup and a slice of cold roast beef were served instead of ices and slices of sponge-cake; and half a score of guests were asked instead of half a hundred. Thackeray avowed a special fondness for these parties, and, living close at hand, was often able to be present. The garden was a well-nigh country garden then, and flycatchers and blackbirds used frequently to build there. The famous Mr [William] Banting [(1796-1878), undertaker and author of* Letter on Corpulence *(1863)], who cured himself of fatness, lived nearly next door, and would send delicious mulberries, fresh gathered from his tree, a few yards only distant. No shrieking trains were near, to make night hideous with their clamour, nor was much traffic audible from what is now the crowded and bus-overburdened road. Indeed, under the weeping ash-tree, where the festive board was spread, all was so cosy and so quiet that you might have heard an "h" drop if a Cockney had been present.*

Those delightful outdoor dinners! Where are such gardens now? Alas! the ash-tree has been sold with the ground whereon it grew, and will soon be rooted up, with all the memories that cling to it. The old house where John Leech lived will be cleared away next year, in order to make room for some new monster brick-and-mortar works; and the garden where we dined will be swept into the "Ewigkeit," just like the famous "barty" that was given by Hans Breitmann [an allusion to a comic verse by Charles G Leland].'

(Henry Silver, 'The Home Life of John Leech', *The Magazine of Art*, 1893, Page 166)

48 Portion of the Armoury, White Tower
Signed
Watercolour
13 x 16 ½ inches
Illustrated: Arthur Poyser (described by), *The Tower of London*,
London: A & C Black, 1908, Facing Page 40

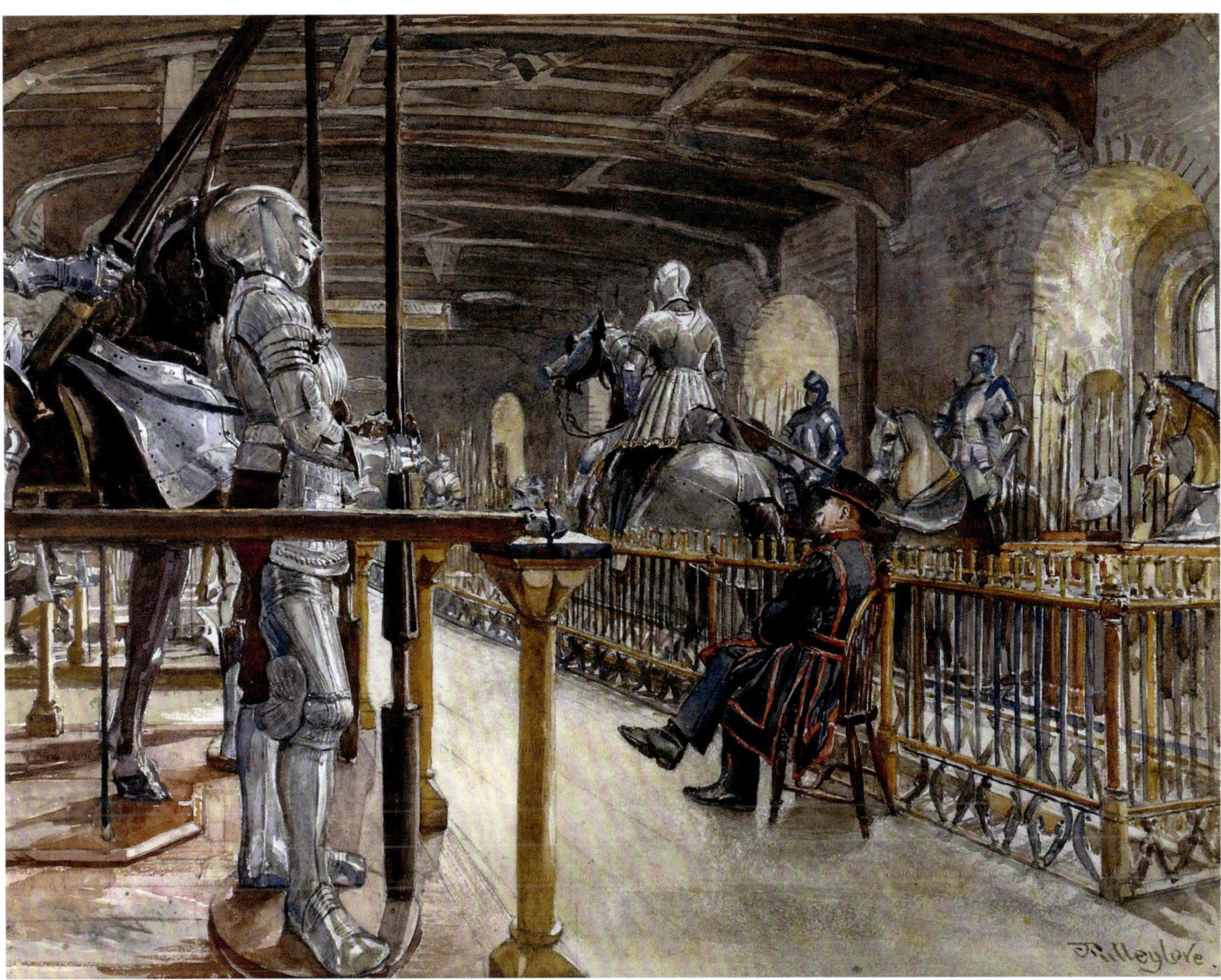

'The White Tower or Keep … is the very heart and centre of the Tower buildings, and all the lesser towers and connecting walls, making the Inner and Outer Wards, and the broad moat encircling all, are but the means of protection and inviolable security of this ancient keep. Within its rock-like walls a threatened king could live in security. Here were provided the elementary necessaries of life – a storehouse for food, a well to supply fresh water, a great fireplace (in the thickness of the wall), and a place of devotion, all within the walls of this one tower …

The large rooms entered from the chapel are the former State apartments, now given over to the housing of a collection of weapons and armour which is described on the show-cases, and therefore need not be detailed here. In these rooms Baliol in the reign of Edward I, and King David of Scotland in that of Edward III, were kept prisoners, but not in the strictest sense. Other notable captives here were King John of France (after the battle of Poitiers), Prince (afterwards King) James of Scotland, and Charles, Duke of Orleans – all of whom have been spoken of in the previous chapter. Several models of the Tower buildings, made at various periods, will be found in these rooms.'

(Arthur Poyser (described by), *The Tower of London*, London: A & C Black, 1908, pages 110 & 112)

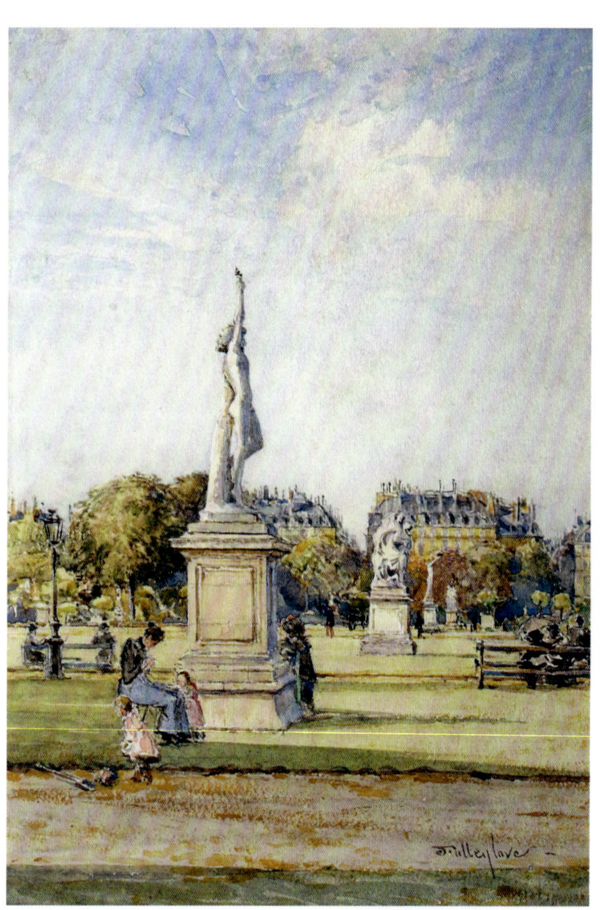

49 In the Tuileries Gardens, Paris
Signed
Watercolour
10 ¾ x 7 ¼ inches

John Fulleylove in Italy

From 1875, John Fulleylove made several sketching trips to Italy, and, from his marriage in 1878, these were made in the company of his artist wife, Elizabeth (the sister of George Samuel Elgood). Given his Classical interests, it is no surprise that Fulleylove went first to Rome, and that that city should prove a favourite, both for such ancient sites as the early second century Temple of Vesta (more accurately the Temple of Hercules Victor) [51] and such atmospheric spots as the Medici Gardens [50]. He also visited Florence on that first trip, and later returned to Tuscany to take in the towns along the Val d'Arno and those further south, notably Siena and San Gimignano. By the time that he contributed to the two volumes of Cassell's *The Picturesque Mediterranean*, which was published in 1889 and 1891, he had become familiar with many of the most important of Italy's coastal towns, including, of course, Venice.

50 The Medici Gardens, Rome
Signed
Inscribed with title below mount
Signed and inscribed with title on backboard
Watercolour
9 x 14 inches

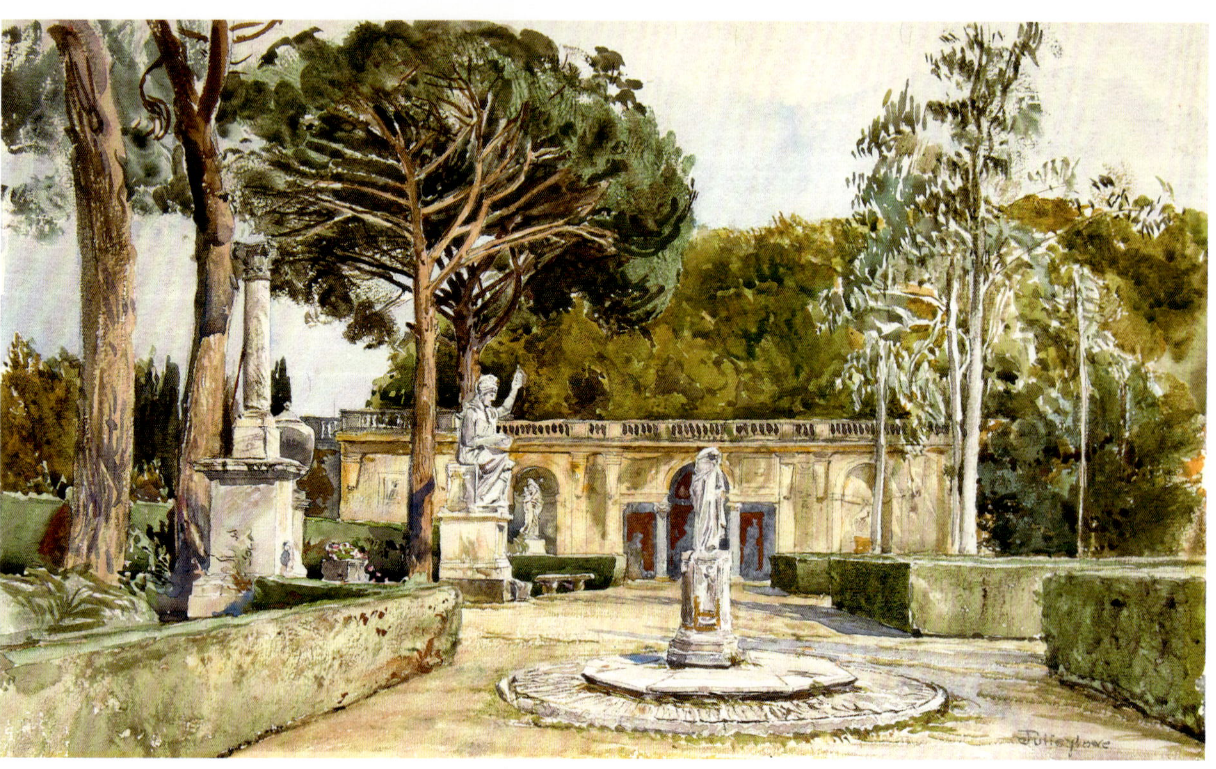

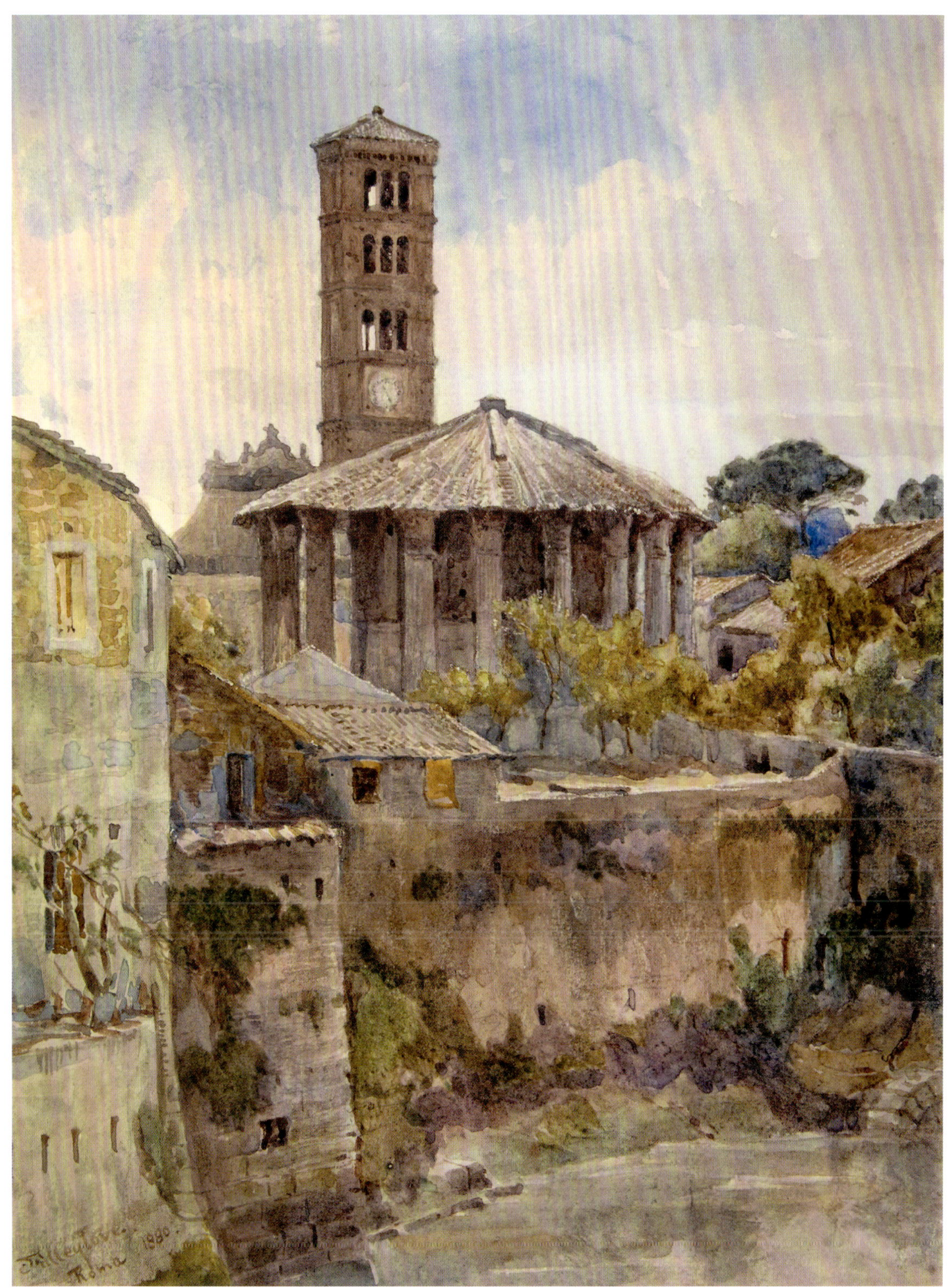

51 Tempio di Vesta, Rome
Signed, inscribed 'Roma' and dated 1880
Watercolour
13 x 10 ¼ inches

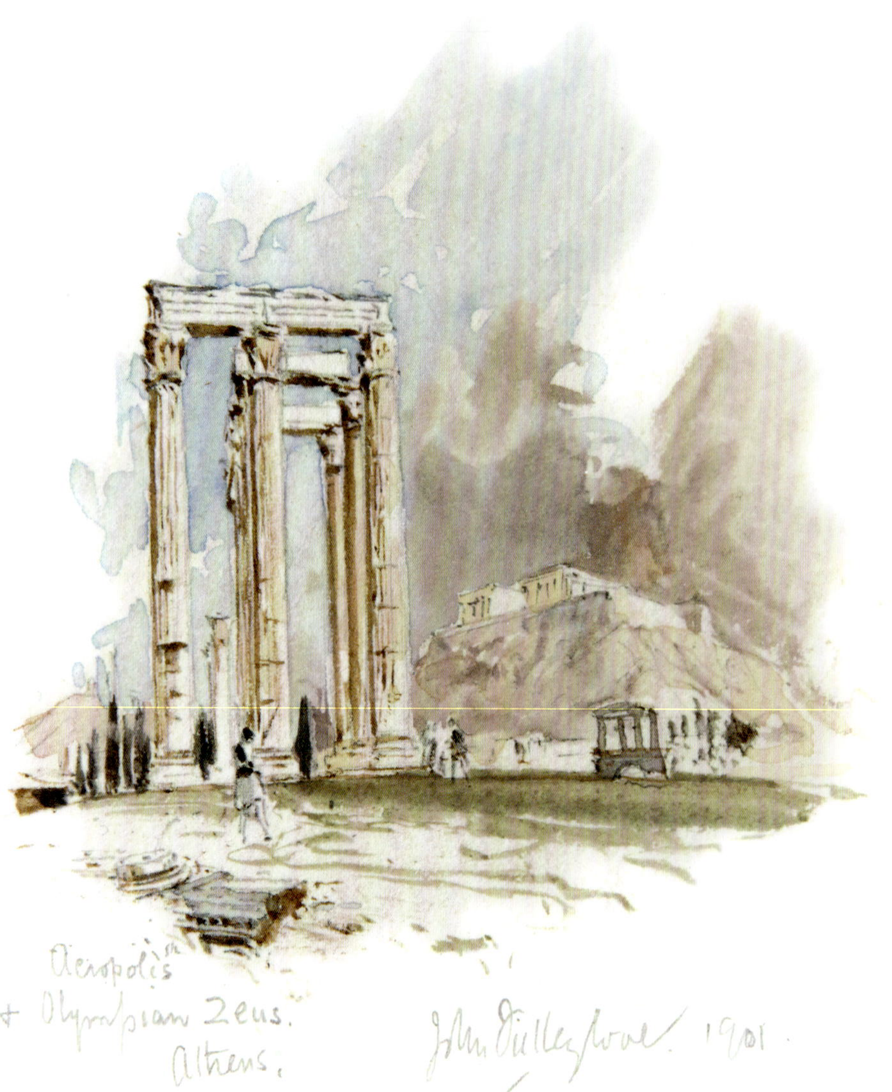

52 Acropolis and Olympian Zeus, Athens
Signed, inscribed with title and dated 1901
Watercolour with pencil
7 x 5 inches

'The emperor [Hadrian]'s greatest monument was the Olympieum, or temple of Olympian Zeus, situated to the south-east of the Acropolis, on the right bank of the Ilissus. The foundation of the temple had been laid by Peisistratus nearly 700 years before, and the work had been considerably advanced by Antiochus Epiphanes nearly 400 years later; but it was reserved to Hadrian to complete the great undertaking, which he did in a munificent style. Unfortunately only fifteen of the hundred or more Corinthian columns of Pentelic marble are now standing, occupying but a small part of the vast platform (about 2200 feet in circumference) on which the temple stood. But such is the grandeur of the columns, rising to a height of nearly 57 feet and fully 5½ feet in diameter, that they form one of the most imposing ruins in the world. Even before the commencement of the temple of Peisistratus, the place was regarded with peculiar veneration as the traditional site of a temple erected by Deucalion, the survivor of the Flood; and in the days of Pausanias a cleft was to be seen in the ground, into which the subsiding waters were said to have sunk, and where, every year, the people cast in wheaten meal kneaded with honey, probably in memory of those who perished in the Deluge.'

(J A M'Clymont, *Greece*, London: A & C Black, 1906, pages 211-212)

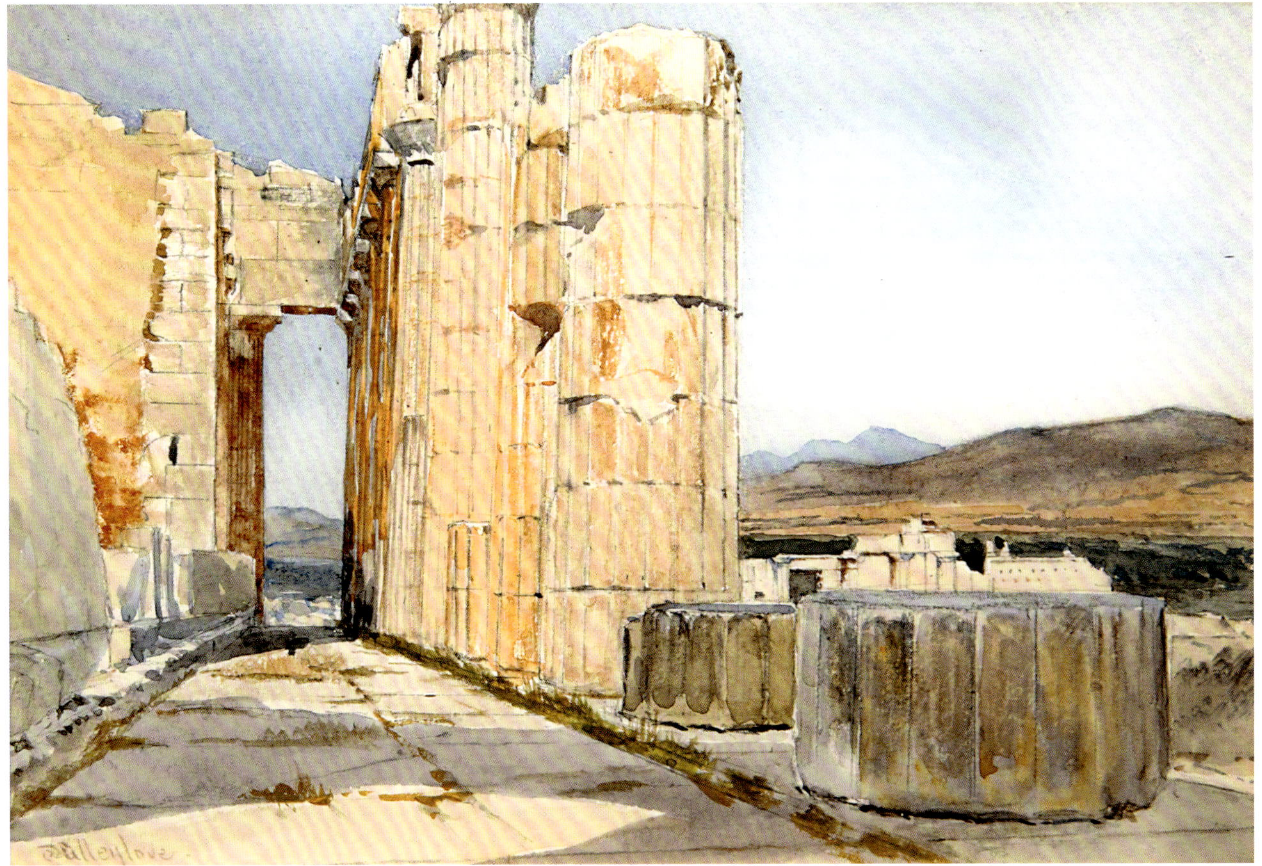

53 **Vista of the Northern Peristyle of the Parthenon, Looking Westward**
Signed
Watercolour with pencil
7 ½ x 10 ¾ inches
Illustrated: J A M'Clymont, *Greece*, London: A & C Black, 1906, Facing Page 146

Vista of the Northern Peristyle of the Parthenon, Looking Westward

John Fulleylove established himself as an expert in Greek topography from the time of his travels in Greece in 1895, which resulted in the 90 drawings that he exhibited in a solo show held at the Fine Art Society, London, in the following year. A decade later, in 1906, he illustrated J A M'Clymont's well-reviewed *Greece*, as the fifth of his projects for A & C Black, and it is among its pages that the present image was reproduced.

The Parthenon is the largest building on the Acropolis of Athens, and the most important surviving building of Classical Greece. Dedicated to the goddess Athena, it was constructed and decorated between 447 and 432 BC. Its fabric was damaged in 1687, during the Ottoman occupation of Greece, when an ammunition dump stored inside it was ignited by a Venetian bombardment.

'Out of the seventeen columns of the northern peristyle the remains of fourteen, more or less perfect, may be counted on the right. Six of them, which have stood unmoved for more than twenty-two centuries, are distinguished by their splendid colour, almost matching in this respect the second column of the west front, which is also visible. The remains of the north cella wall are seen to the left. The two drums of columns in shadow in the foreground reflect the pure blue of the early morning sky. Over their tops may be seen part of the Propylæa, and the mountains of Daphni and Megara.'

(J A M'Clymont, *Greece*, London: A & C Black, 1906, facing page 146)

'This spring, which is at the extreme southern end of the village, is in an arched recess of modern Turkish construction. The hour is about seven in the morning, when water is drawn by the villagers for the day's consumption. The brilliancy and variety of costume are peculiar to the women of Nazareth. Across the road to the left is a hut covered with boughs, the leaves of which have turned brown. Such huts are common in this district, to afford shelter to the watchmen who guard the crops.'

(John Kelman (described by), *The Holy Land*, London: A & C Black, 1912, facing page 73)

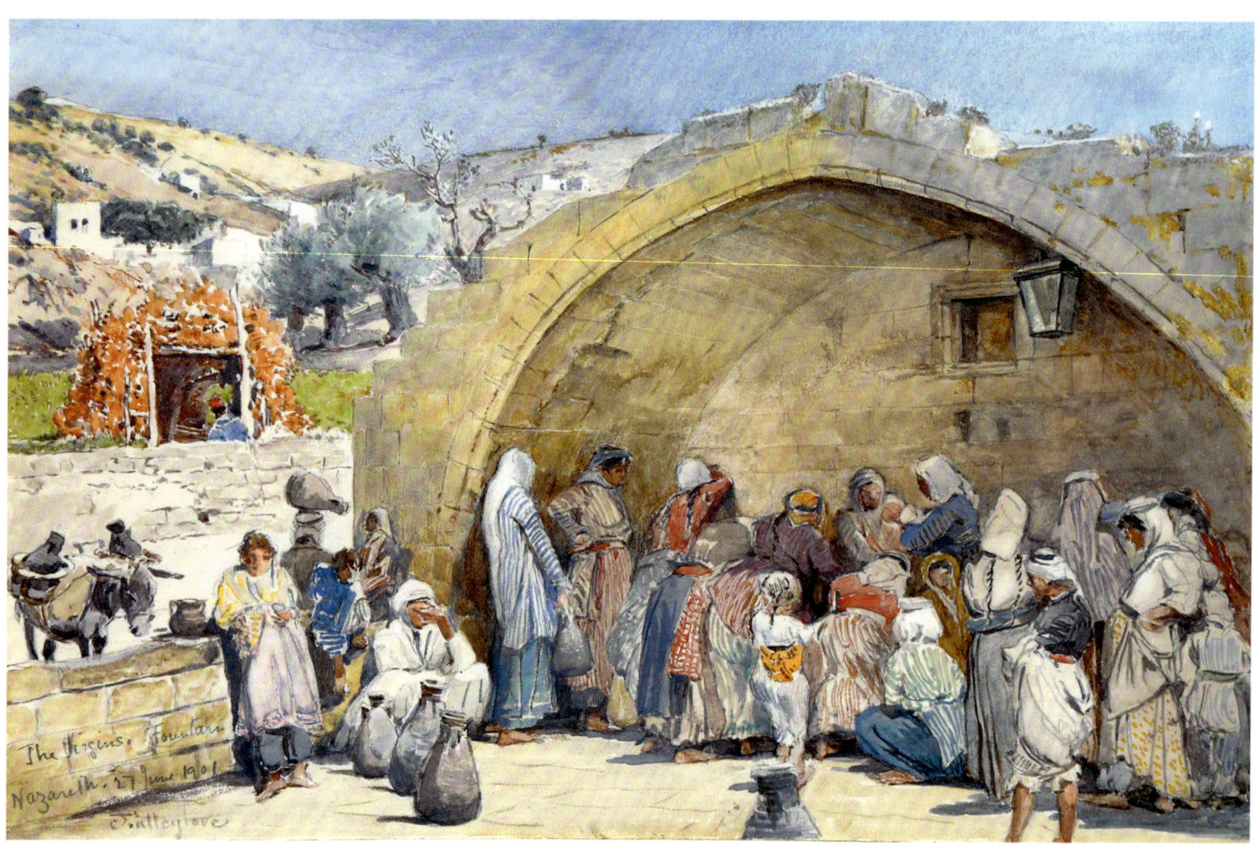

54 The Fountain of the Virgin at Nazareth
Signed, inscribed 'The Virgin's Fountain, Nazareth' and dated '27 June 1901'
Watercolour
10 x 14 inches
Illustrated: John Kelman (described by), *The Holy Land*, London: A & C Black, 1912,
Facing Page 73

LOUISA ANNE BERESFORD, MARCHIONESS OF WATERFORD

Louisa Anne Beresford, Marchioness of Waterford (née Stuart) (1818-1891)

Though largely untutored, Louisa Anne Beresford, Marchioness of Waterford, became one of the best-known amateur painters of her time. Working mainly in watercolour, she produced images that, ranging in mood and scale, reflected her interests in religion and philanthropy. She was influenced by artists of the Italian Renaissance, and encouraged by John Ruskin and members of the Pre-Raphaelite Brotherhood.

For a biography of Louisa Anne Beresford, Marchioness of Waterford, please refer to page 106.

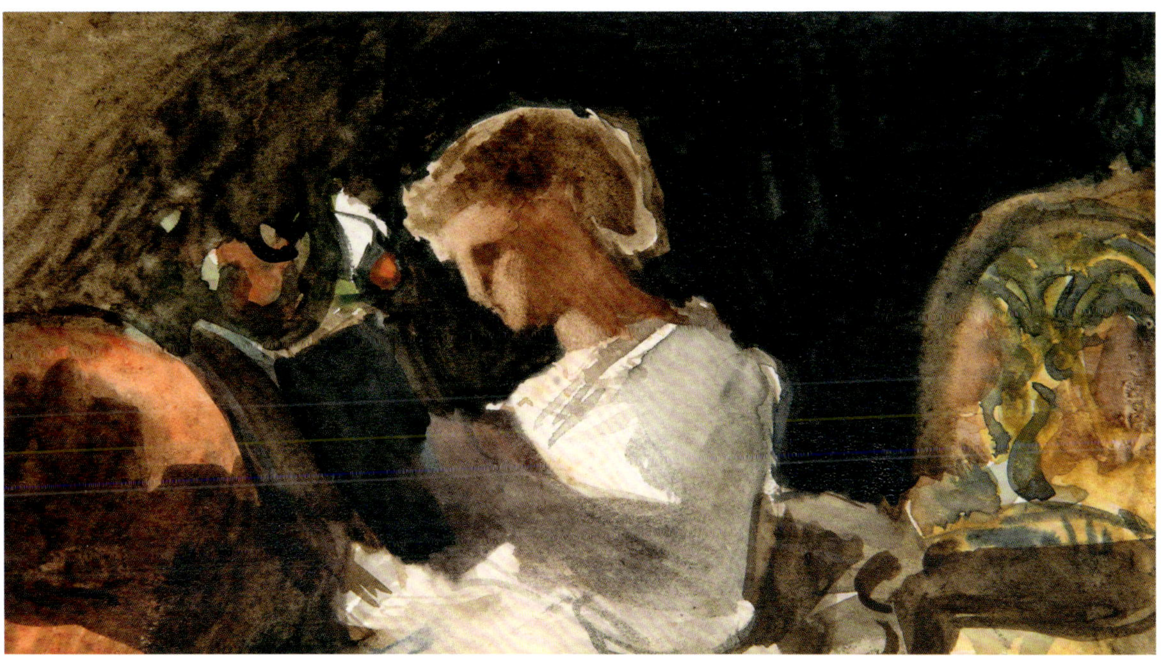

55 The Young Reader
Inscribed 'Miss Leslie' and 'Highcliffe June ...' on reverse
Watercolour
3 ½ x 6 inches

The Young Reader

The reverse of the present watercolour is inscribed 'Miss Leslie' and 'Highcliffe June'. This suggests that the young reader is Christiana Leslie, the fiancée, and later the wife, of John Beresford, Louisa Anne's brother-in-law. On the death of Louisa Anne's husband in 1859, John became the 4th Marquess of Waterford. If the sitter is Christiana Leslie, then the work can be dated to a visit to Highcliffe Castle, the Beresford family seat, in June 1842, a few months before her marriage on 20 February 1843.

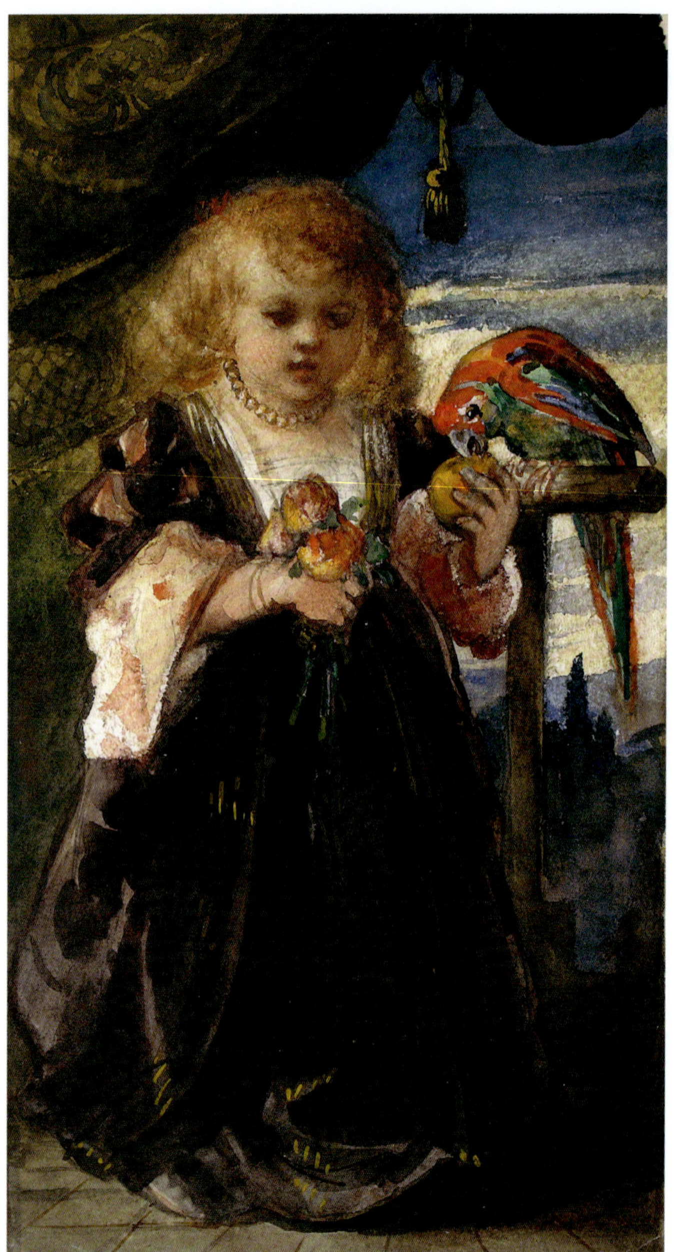

56 **Fruit for the Parrot**
Watercolour
13 x 6 ¾ inches

57 **Red Dress and Lilies**
Watercolour with bodycolour
7 ¼ x 3 ¾ inches

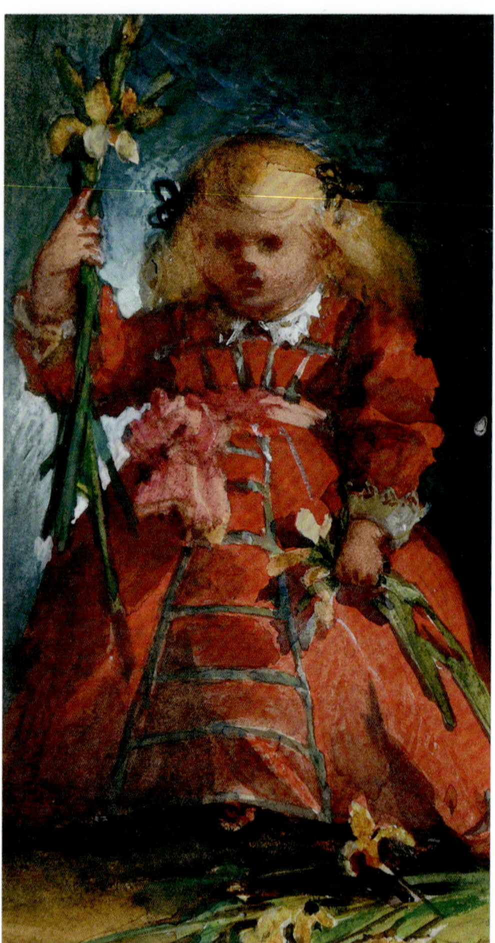

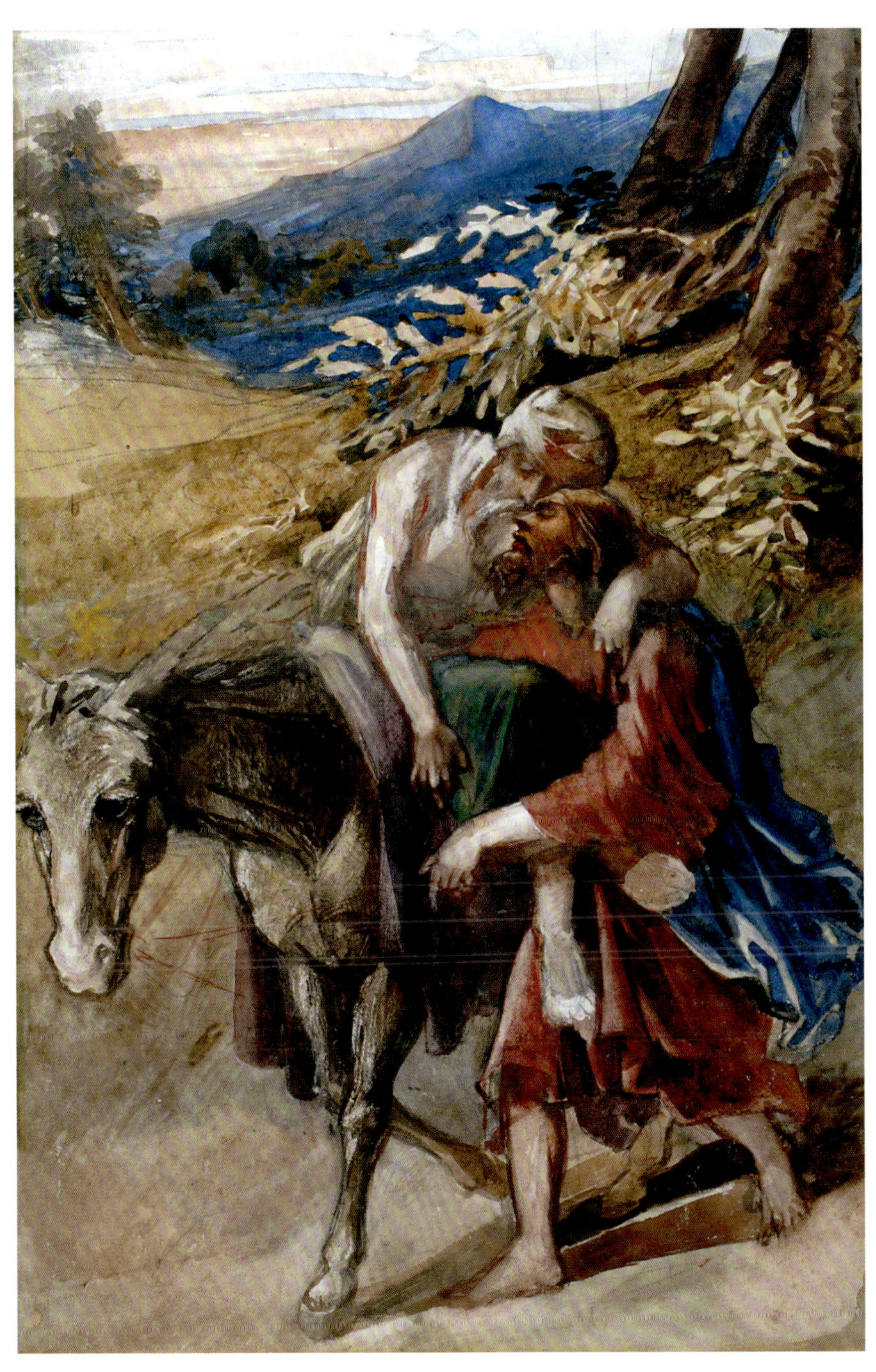

58 The Good Samaritan
Watercolour
17 ¼ x 11 ½ inches

CHARLES GREEN

Charles Green, RI (1840-1898)

Charles Green was a painter and illustrator of genre and historical subjects. He is now best remembered for images illustrating, or inspired by, the work of Charles Dickens.

For a biography of Charles Green, please refer to *Chris Beetles Summer Show*, 2020, page 114.

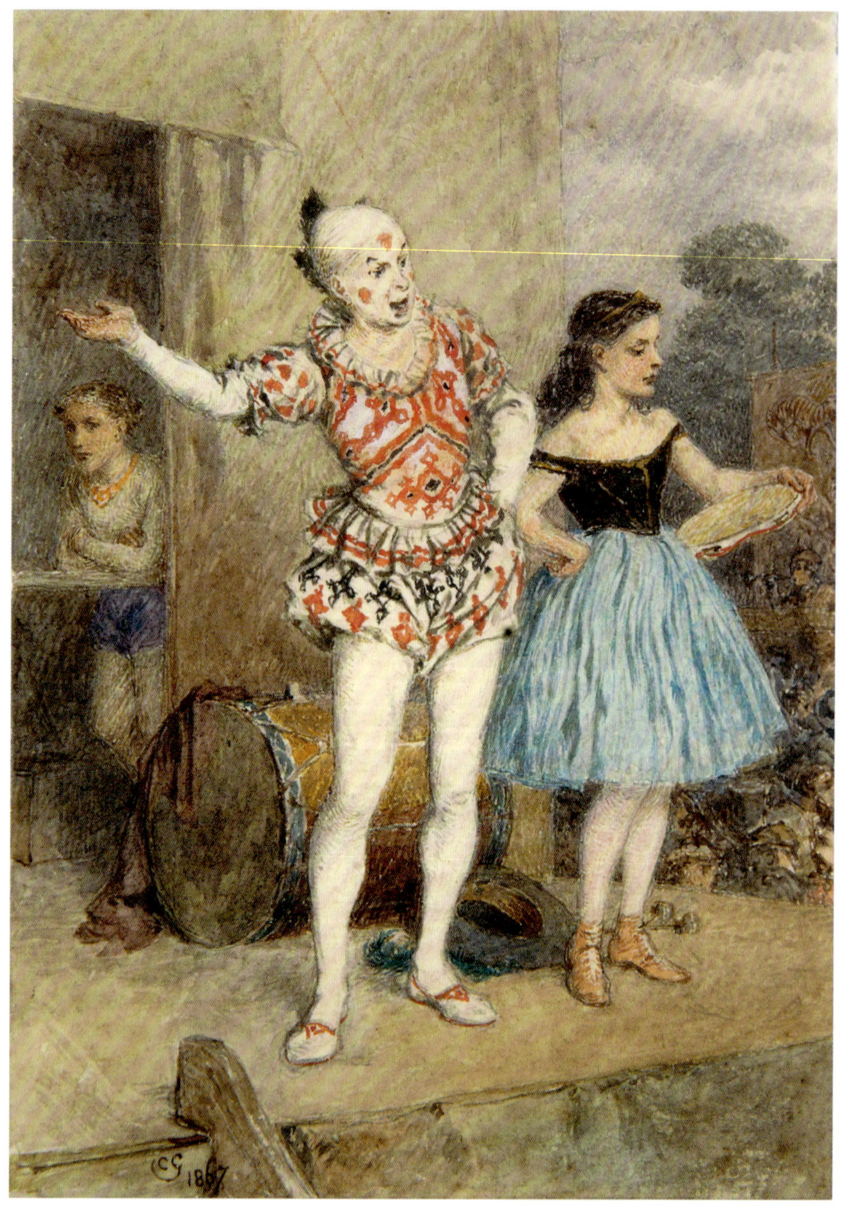

59 **Performing at the Fair**
Signed with monogram and dated 1867
Watercolour with bodycolour
6 x 4 ½ inches

Provincial Players

Charles Green was well known for his images of performers, including clowns at work in both theatres and circuses. The most famous of these is probably the watercolour generally known as *Her First Bouquet: The Lane Family with the Clown George Lupino at the Britannia Theatre, Hoxton* (1868, Private Collection), the Britannia Theatre in the East End of London being renowned for its spectacular pantomimes and melodramas. However, as Professor Jim Davis has pointed out, 'if this is indeed a representation of the Britannia Theatre, then it most likely is Jean Louis who is depicted here' as he was 'The Clown in both the 1867-68 and 1868-9 pantomime' ('First Bouquets, Big Heads and Obstinate Horses: Illustrating the Victorian Pantomime', *Popular Entertainment Studies*, vol 3, issue 2, 2012, page 5).

Though the present watercolours were produced by Green in 1867, just a year before *My First Bouquet*, the clowns shown in them are of a very different ilk from Jean Louis (active 1853-75). They are provincial, and possibly travelling, players, who advertise their talents on an external platform at a fair, in the hope of attracting an audience to a more substantial performance inside their temporary theatre. The engagement between the figures suggests close familiarity and even familial relationships, such as the father initiating his son into his own profession.

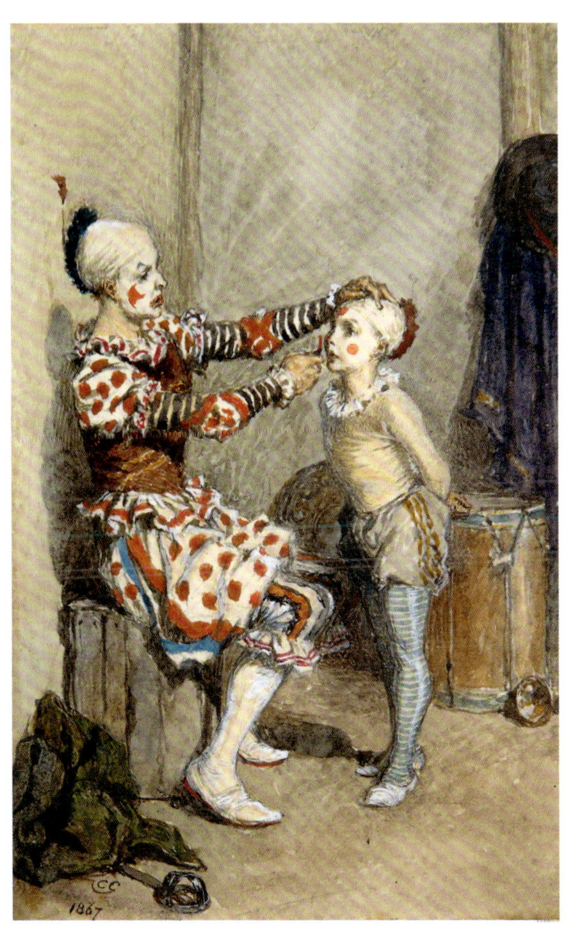

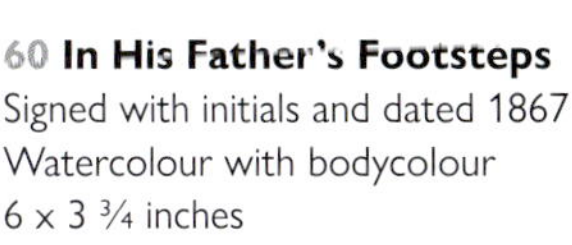

60 In His Father's Footsteps
Signed with initials and dated 1867
Watercolour with bodycolour
6 x 3 ¾ inches

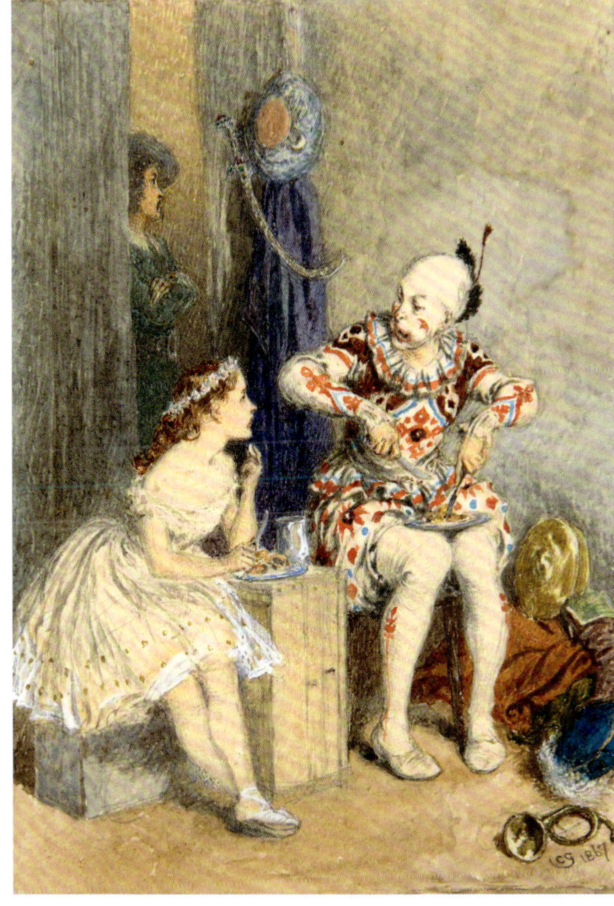

61 Backstage
Signed with monogram and dated 1867
Watercolour with bodycolour
6 x 4 ½ inches

SPY

Sir Leslie Ward, RP (1851-1922), known as 'Spy'

For almost forty years, the caricaturist, Leslie Ward, was synonymous with the society paper, *Vanity Fair*. His 'character portraits' were invariably well observed and witty, but rarely cruel.

For a biography of Spy, please refer to page 107.

His work is represented in the collections of the National Portrait Gallery.

Further reading:

Peter Mellini, 'Ward, Sir Leslie [pseud. Spy] (1851-1922)', H C G Matthew and Brian Harrison (eds), *Oxford Dictionary of National Biography*, Oxford University Press, 2004, vol 57, pages 325-326

Mr Walter Herries Pollock

The second son of Sir William Frederick Pollock, Walter Herries Pollock (1850-1926) was best known as the editor of the London weekly newspaper, the *Saturday Review*, from 1884 to 1894. On leaving the position, he moved to Chawton to devote himself to his writing and, in 1899, produced a major study of Jane Austen, a previous resident of that Hampshire village. His wide-ranging output included essays, novels, plays and poems, as well as translations from French, and he numbered Egerton Castle and Rudyard Kipling among the members of his wide literary circle.

In addition, Pollock participated in the first revival of historical fencing in Britain, and gained repute as the finest amateur fencer in the country. In 1897, he contributed to *Fencing, Boxing and Wrestling* for the Badminton Library of Sports and Pastimes published by Longmans, Green & Company.

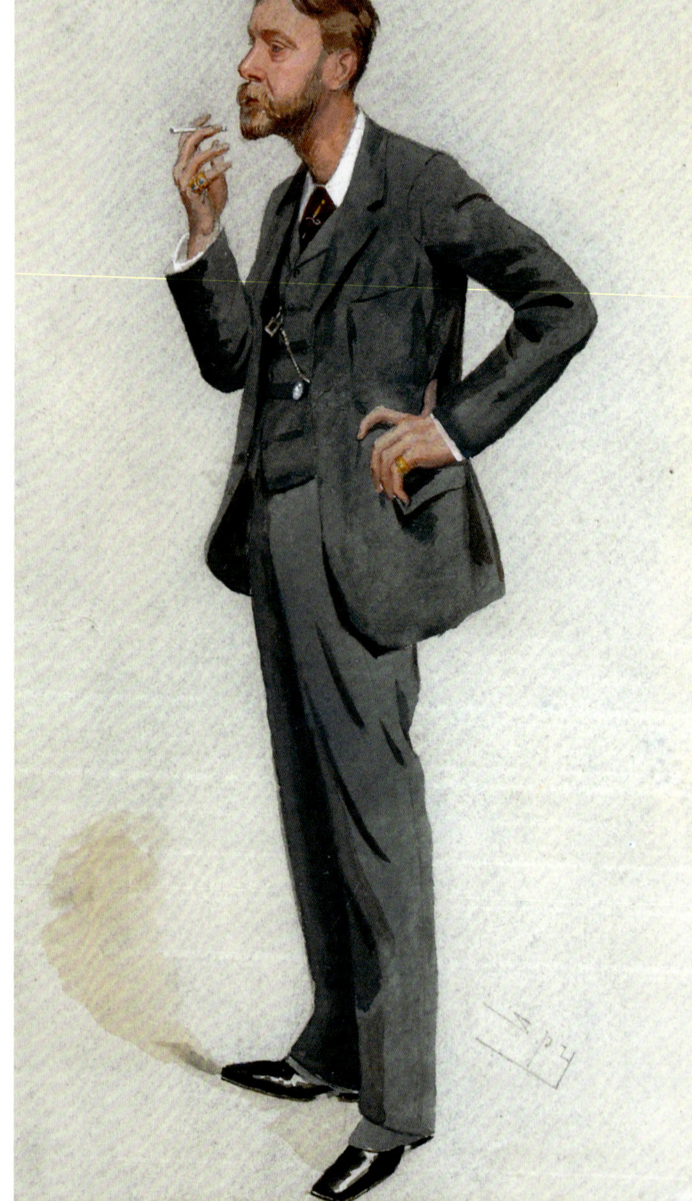

62 **Mr Walter Herries Pollock**
Signed
Watercolour with bodycolour and pencil on tinted paper
12 ¾ x 7 ¾ inches
Illustrated: *Vanity Fair*, 31 December 1892, Men of the Day No 553, 'The Saturday Review'
Exhibited: 'The Long Nineteenth Century: Treasures and Pleasures', Chris Beetles Gallery, March-April 2014, No 141

HM George, King of Greece

Spy's caricature of King George is a reminder of British, and generally international, involvement in the governance of Greece following its independence from the Ottoman Empire in 1830. The 'Great Powers' – Britain, France and Russia – recognised the country's autonomy as early as 1828 and, at the London Conference in 1832, established a monarchy in Greece under the Bavarian prince, Otto. He reigned for 30 years, but became increasingly unpopular with native Greek politicians, and was deposed in 1862.

As a replacement for Otto, the Great Powers suggested the Danish prince, William (1845-1913), the seventeen-year-old second son of Prince Christian of Schleswig-Holstein-Sonderburg-Glücksburg. He was elected the King of the Hellenes by the Greek National Assembly in 1863, and took the regnal name of *George*. At his urging, Greece adopted a more democratic constitution, and greatly developed its parliamentary process, though the country struggled economically until late in the century.

In 1863, the year that George became King of Greece, his sister, Alexandria, married (Albert) Edward, the Prince of Wales and future Edward VII. In 1868-69, the Prince and Princess of Wales undertook a six-month international tour that included visits to George in Greece. Then, in 1875, Edward again visited George, while travelling *en route* to India on HMS Serapis. These personal bonds further strengthened relations between Britain and Greece, and helped maintain George's reputation among the British people, as exemplified by Spy's gentle caricature, which was published in 1876.

A recurrent issue in Greek politics through the nineteenth century was the desire to unify all areas that had been historically inhabited by the ethnically Greek people. So, in 1897, the Greek population of Crete rose up against its Ottoman rulers, and the Greek Prime Minister, Theodoros Diligiannis, mobilised troops, which invaded Crete and crossed the Macedonian border into the Ottoman Empire. When Greece lost the war that followed, King George considered abdicating. However, when he survived an assassination attempt in 1898, his subjects began to hold him in greater esteem. Then the death of Queen Victoria in 1901 made him the second-longest-reigning monarch in Europe.

George and his family lost some power during the opening decade of the twentieth century, as the politician, Eleftherios Venizelos, collaborated with a military league to force a revision of the constitution. Nevertheless, following the election of Venizelos as Prime Minister, in 1910, he and King George united to strengthen Greece's military capability. So, when, in 1912, the Kingdom of Montenegro declared war against the Ottoman Empire, the Greek army was ready to offer support, so instigating what became known as the First Balkan War. Crown Prince Constantine led the Greek forces, which won victory after victory. In November 1912, King George joined Constantine in Thessaloniki, and together they rode through the streets in triumph. George planned to abdicate in favour of his son immediately after the celebration of his Golden Jubilee in October 1913. However, while walking in Thessaloniki on 18 March 1913, he was assassinated by the anarchist, Alexandros Schinas. Constantine succeeded to the throne.

63 **HM George, King of Greece**
Signed
Watercolour and bodycolour with pen and ink on tinted paper
12 x 7 ¼ inches
Illustrated: *Vanity Fair*, 21 October 1876, Sovereigns No 12

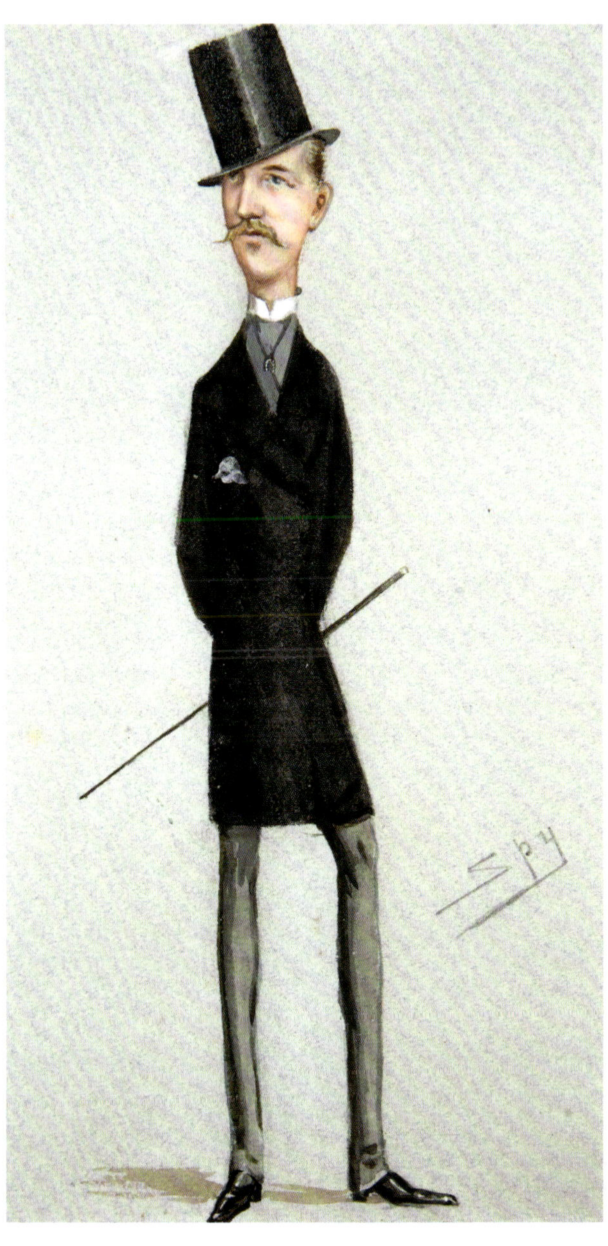

64 Joseph Armitage Robinson
Dean of Westminster
Signed
Watercolour with bodycolour and pencil
on tinted paper laid on board
14 ½ x 10 ½ inches
Illustrated: *Vanity Fair*, 14 December 1905,
Men of the Day No 993, 'An Erudite Dean'

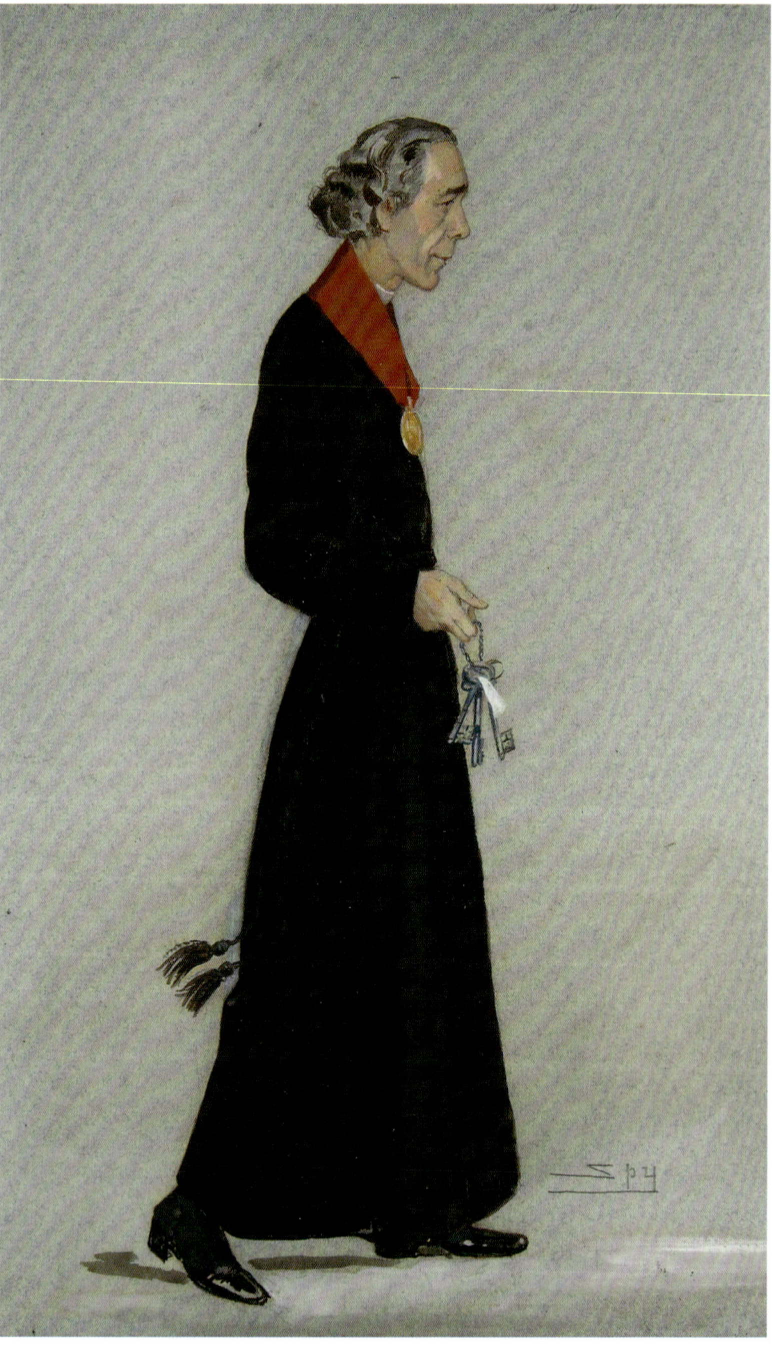

Joseph Armitage Robinson, Dean of Westminster

Joseph Armitage Robinson (1858-1933) was one of the leading Anglican clerics and theological scholars of the late nineteenth and early twentieth centuries. He was educated at Cambridge, and, as a fellow of Christ's College, taught and researched, while also taking up various positions, including that of domestic chaplain to J B Lightfoot, the Bishop of Durham and probably the leading European scholar of patristics (1883-84). His positions at Cambridge included Dean of Christ's College (1884-90) and Norrisian Professor of Divinity (1893-99). In 1891, he became editor of the first of a new series of Cambridge 'Texts and Studies', and was a key contributor to later numbers. As early as 1894, his impact on international scholarship was marked by honorary degrees from Göttingen and Halle universities.

In 1899, Robinson moved to London to become Rector of St Margaret's Westminster (1899-1900) and then Dean of Westminster (1902-11), the role in which Spy here presents him. The cathedral chapter sometimes considered his actions autocratic, and so it sought, unsuccessfully, to limit his powers. While at Westminster, he continued to publish, and distinguished himself as both a theologian and a historian. Especially important was his landmark commentary of St Paul's Epistle to the Ephesians (1908).

In 1911, Robinson became Dean of Wells, in Somerset (which was already familiar to him as he had held the prebend of Compton Bishop during the late 1890s). Wells Cathedral stimulated his antiquarian interests, and the county of Somerset inspired further publications. During the 1920s, he became an active participant in the five Malines Conversations, which explored the possibilities of reunion between the Roman Catholic Church and the Church of England.

Mr H J Cockayne-Cust, MP
Editor of 'The Pall Mall Gazette'

Harry Cockayne-Cust (1861-1917) entered Parliament in 1890 as the Unionist MP for Stamford, Lincolnshire, and a decade later served as the MP for Bermondsey. In 1892, he became editor of the *Pall Mall Gazette*, on the invitation of its owner, William Waldorf Astor, and transformed it into the best evening newspaper of the age by employing such significant writers as Rudyard Kipling and H G Wells. However, he annoyed Astor by disagreeing with him over politics and by rejecting his literary submissions; as a result, he was dismissed in 1896. His own literary output included the once popular poem, 'Non nobis domine'.

Handsome and witty, Cockyane-Cust developed a reputation as a womaniser. His mistresses included the Duchess of Rutland, who, in 1892, gave birth to their daughter, Lady Diana Manners – better known as the socialite and philanthropist, Lady Diana Cooper. It was as the result of a suspected pregnancy that, in 1893, he married 'Nina' Welby-Gregory, an artist and translator. They never had any children.

Following the outbreak of the First World War, Cockayne-Cust founded the Central Committee for National Patriotic Organizations, and became active in propaganda on behalf of the British government. However, in 1917, he died of a heart attack at his home at Hyde Park Gate, London. He was heir apparent to the barony of Brownlow, the Cust baronetcy and their estates.

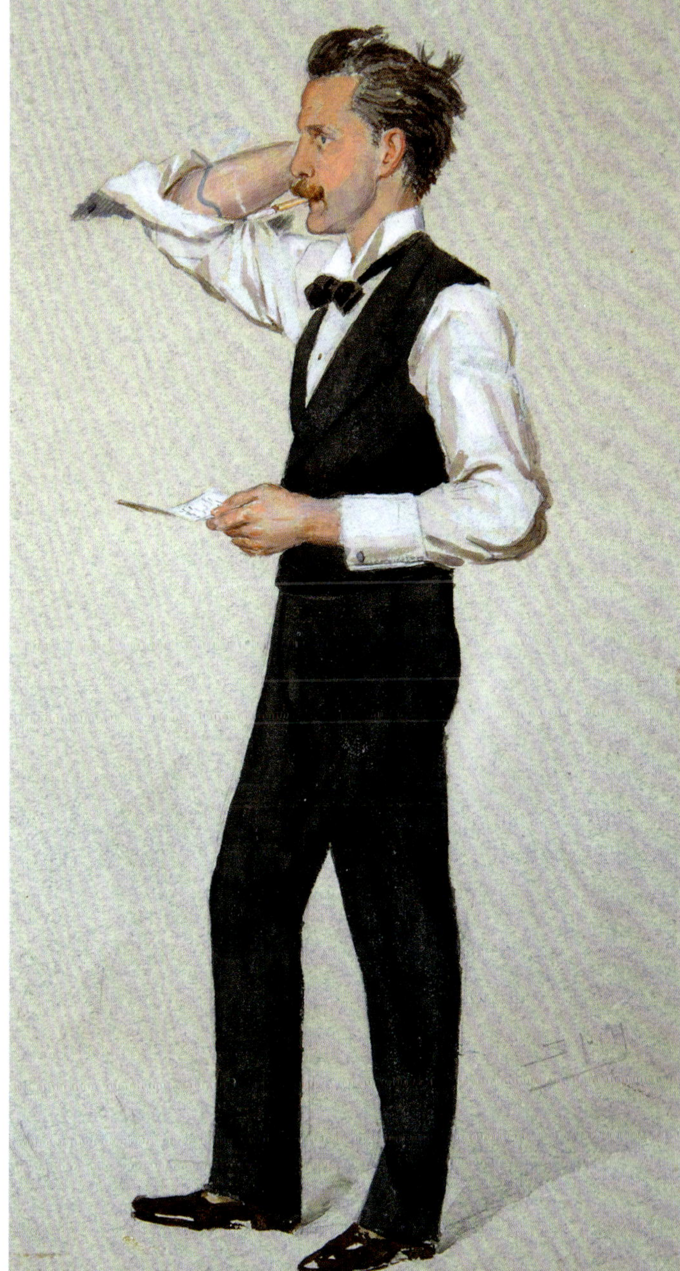

65 **Mr H J Cockayne-Cust, MP**
Editor of 'The Pall Mall Gazette'
Signed
Watercolour and bodycolour on board
17 ¾ x 13 ¾ inches
Illustrated: *Vanity Fair*, 15 February 1894,
Statesmen No 632, 'Pall Mall Gazette'

WILLIAM HENRY MARGETSON

William Henry Margetson, RI RMS ROI (1861-1940)

Best known as a figurative artist, William Henry Margetson was equally successful as a painter and an illustrator. He became popular as an illustrator of adventure stories and fairy tales in the 1890s, and then gained a reputation as a painter of beautiful young women, sitting or standing in contemplation, at home or in the garden.

For a biography of William Henry Margetson, please refer to page 108.

Spring Love

Though this oil on canvas is – somewhat puzzlingly – dated 1873, when William Henry Margetson would have been only 12 years of age, it is likely to have been painted at the height of the artist's fame, during the first two decades of the twentieth century. By that time, he had become well known for his paintings of beautiful young women, sitting or standing in meditative isolation. It is likely that he used his daughters as models, and his own houses in Blewbury, then in Berkshire, for many of the settings. While some of the subjects are resolutely modern, with suggestions of the New Woman or even the Flapper, others evoke the Georgian or Regency period. So, the present work might represent a scene from a novel by Jane Austen, and could be compared to the work of Hugh Thomson and the Brothers Brock, Margeston's contemporaries in the field of illustration. However, though Margetson was himself a highly able narrative illustrator, he was more interested – in his paintings – in creating a mood, through careful arrangements, delicate harmonies of colour and subtle effects of light.

66 **Spring Love** (opposite)
Twice signed and
incorrectly dated 1873
Oil on canvas
40 x 24 inches

Details of **66**

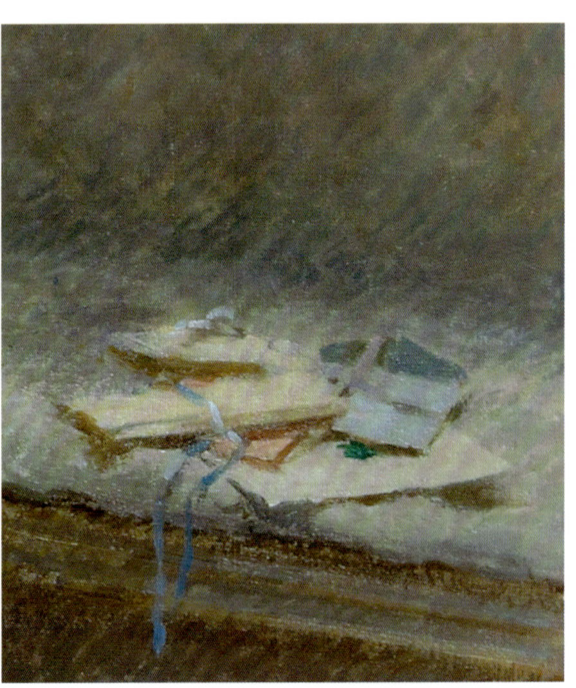

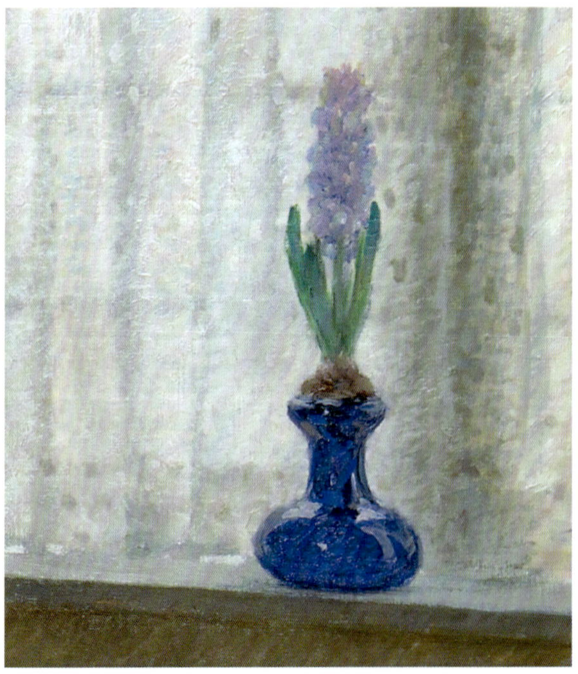

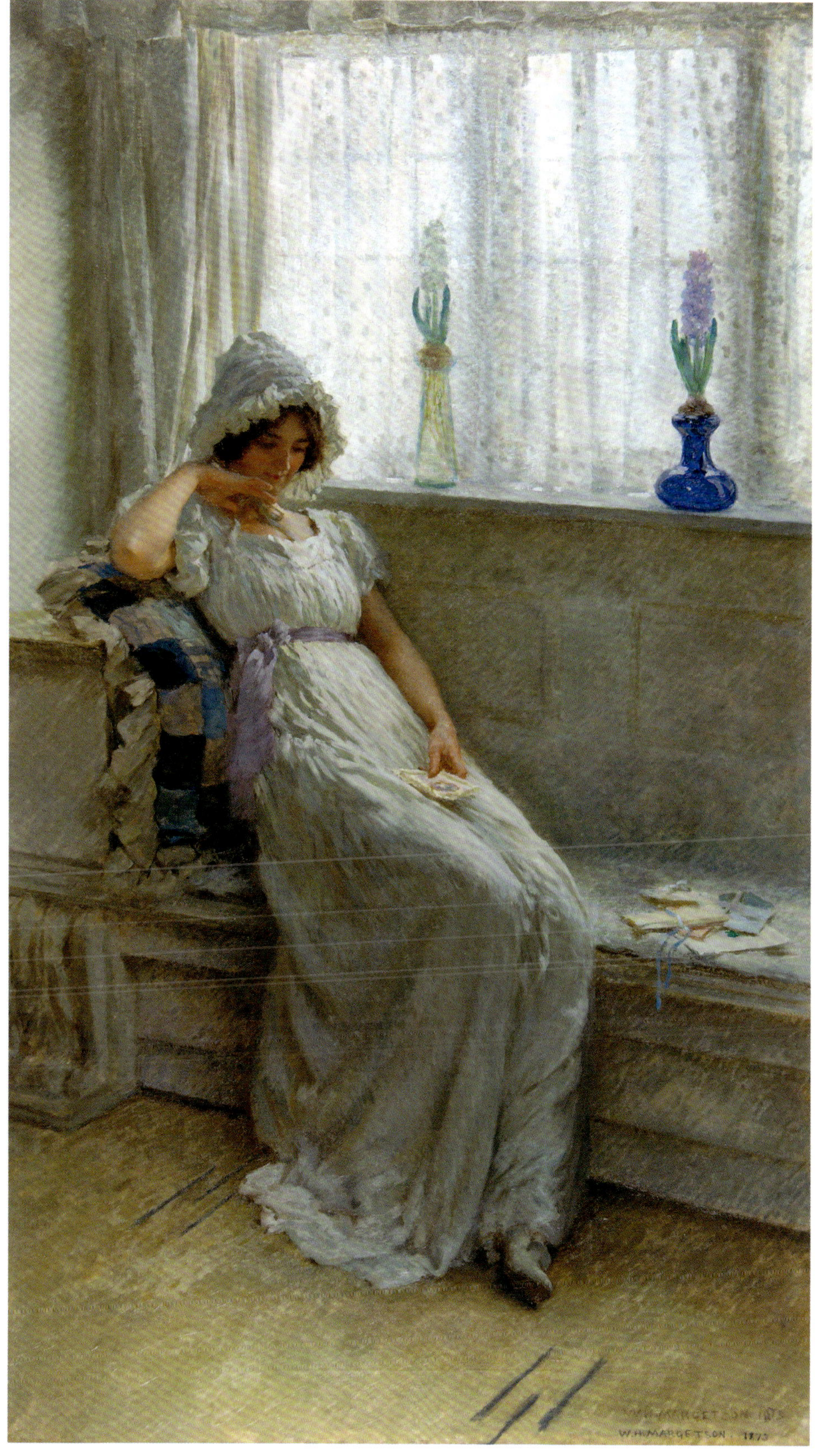

GEORGE COLE

George Cole, VPSBA (1810-1883)

Essaying a number of genres early in his career, and most notably animal portraiture, George Cole concentrated on landscape painting from about 1850. His most characteristic works show the rivers, coasts and – especially – the downs of Southern England, enlivened by farm workers and their livestock, and enhanced by atmospheric effects. He and his son, George Vicat Cole, strongly influenced each other, and rivalled each other in popularity.

For a biography of George Cole, please refer to page 109.

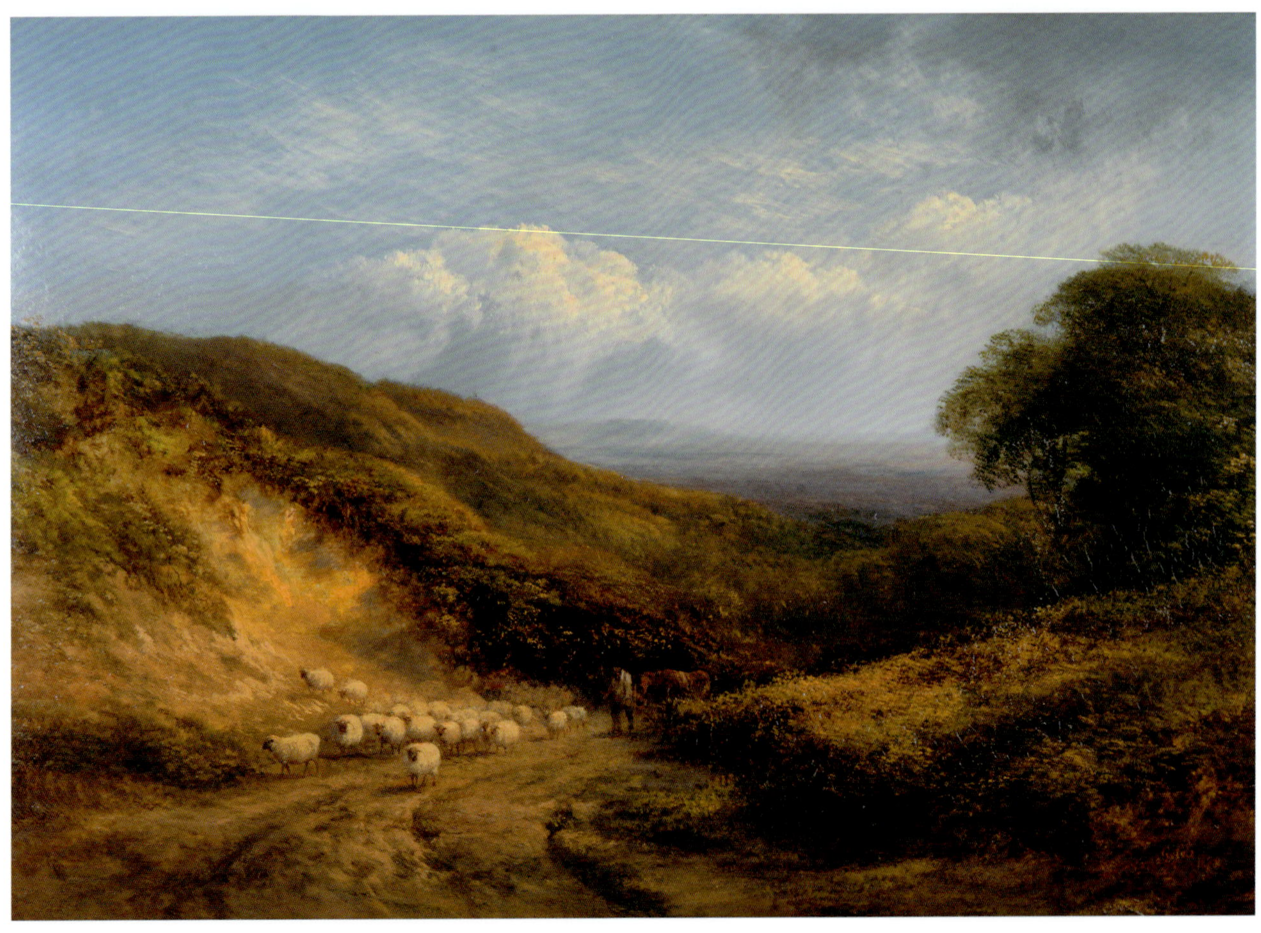

67 **Sunset in Surrey**
Signed and dated 1878
Oil on board
17 x 24 inches

This work is similar to *Landscape with Sheep* (1876), in the collections of Brighton and Hove Museums and Art Galleries.

EDMUND GEORGE WARREN

Edmund George Warren, RI ROI (1834-1909)

Edmund George Warren was perhaps the best known of all Victorian watercolourists to specialise in arboreal landscapes and woodland scenes. He painted minutely detailed views of shady glades and the forest floor, and also delighted in describing the effects of sunlight breaking through the canopy of leaves. He also enjoyed painting harvest scenes in the company of George Vicat Cole.

For a biography of Edmund George Warren, please refer to page 110.

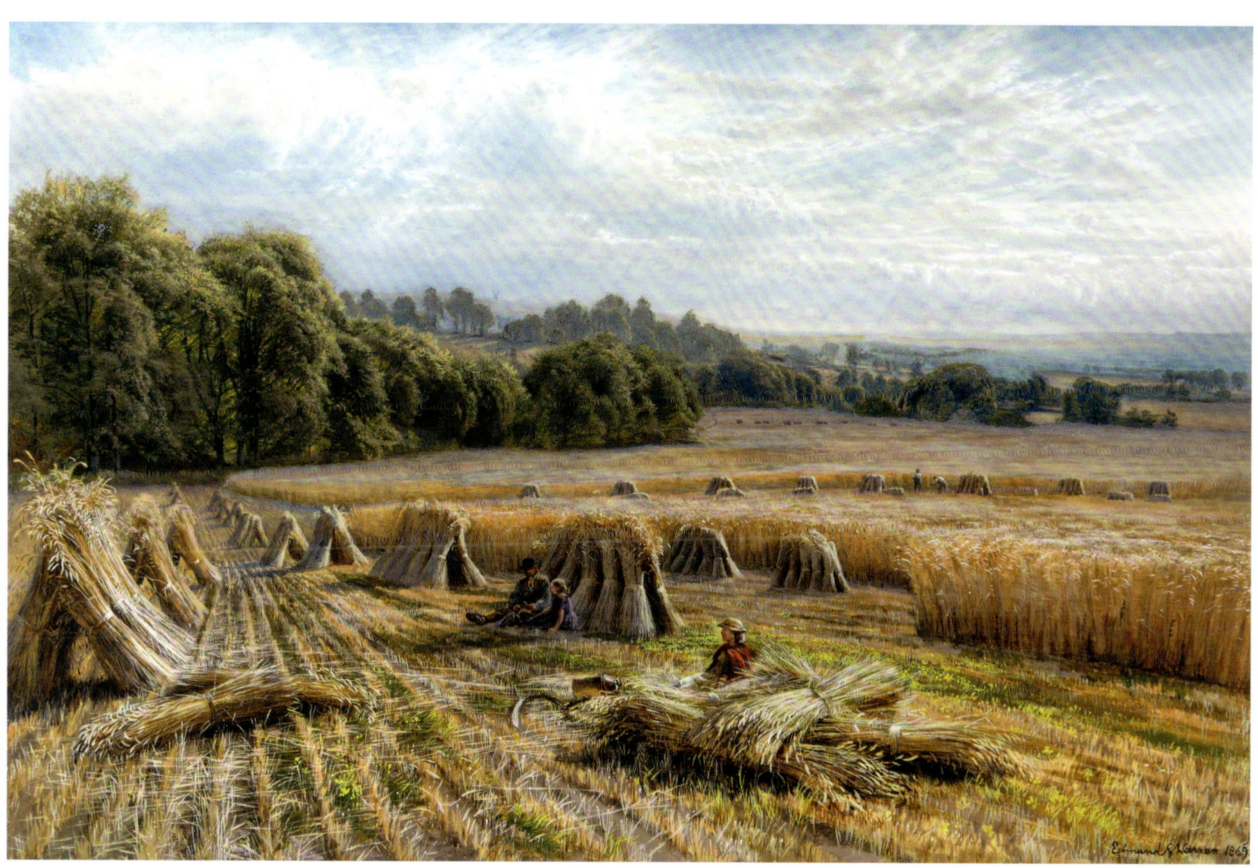

68 **High Summer Harvest**
Signed and dated 1869
Watercolour and bodycolour
20 x 29 ½ inches

BIRKET FOSTER

Myles Birket Foster, RWS (1825-1899)

Myles Birket Foster was one of the most popular artists of the Victorian period, achieving success first as an illustrator and then as an exhibition watercolourist. In both disciplines, he conveyed a gentle naturalism through mastery of technique.

For a biography of Birket Foster, please refer to *Chris Beetles Summer Show*, 2017, page 65.

69 **Sheep Watering at Sunset**
Signed with monogram
Watercolour with bodycolour
6 x 9 inches

70 **A Surrey Lane** (opposite)
Signed with monogram
Inscribed with title on reverse
Watercolour with bodycolour
10 x 7 inches

A Surrey Lane (opposite)

'A Surrey Lane' is a description that would suit many of the scenes of Birket Foster, and the artist used it as the title of at least three works, including the present one.

In 1869, a work by Foster entitled *A Surrey Lane* was exhibited at the Royal Academy of Arts, as No 829. It was purchased by the famous London art dealer, Ernest Gambart, and was one of the items of his stock that was sold at Christie's on his retirement in 1871. It was purchased by a Mr Cubitt for 250 guineas.

By 1872, a portrait-format work by Foster entitled *A Surrey Lane* was published as a chromolithograph by George Rowney & Co, of 52 Rathbone Place and 29 Oxford Street, London, and priced at 12 shillings. The chromolithograph was exhibited as No 3385 in the 'London International Exhibition of 1873', in the section shown at the Royal Albert Hall, Kensington.

It is very likely that the work exhibited at the RA in 1869 is that which was reproduced as a chromolithograph, and that it also equates to the present watercolour.

Foster produced two further works entitled *A Surrey Lane* in 1889 and 1891, and exhibited the second at the Royal Society of Painters in Water-Colours in 1891, as No 215.

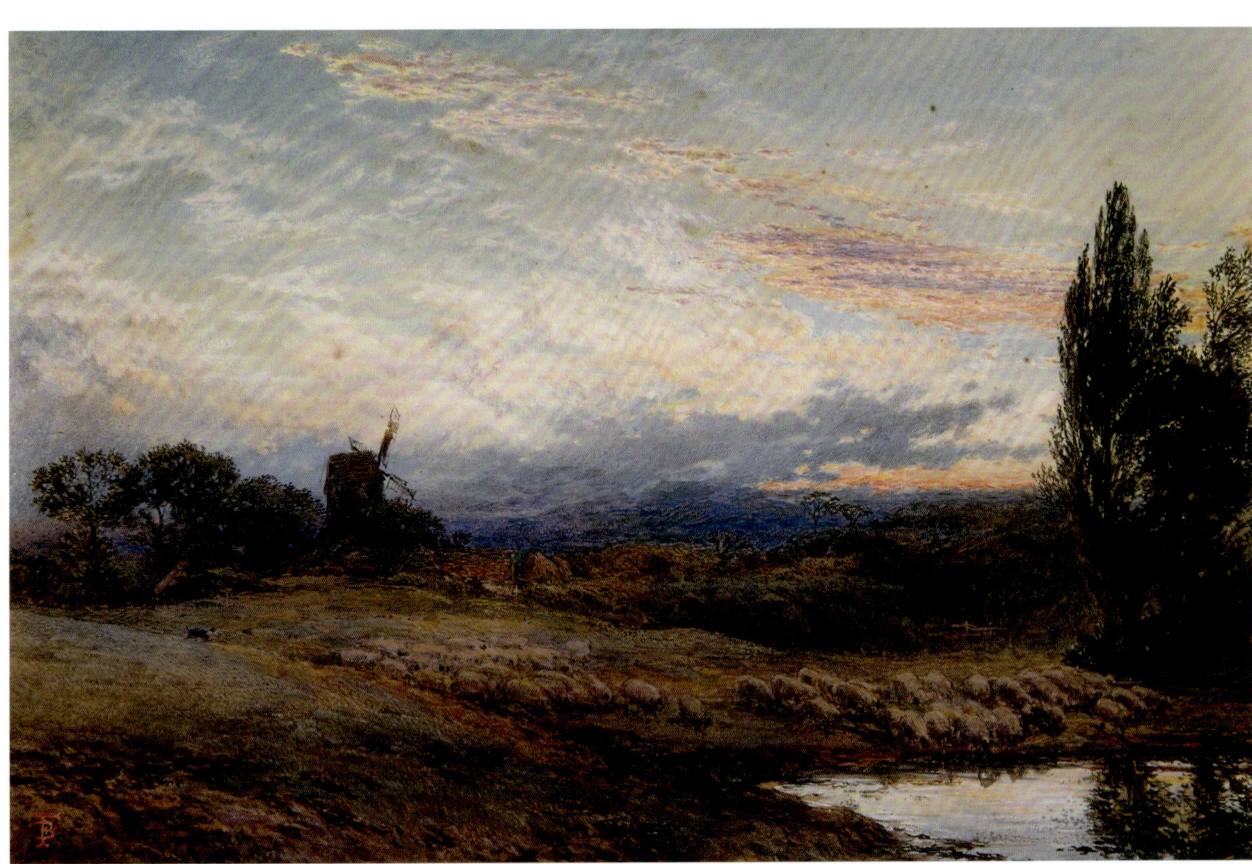

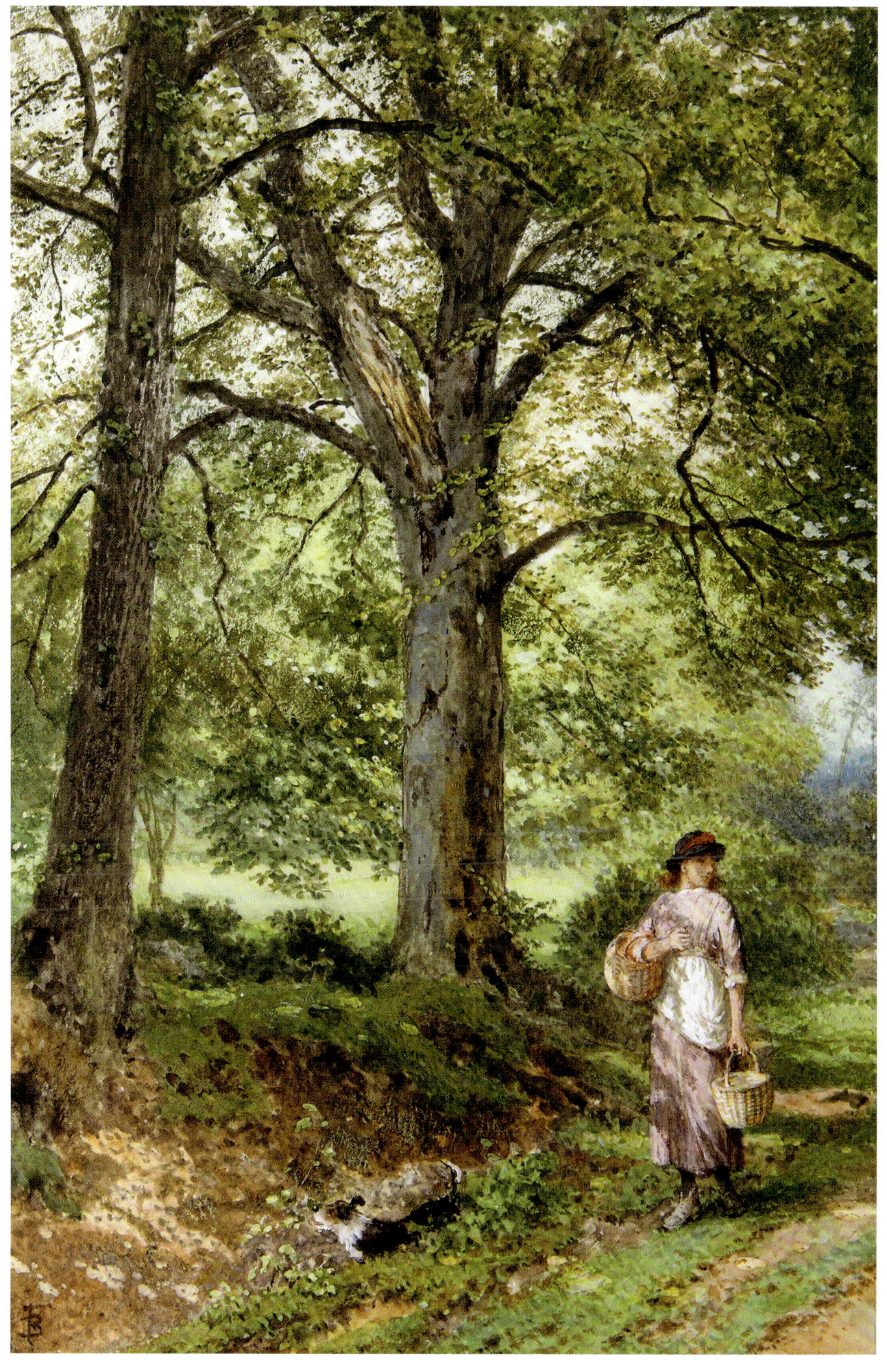

ALFRED PARSONS

Alfred William Parsons, RA PRWS RSW RI HRMS ROI NEAC (1847-1920)

Alfred Parsons became an expert in various branches of the art of the garden. He used watercolour to produce fresh portraits of gardens and accurate illustrations of botanical specimens. Having collaborated on books with the famous gardener, William Robinson, he went on to become a designer of gardens in Britain and the United States. His transatlantic connections were strengthened through his membership of the Anglo-American 'Broadway Group' of artists and writers that included Henry James and John Singer Sargent. He further broadened his horizons and deepened his knowledge through trips to Japan in the period 1892-94.

For a biography of Alfred Parsons, please refer to *Chris Beetles Summer Show*, 2016, pages 21-22.

The Tithe Barn, Bredon

Alfred Parsons became a member of the 'Broadway Group' of artists and writers in the 1880s, and then worked extensively in Bredon and other villages of southern Worcestershire. His illustrations to Arthur Quiller-Couch's *The Warwickshire Avon* (1892) include one of Bredon's 'huge tithe-barn … with a chamber over its doorway, doubtless for the accountant'. The building was commissioned by one of the Bishops of Worcester – probably Wulstan Bransford – in the mid fourteenth century. It was long thought to be a tithe barn, for the storage of crops taken as taxes for the church and clergy. However, it is now known to have been a manorial barn, for the storage of crops belonging to the Bishops of Worcester, who were the local landowners.

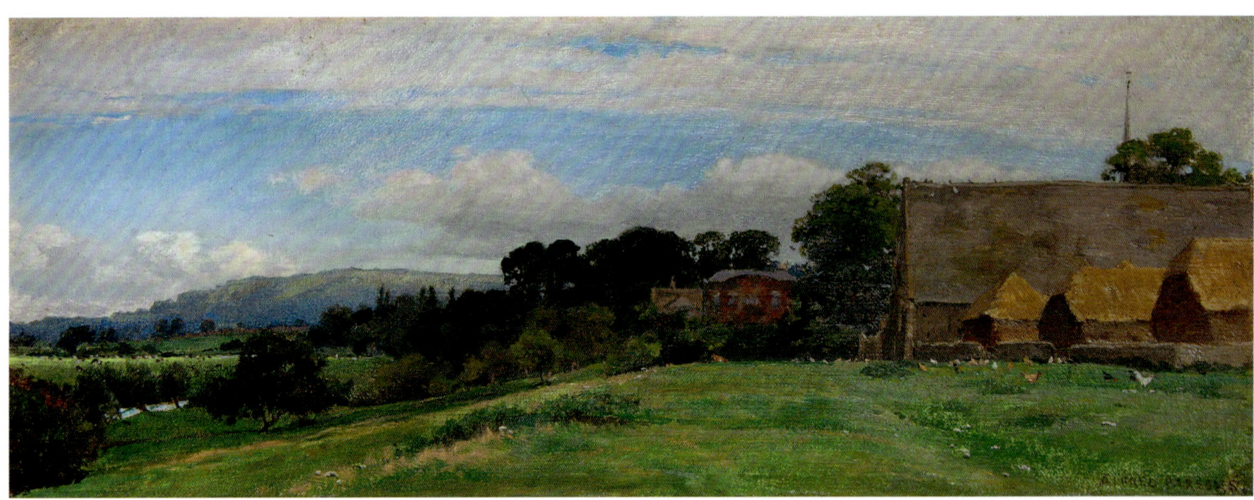

71 **The Tithe Barn, Bredon**
Signed
Inscribed with title on label on reverse
Oil on canvas laid on board
4 ¾ x 12 ½ inches
Exhibited: The Leicester Galleries, London, February 1909, No 19

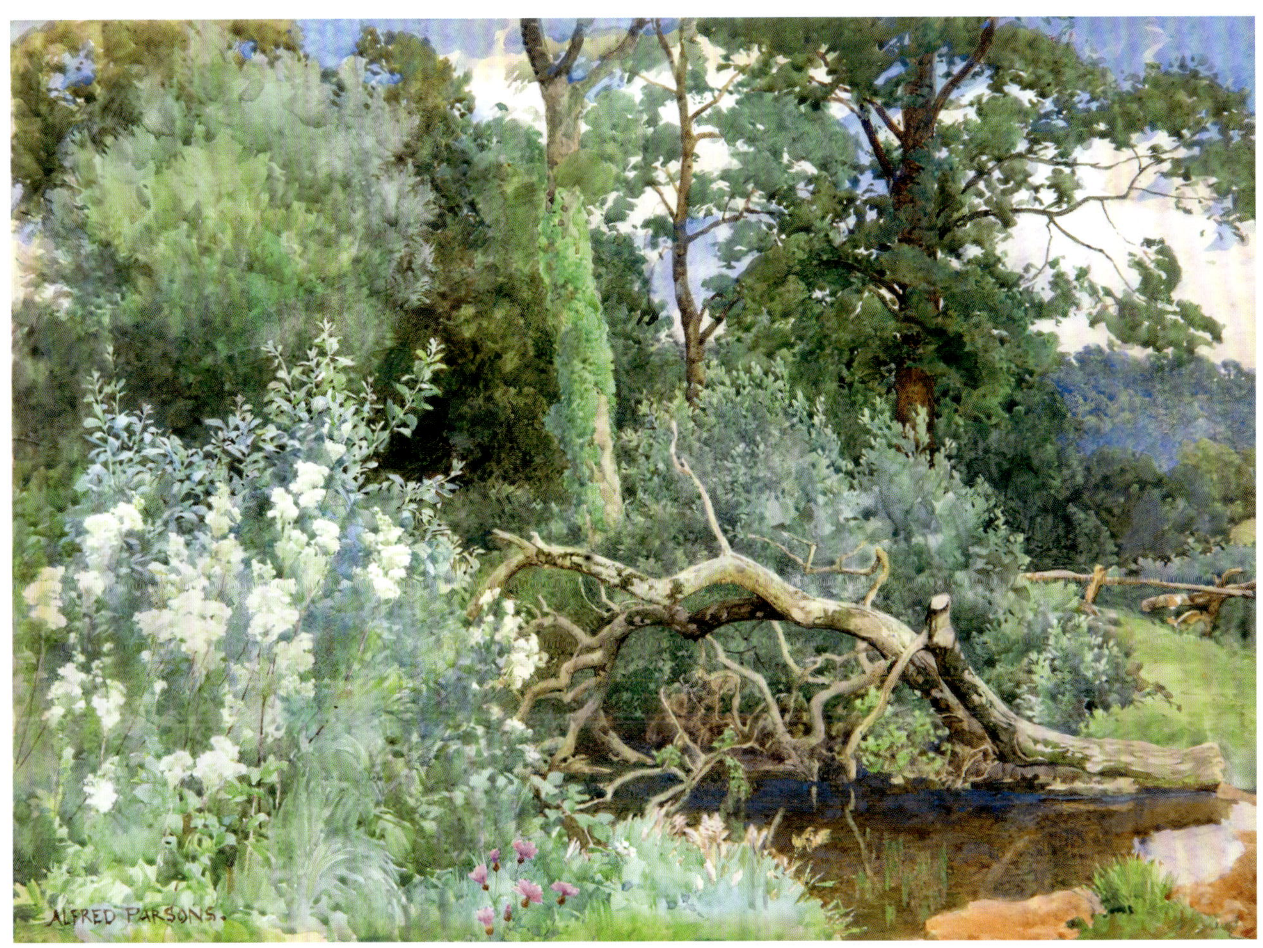

72 **On the Windrush**
Signed
Watercolour
10 ½ x 14 inches

HECTOR CAFFIERI

Hector Edward Philippe Caffieri, RBA RI ROI
(1847-1931)

Though he is best known for his sensitive, atmospheric studies of fisherfolk – in ports that include his adopted home of Boulogne – Hector Caffieri was a wide-ranging painter of landscapes and genre scenes in the tradition of French academic naturalism.

For a biography of Hector Caffieri, please refer to page 111.

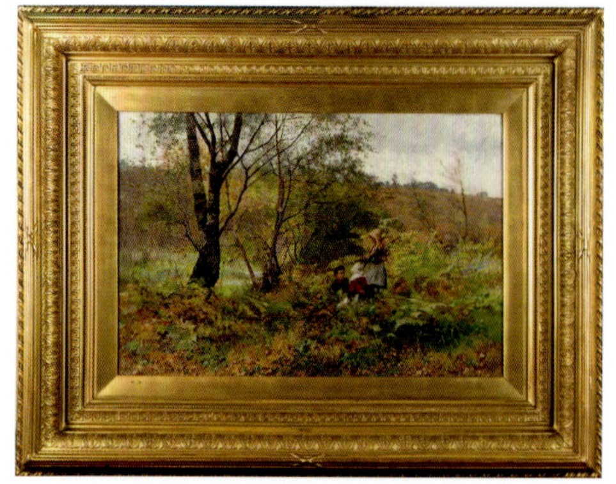

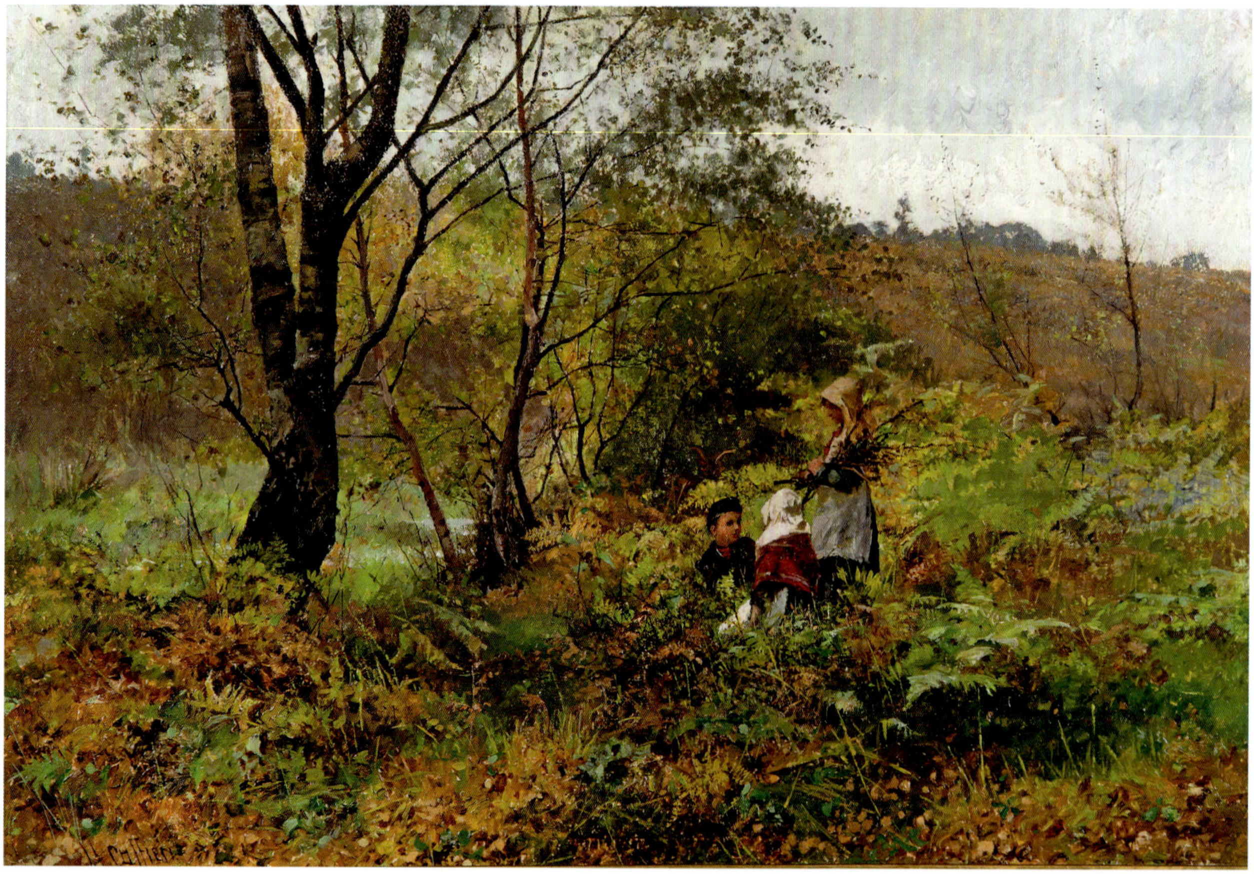

73 Children Gathering Firewood
Signed
Oil on canvas
16 x 24 inches
Exhibited: This is possibly the work exhibited at the Society of British Artists in 1879/80, as No 7, 'Getting Firewood'.

HELEN ALLINGHAM

Helen Mary Elizabeth Allingham (née Paterson), RWS (1848-1926)

One of the most successful women artists of the Victorian age, Helen Allingham produced archetypal watercolour images of cottages and gardens.

For a biography of Helen Allingham, please refer to *Chris Beetles Summer Show*, 2016, page 18.

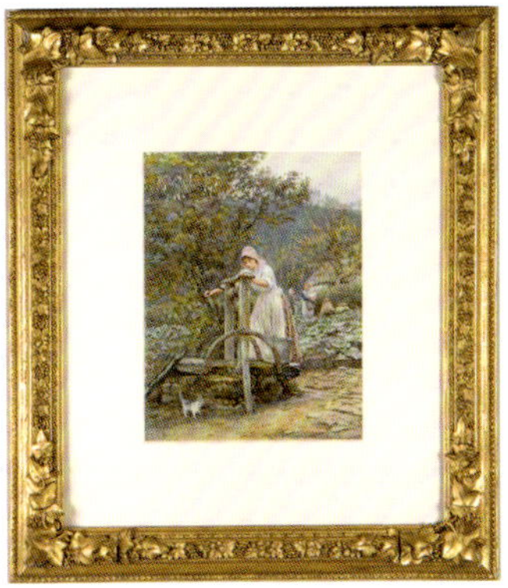

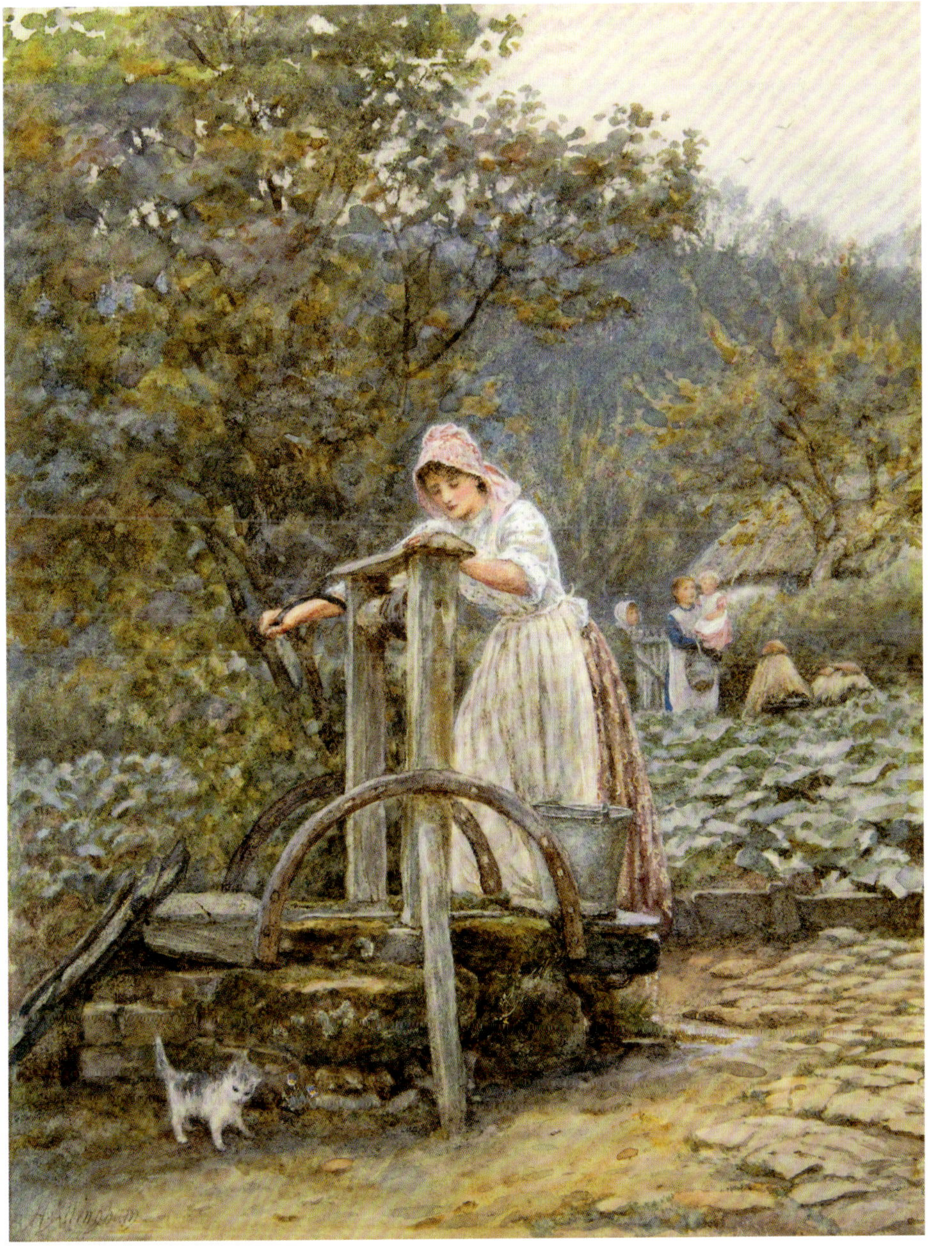

74 A Drink from the Well
Signed
Watercolour with bodycolour
8 ¾ x 6 ¾ inches

WALTER TYNDALE

Walter Frederick Roope Tyndale, RBC RI (1855-1943)

Walter Tyndale was one of the most popular and influential topographical watercolourists working at the turn of the century. He was also one of the first to benefit from the printing revolution of 1901 when his publishers, A & C Black, pioneered the use of three colour half-tone plates. The ensuing publishing boom led to a wealth of commissions for Tyndale for illustrated travel books, which took him from the Wessex countryside to Europe and the Far East.

For a biography of Walter Tyndale, please refer to page 112.

In Spring 2022, Chris Beetles Gallery is to mount a major retrospective of the work of Walter Tyndale, surveying the full range of his work as a topographical watercolourist, and including images of Egypt and Japan, as well as England and Continental Europe.
It will be accompanied by a substantial, fully illustrated catalogue, which will include details of his life, work and travels, including essays and notes, a chronology, a list of exhibitions, and extracts from his journals.

75 **A River Flowing through the Dunes**
Signed and dated 95
Watercolour
6 ½ x 9 ½ inches

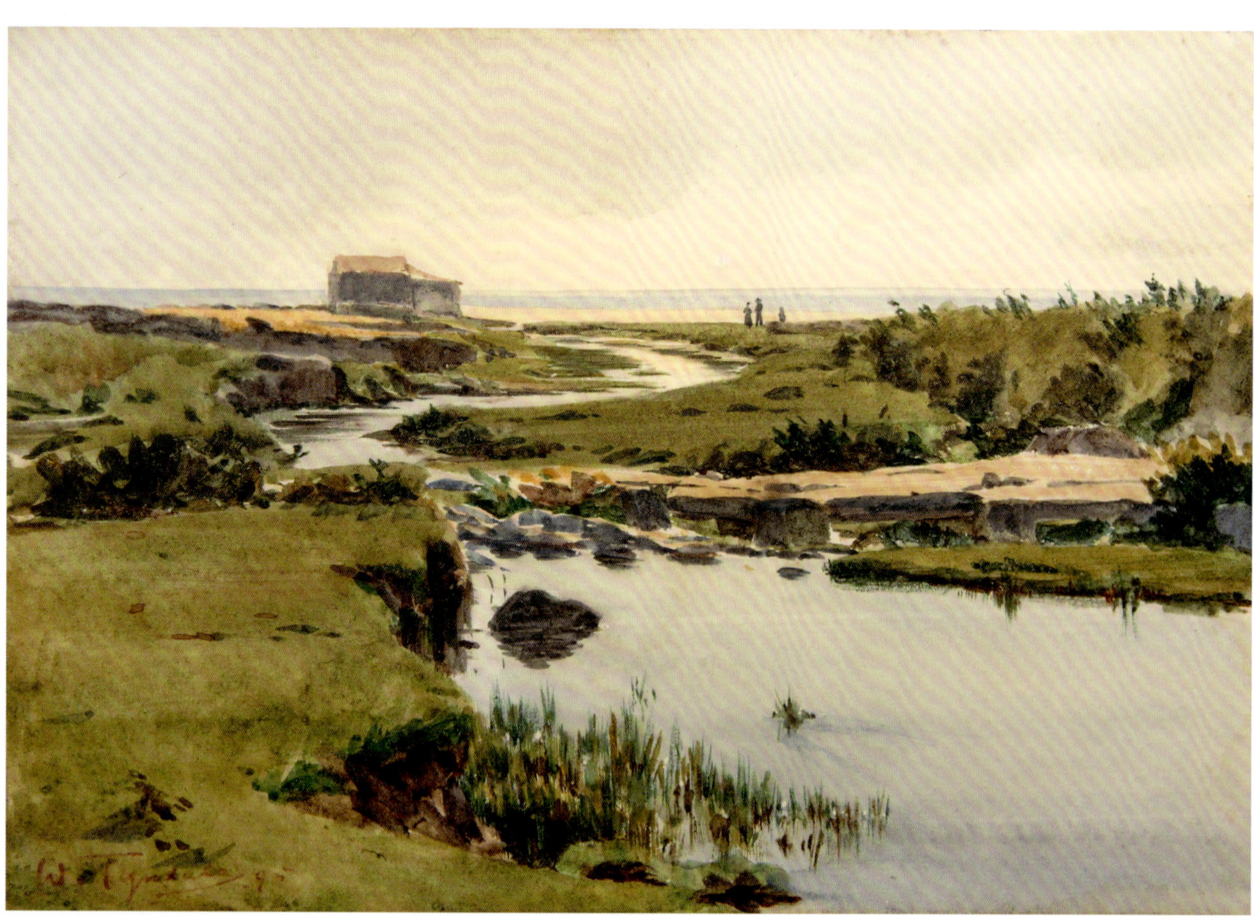

ERNEST ALBERT CHADWICK

Ernest Albert Chadwick, RBSA RCamA RI NSA
(1876-1956)

The landscape watercolours of E A Chadwick are detailed, realistic and carefully composed, but also gentle in both handling and mood. His best known works depict rural life in his native Warwickshire and surrounding counties, but he travelled widely by bicycle across England and Wales in order to discover suitable subjects.

For a biography of Ernest Albert Chadwick, please refer to page 113.

76 **Old Berry Hall, Solihull**
Signed
Signed and inscribed 'Old Berry Hall' on reverse
Signed and inscribed with title on back label on original backboard
Watercolour
6 x 7 ½ inches

Old Berry Hall, Solihull
Old Berry Hall, like many of the subjects painted by E A Chadwick, is one of the most picturesque places in Warwickshire. A moated, half-timbered house to the east of Solihull, it was built in the late fifteenth century, and extended during the sixteenth and seventeenth centuries, while in the ownership of the Waring family. Originally known as Berry Hall, it was renamed Berry Hall Farm by the Birmingham pen manufacturer, Joseph Gillott junior, when he acquired the estate in 1870, and built a large new house, to designs by J A Chatwin, which he wished to call Berry Hall. However, the two buildings were generally known to locals as New and Old Berry Hall until the newer one was demolished in the late 1980s. The old hall survives to this day as a private residence.

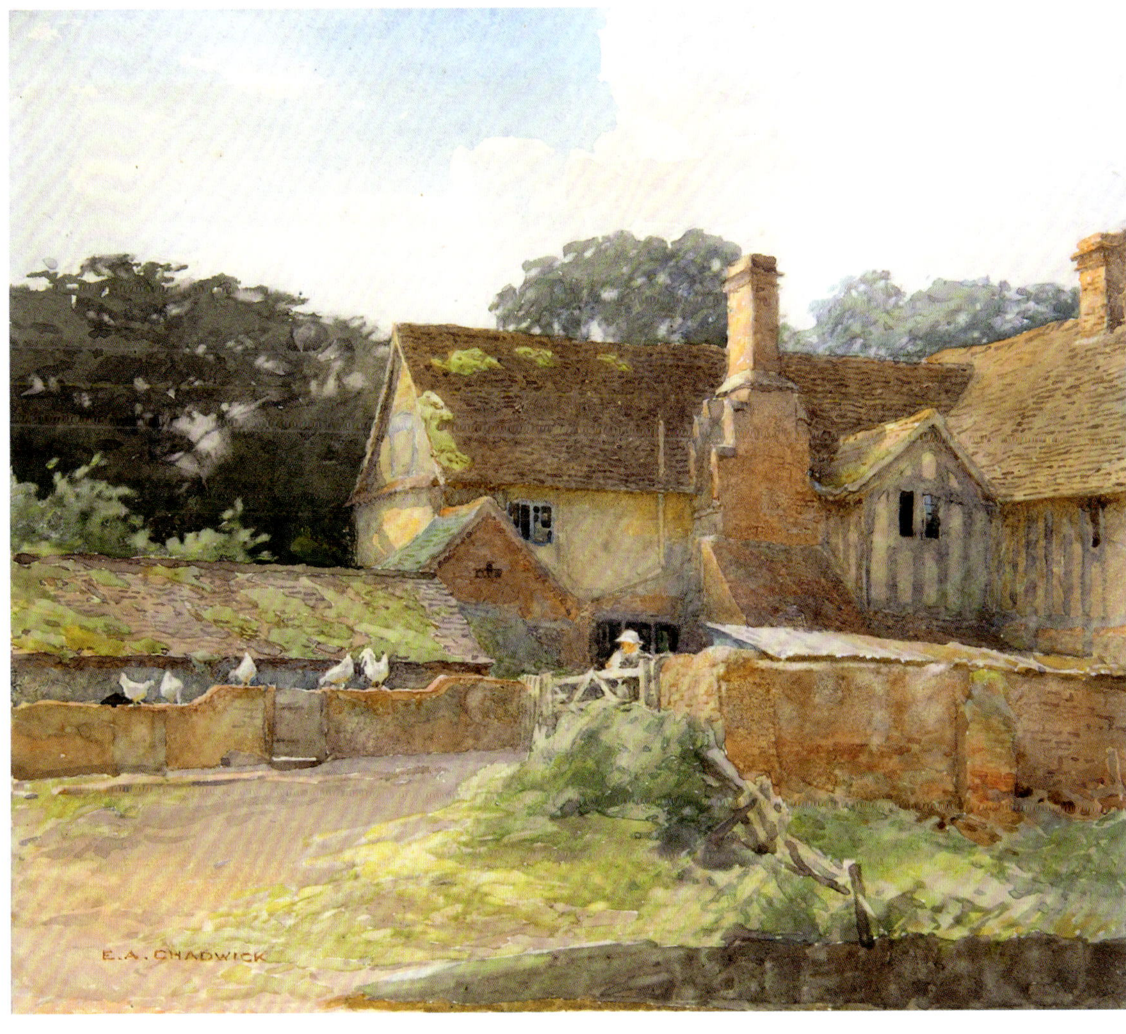

JAMES AUMONIER

James Aumonier, RI ROI NEAC PS (1832-1911)

Though he did not take up painting professionally until he was over 30, James Aumonier soon distinguished himself with his peaceful landscapes of Southern England, and especially his pastorals and river scenes.

For a biography of James Aumonier, please refer to page 114.

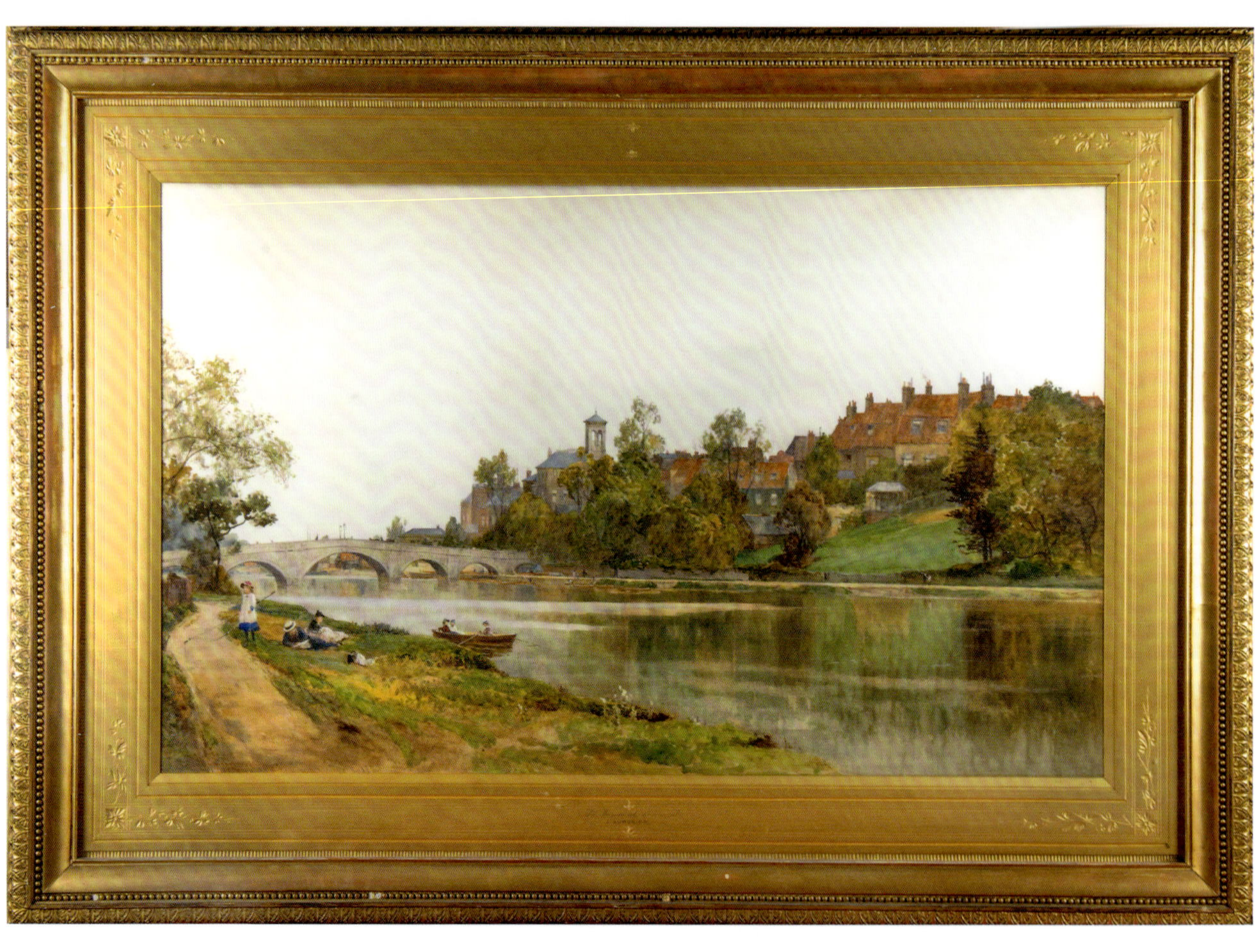

77 Richmond Bridge
Signed and dated 1883
Watercolour with bodycolour
22 ½ x 38 ¼ inches

WILLIAM WALCOT

William F Walcot, RBA RE (1874-1943)

Working as a painter and printmaker, William Walcot became the most celebrated architectural artist in England during the 1920s and 30s.

For a biography of William Walcot, please refer to *Chris Beetles Summer Show*, 2014, pages 42-43

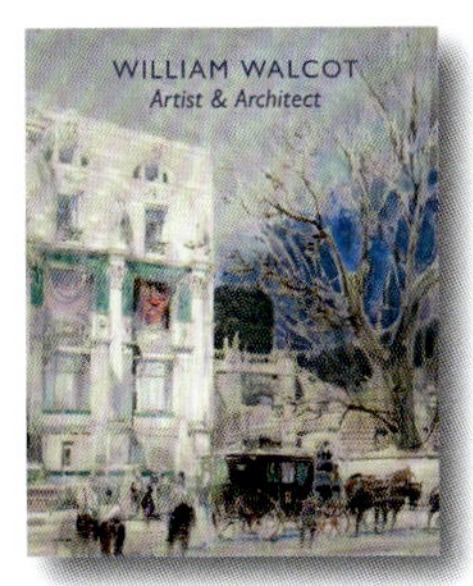

In 2018, Chris Beetles Gallery mounted a major retrospective of the work of William Walcot. It was accompanied by this beautifully designed, fully-illustrated, 50-page catalogue, which includes biographical information and a topographical index, and is still available for sale.

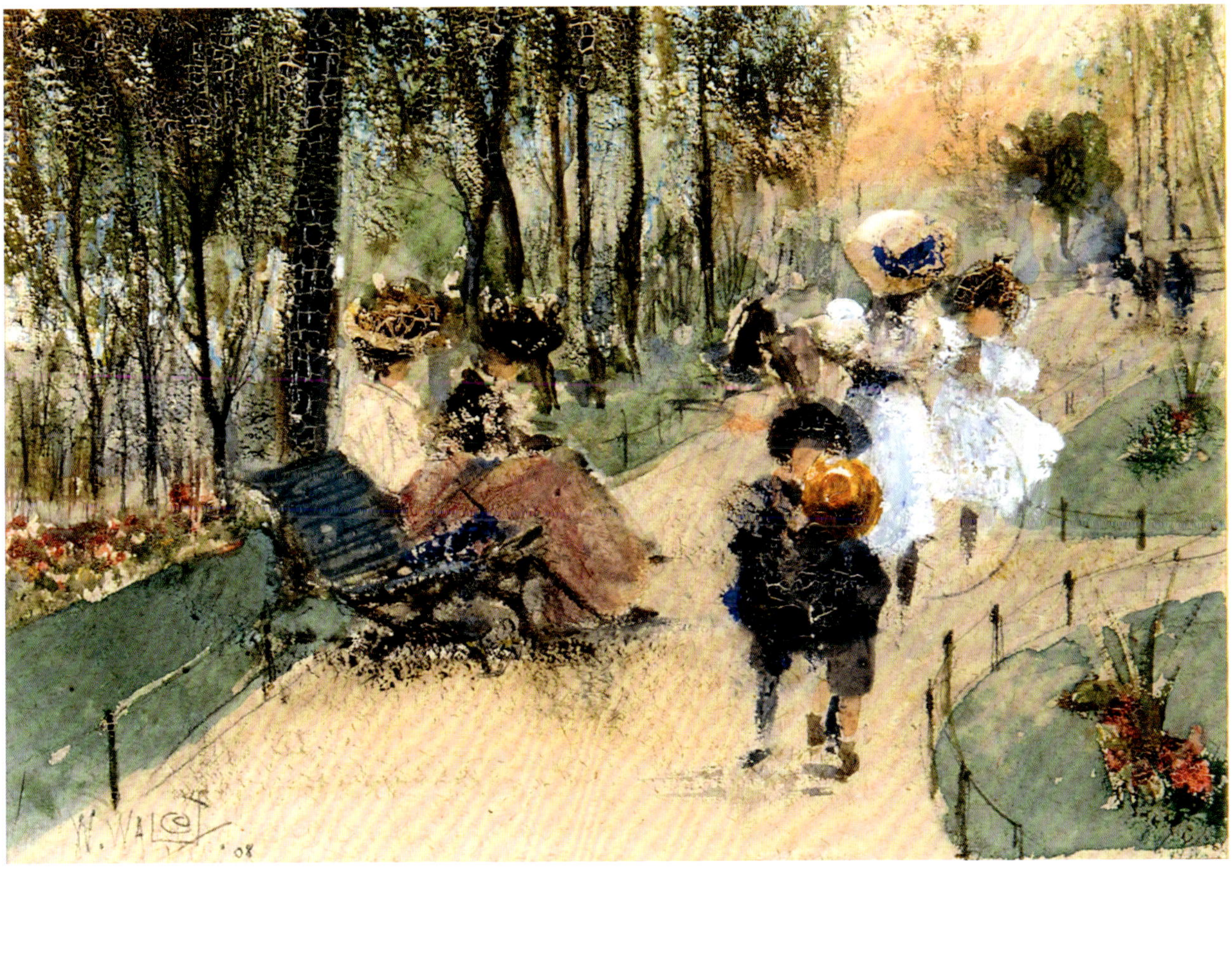

78 **Women and Children in a Park**
Signed and dated 08
Watercolour with bodycolour, gum arabic and pencil
8 x 10 ¼ inches

ALBERT GOODWIN

Albert Frederick Goodwin, RWS (1845-1932)

In synthesising the influences of J M W Turner and the Pre-Raphaelites, Albert Goodwin may be considered one of the most Ruskinian of Victorian landscape painters. Indeed, he was taken up by John Ruskin and, in 1872, given the opportunity to travel with him on an intensive tour of Italy and Switzerland. This set the pattern for many further and extensive travels. Like Ruskin, Goodwin responded to landscape with a religious fervour and understanding; but he interpreted it with even greater eclecticism than did his mentor, even experimenting with the style of James McNeill Whistler, Ruskin's adversary in the field of aesthetics.

For a biography of Albert Goodwin, please refer to *Chris Beetles Summer Show*, 2014, page 26.

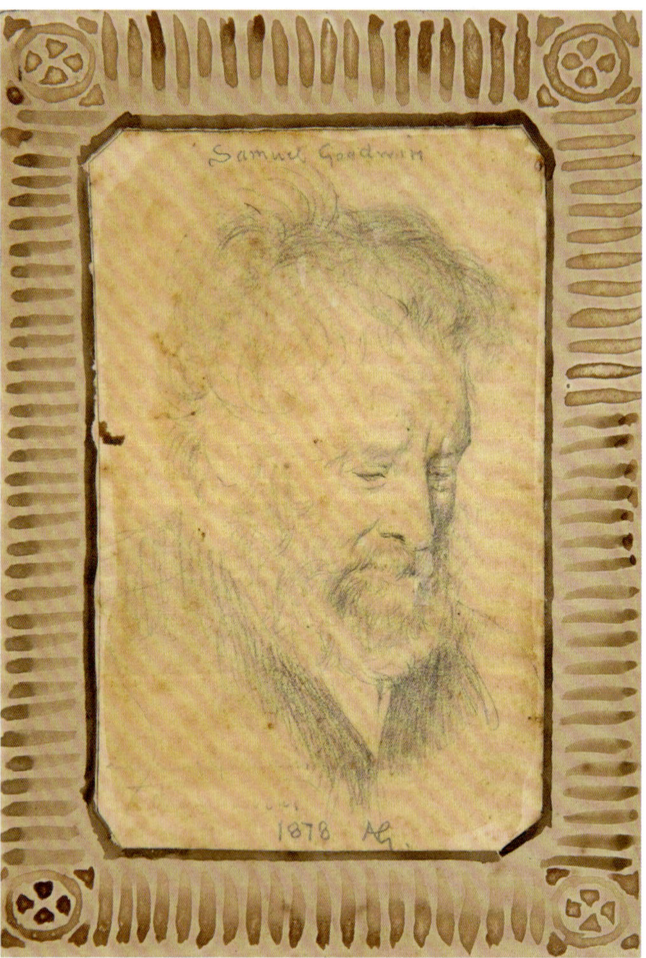

St Anthony's Works, Newcastle upon Tyne
(opposite below)
In September 1864, as the result of the personal recommendations of his teachers, Ford Madox Brown and Arthur Hughes, Goodwin visited Newcastle upon Tyne, in order to meet the industrialist and collector, James Leathart. In the event, he seems to have been too shy to call on him, though he did make contact with the painters, William Bell Scott and George Price Boyce – and may actually have been travelling with Boyce. However, it was not a wasted trip, as he returned from Newcastle with a 'host of material for delineating the Tyne and all things in her neighbourhood' (as he wrote in a letter of 20 September). He also visited Durham and Whitby while in the area, both of which would become favourite subjects.

James Leathart would eventually own at least five of Goodwin's watercolours, four dating to 1864, including the present work, which depicts the smelting works that came under the direction of Leathart, as managing partner of the lead manufacturers, Locke, Blackett & Co.

Samuel Goodwin
Albert Goodwin was the seventh of the eight surviving children of the builder, Samuel Goodwin (died 1877). A devout Baptist, Samuel had built the Bethel Chapel, Maidstone, Kent in which he worshipped and sometimes preached, and also its Sunday school. He is seen here in a posthumous drawing by Albert, with one of the artist's characteristic decorative borders.

79 **Samuel Goodwin**
Signed with initials, inscribed with title and dated 1878
Pencil enclosed by a decorative border in watercolour
5 ½ x 4 inches

80 Whitby
Signed, inscribed with title
and dated 1905
Watercolour with bodycolour
5 x 6 ¾ inches

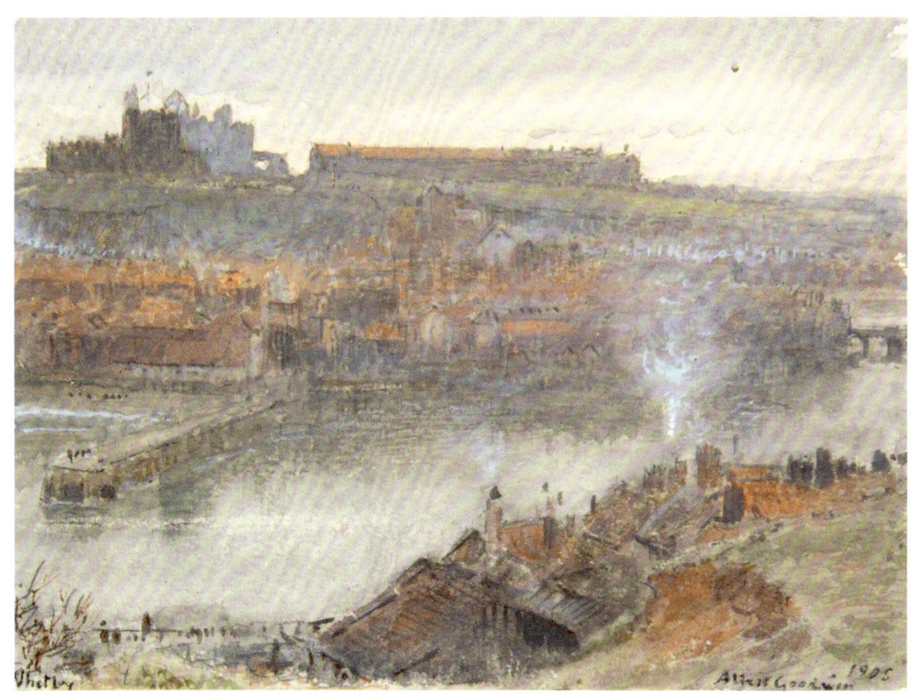

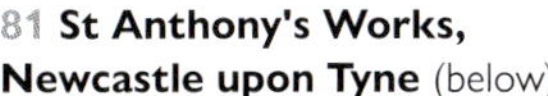

81 St Anthony's Works, Newcastle upon Tyne (below)
Signed with monogram
and dated /64
Watercolour
9 ¼ x 13 ¾ inches
Provenance: James Leathart
Literature: Hammond Smith,
Albert Goodwin, RWS 1845-1932,
Leigh-on-Sea: F Lewis, 1977,
Plate 44

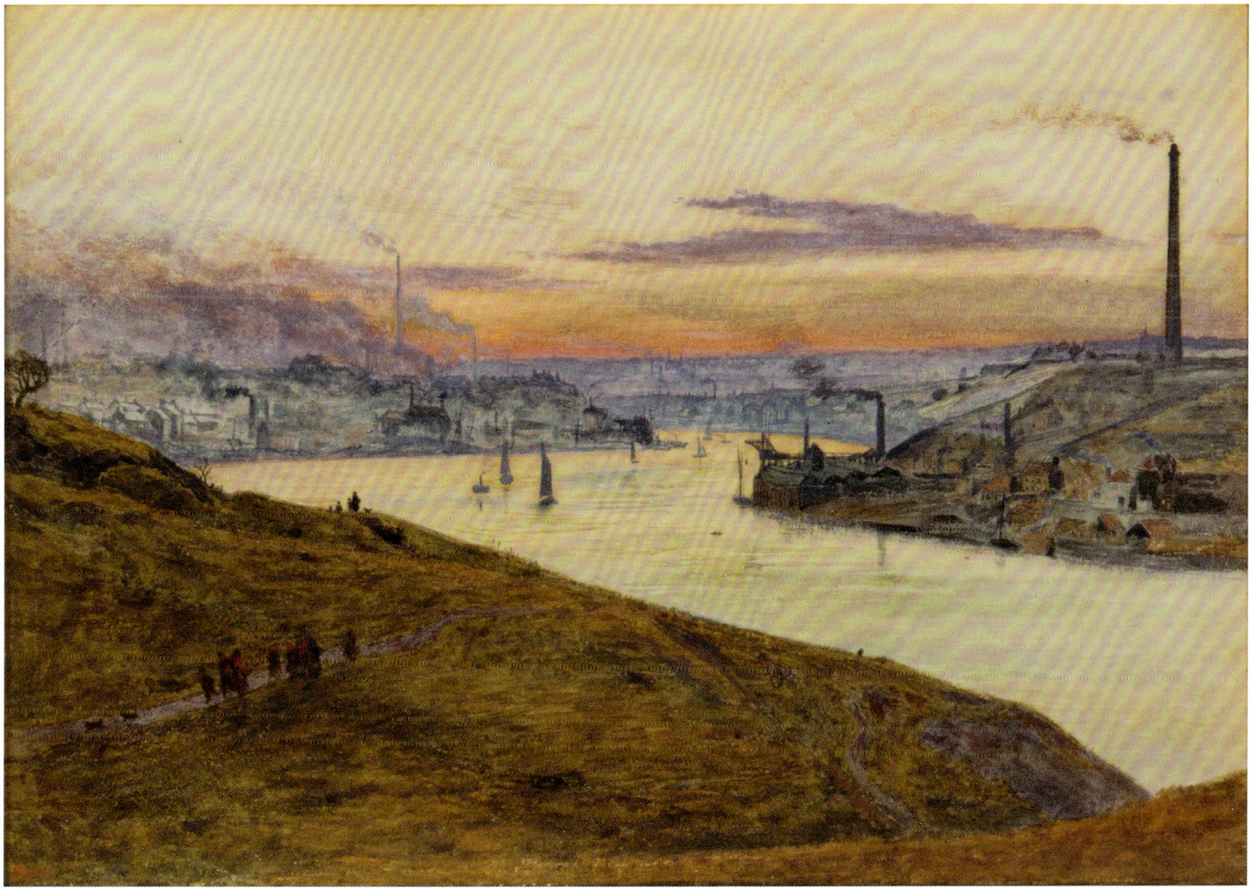

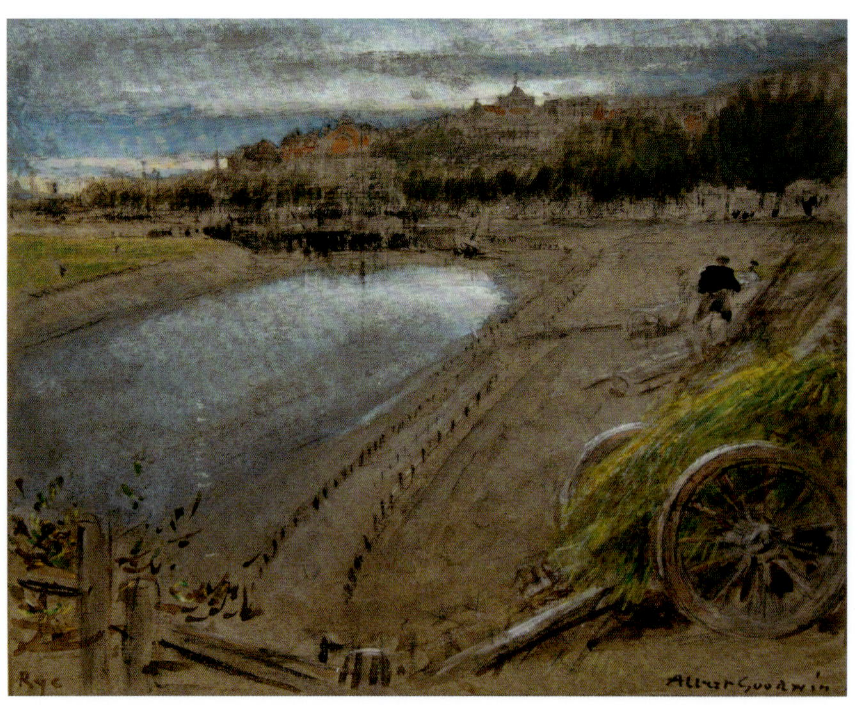

82 Rye by Moonlight
Signed and inscribed 'Rye'
Watercolour and bodycolour
on tinted paper
10 x 12 inches
Literature: *Albert Goodwin RWS, 1845-1932*, London: Chris Beetles Ltd, 1986, Limited Edition of 1000, Plate 130
Exhibited: 'Albert Goodwin, RWS (1845-1932)', Chris Beetles Gallery, May-June 1996, No 112

83 Winchester College
Signed and inscribed with title
Pen ink, watercolour and
bodycolour on tinted paper
10 ¼ x 15 inches
Literature: *Albert Goodwin RWS, 1845-1932*, London: Chris Beetles Ltd, 1986, Limited Edition of 1000, Plate 117

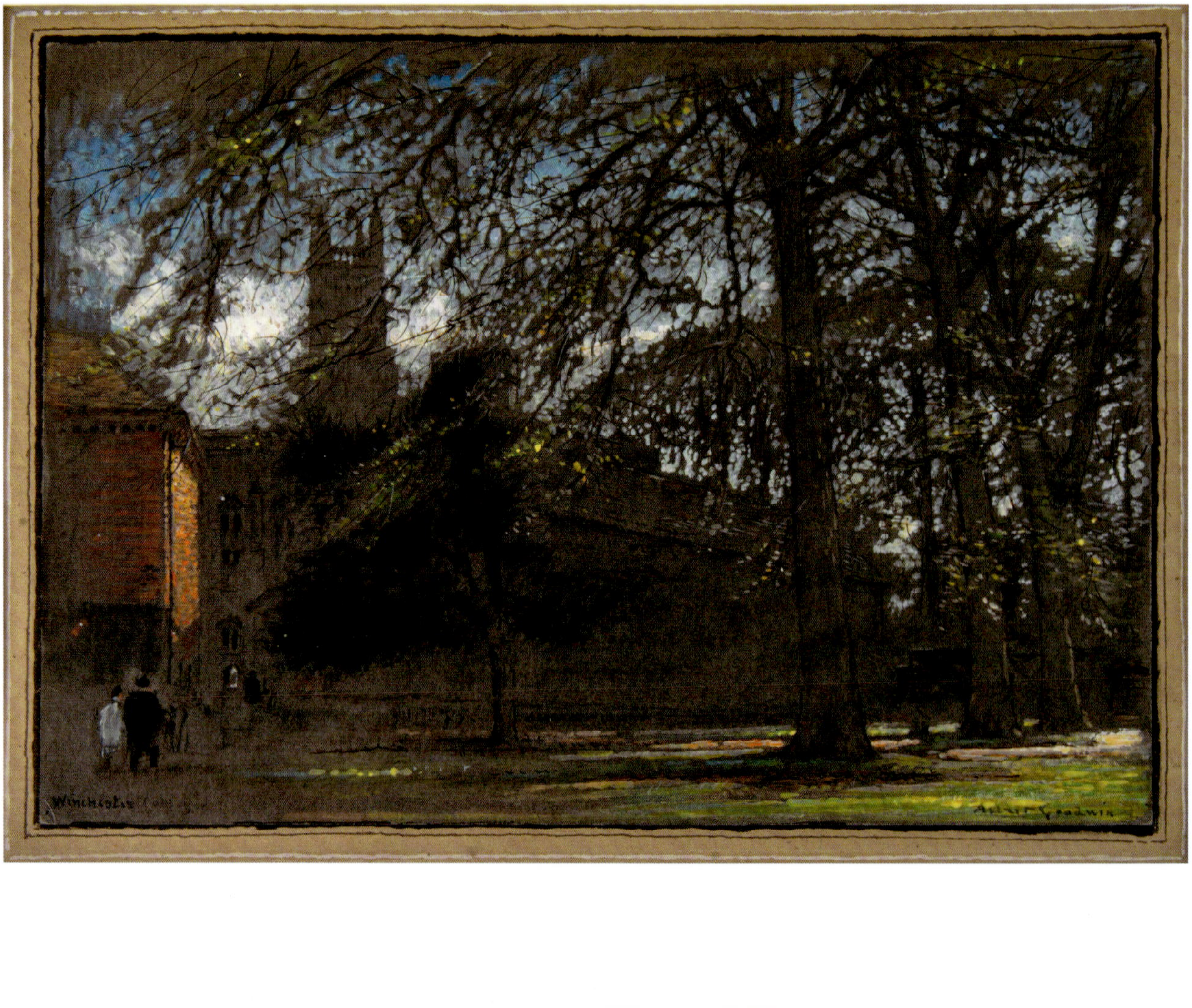

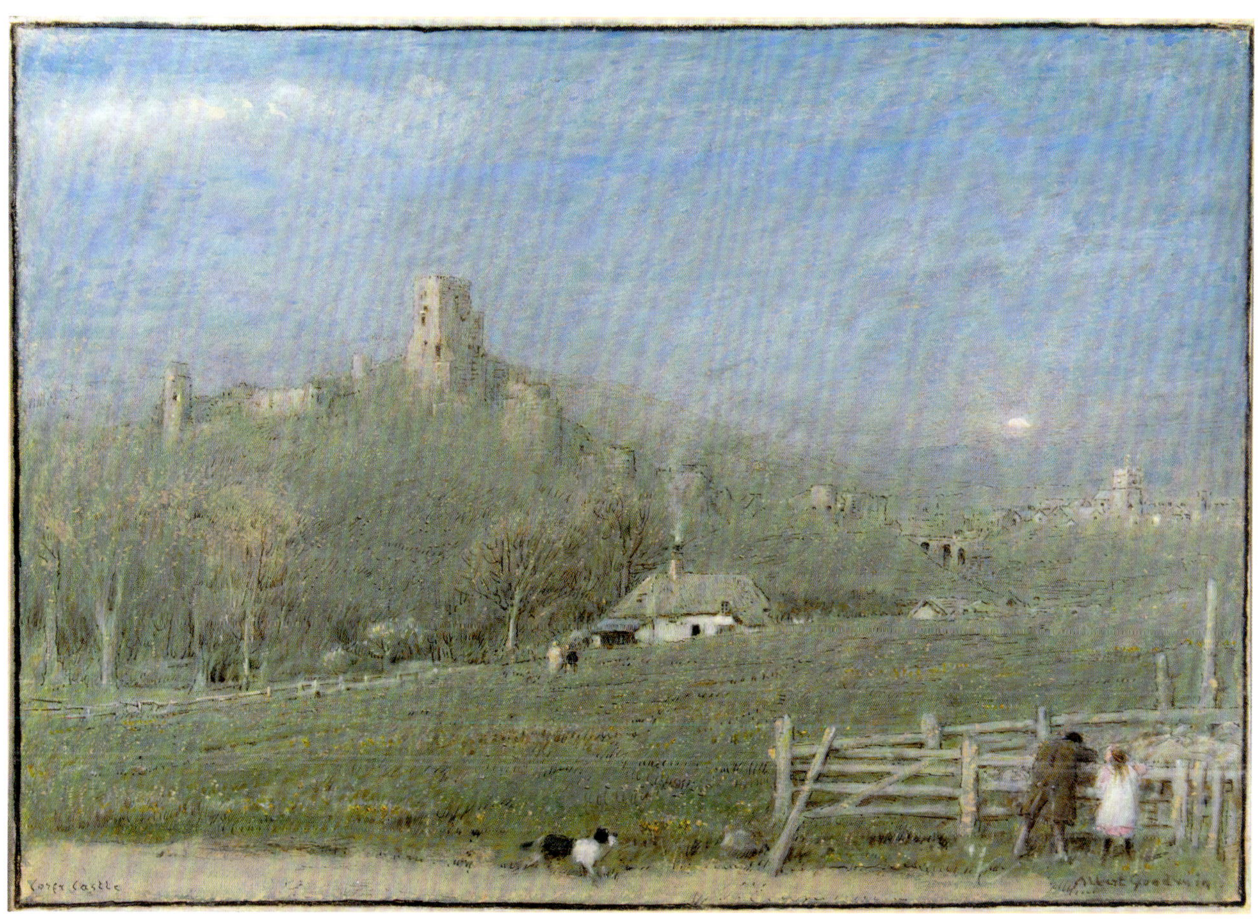

84 **Corfe Castle**
Signed and inscribed with title
Watercolour with pen ink and bodycolour
15 ¼ x 22 ¼ inches
Exhibited: 'Albert Goodwin RWS (1845-1932). An Exhibition of Watercolours to commemorate the fiftieth anniversary of the artist's death', Southgate Gallery, Wolverhampton, 1-14 May 1982, No 40

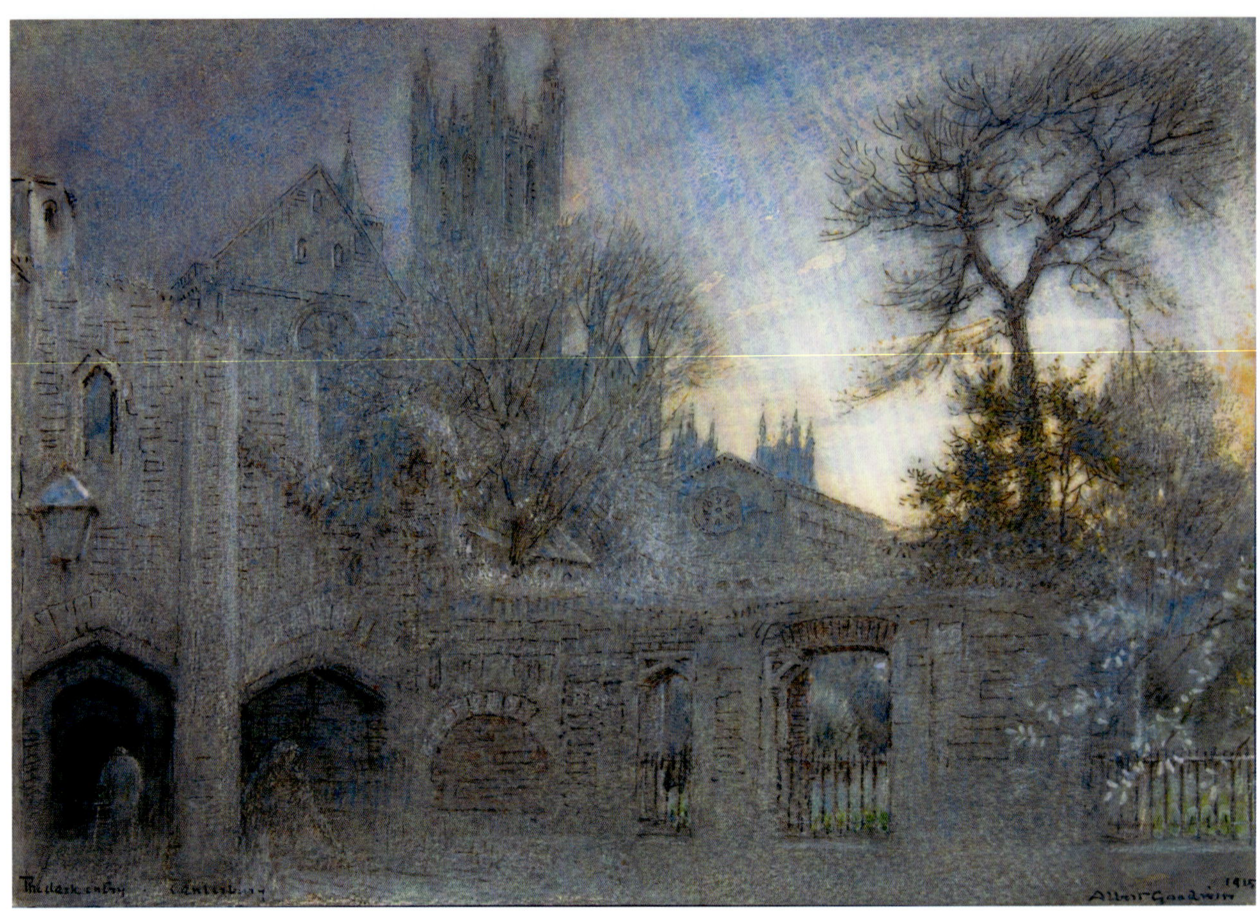

85 The Dark Entry. Canterbury
Signed, inscribed with title and dated 1915
Waterclour with pen and ink and bodycolour
10 ½ x 14 ½ inches

Gathering Storm

When this work was exhibited at the Royal Society of Painters in Water-Colours in Winter 1908, its listing in the catalogue was accompanied by the following quotation from the Biblical Book of Ezekiel:

As a shepherd seeketh out his flock in the day he is among the sheep that are scattered; so I will seek out my sheep, and will deliver them out of all places where they have been scattered in the cloudy dark day
(Ezekiel, xxxiv 12)

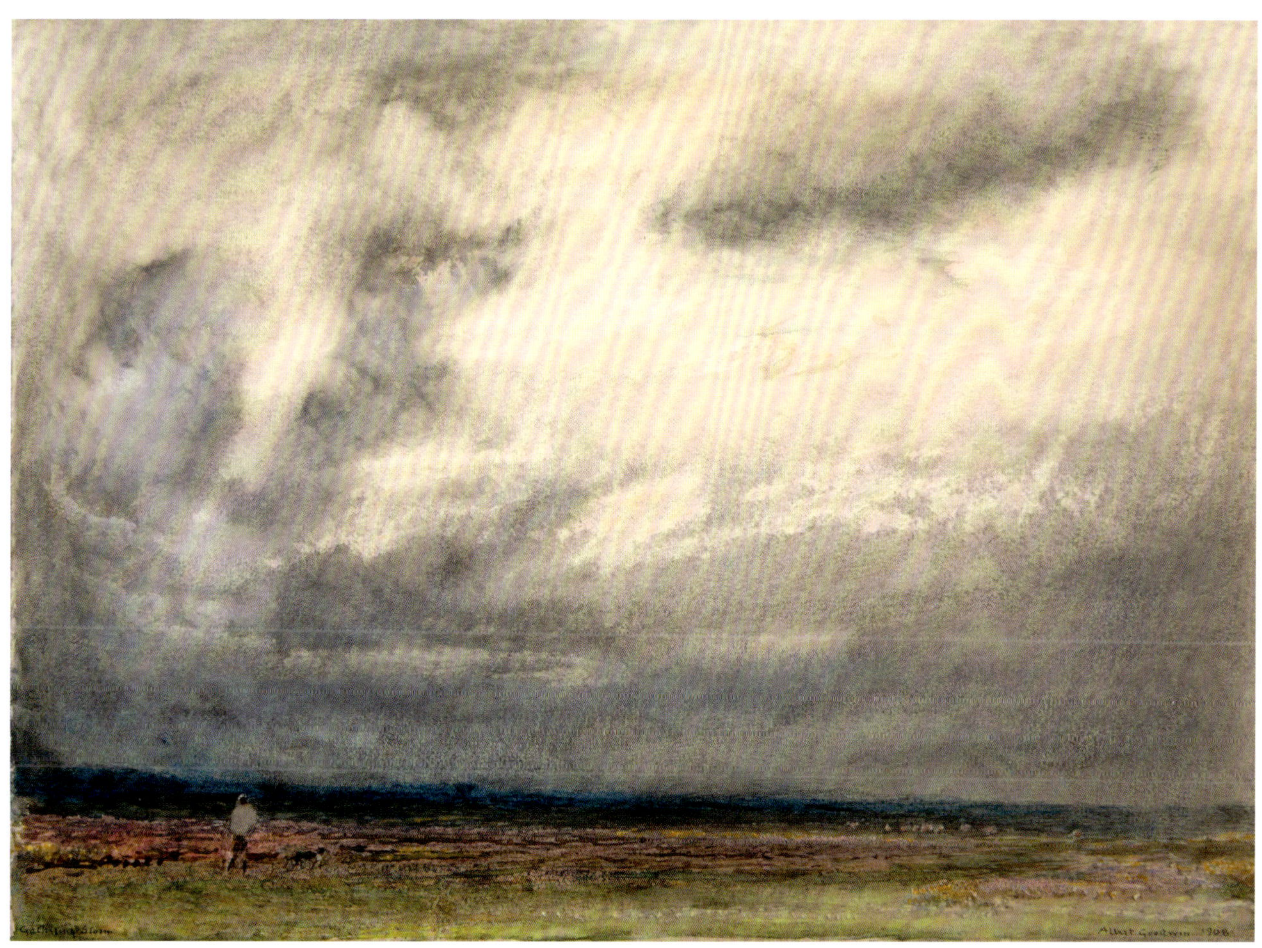

86 **Gathering Storm**
Signed, inscribed with title and dated 1908
Watercolour
10 ½ x 14 ½ inches
Literature: *Albert Goodwin RWS, 1845-1932*, London: Chris Beetles, 1986, Limited Edition of 1000, Plate 105
Exhibited: Royal Society of Painters in Water-Colours, London, Winter 1908, Cat No 34;
'Albert Goodwin RWS (1845-1932). An Exhibition of Watercolours to commemorate the fiftieth anniversary of the artist's death', Southgate Gallery, Wolverhampton, May 1982, No 35 (on loan)

Peter & John at the Gate of the Temple, San Marco, Venezia

Albert Goodwin first visited Venice in June 1872, as a member of a party headed by the leading art critic, John Ruskin. Ruskin encouraged his friends to enthuse about its major sights, though was amused that Goodwin should liken the Byzantine splendour of the Basilica of San Marco to a 'travelling show' (as Arthur Severn, another of the party, would recall in his memoir of Ruskin).

The present watercolour is one of at least two versions of a composition that Goodwin completed soon after his visit to Venice in 1872. It shows how quickly the artist absorbed the view of his mentor, Ruskin, on the beauty and importance of San Marco. It depicts the northwest corner of the basilica, and includes the Arch of Sant'Alipio, which contains the only surviving Byzantine mosaic of the original façade, representing the removal of the body of St Mark from the building. To the left of the building is the Piazzetta dei Leoncini, named after the statues of lions that it contains.

In the foreground of the watercolour, a small child seems to proffer a flower to two Franciscan friars. These friars suggested to Goodwin 'Peter and John at the gate of the Temple', an episode recorded in Chapter 3 the Biblical book of The Acts of the Apostles in which Saint Peter and Saint John heal a lame man outside the Temple of Jerusalem. The best known artistic representations of the story are probably Raphael's tapestry cartoon, designed in about 1515 for the Sistine Chapel, in the Vatican, and Rembrandt's etching of 1659.

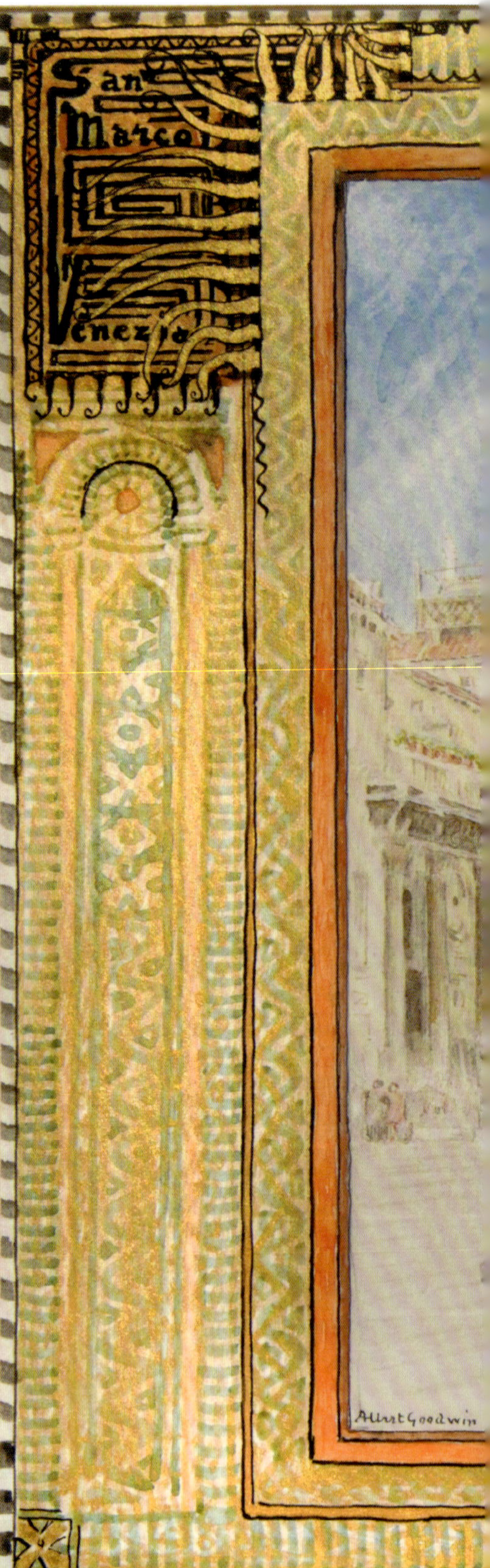

87 **Peter & John at the Gate of the Temple, San Marco, Venezia**
Signed
Inscribed with title on decorative border
Watercolour enclosed by a decorative border in pen ink, gold paint and watercolour
8 ¾ x 10 inches
Literature: Hammond Smith, *Albert Goodwin, RWS 1845-1932*, Leigh-On-Sea: F Lewis, 1977, Plate 42

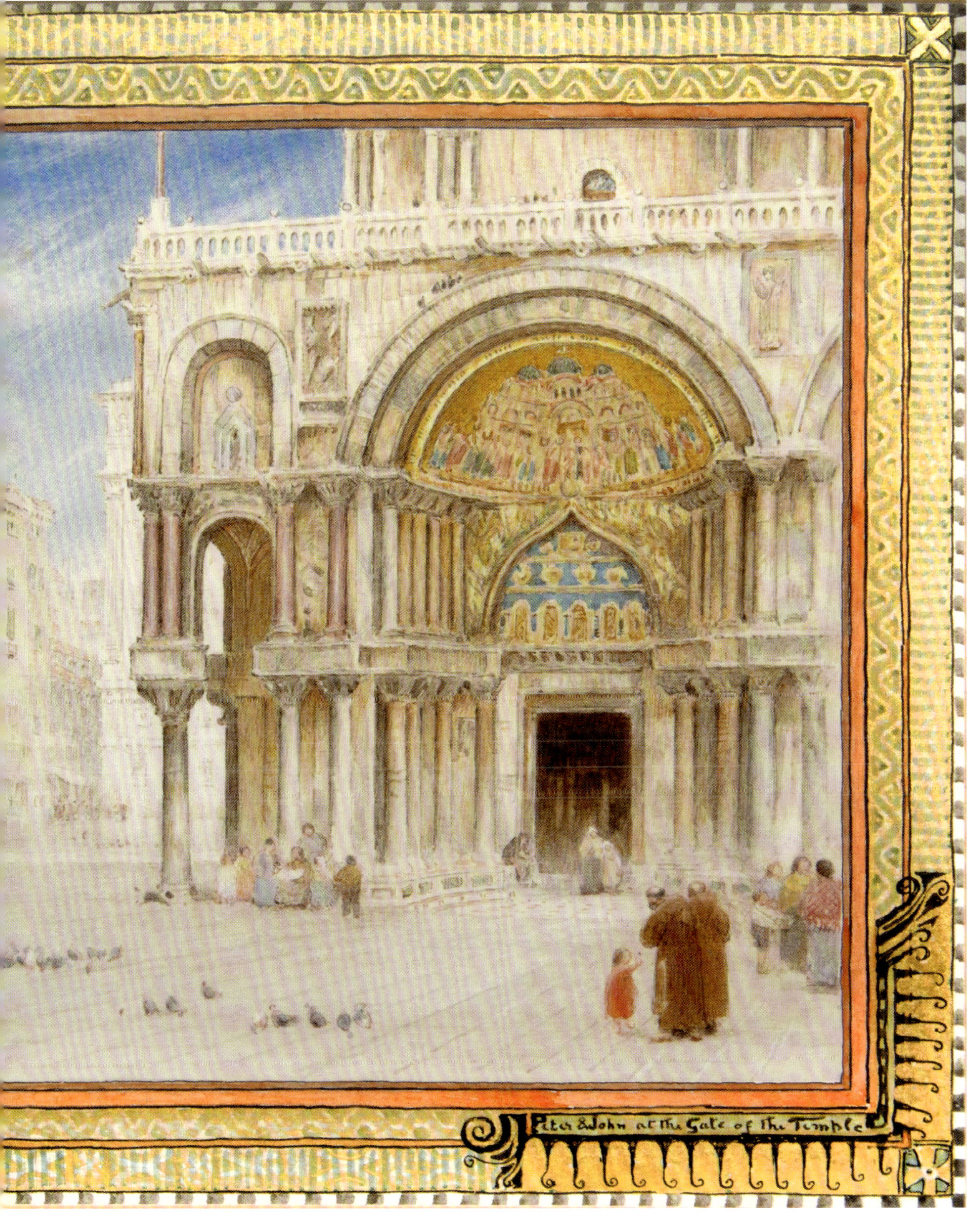
Peter & John at the Gate of the Temple

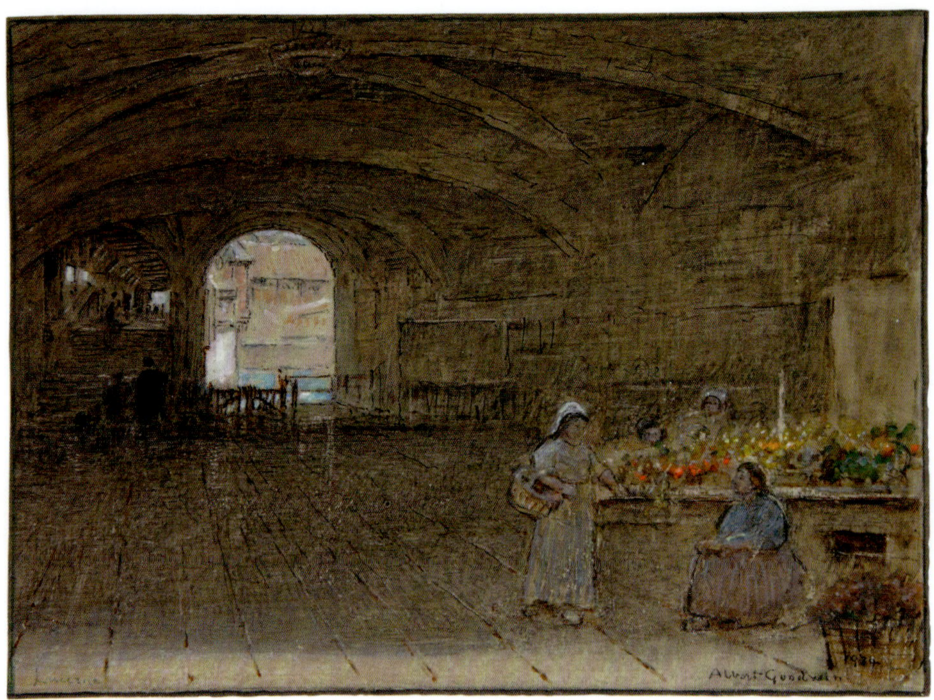

88 **Lucerne**
Signed, inscribed with title and dated 1924
Watercolour with pen ink and bodycolour
7 ¾ x 10 ½ inches

89 **Stanstadt. Lake Lucerne**
Signed and inscribed with title
Watercolour with bodycolour enclosed by a decorative border
6 ¼ x 8 inches
A work of this title was exhibited at the Royal Society of Painters in Water-Colours, Summer 1888, No 241

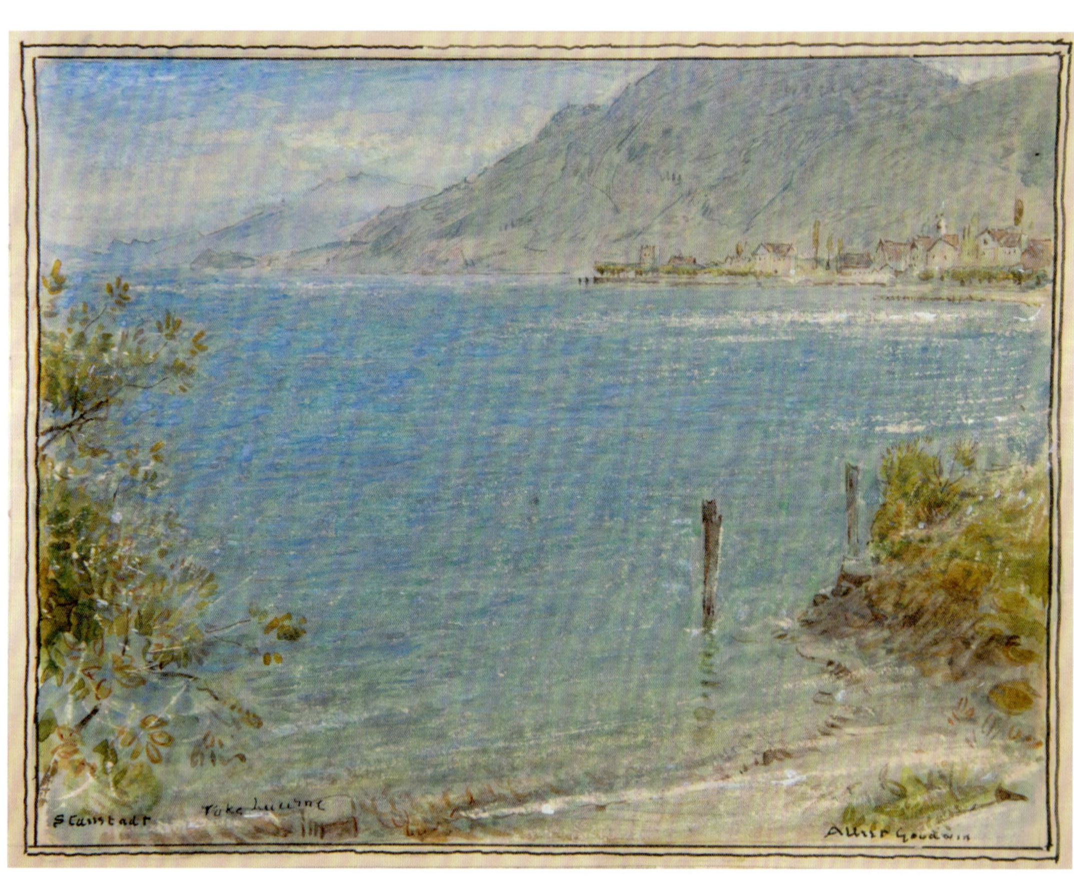

Albert Goodwin in Switzerland

During his first extensive tour of Continental Europe, with John Ruskin in 1872, Albert Goodwin was introduced to Switzerland, as he was to Italy. If Italy provided a primer in art and architecture, Switzerland offered awe-inspiring mountain scenery, which, for the artist, was evidence of God's majesty. He would return to the country frequently throughout his career, and paint in many of its cantons, from Geneva in the west [94] to Grisons in the east, which borders the Tyrol [93]. His favourite sketching grounds included Lake Lucerne, of which three examples are included here. His watercolour of *The Rigi from Lucerne* [90] was undoubtedly painted in emulation of three famous similar compositions by J M W Turner.

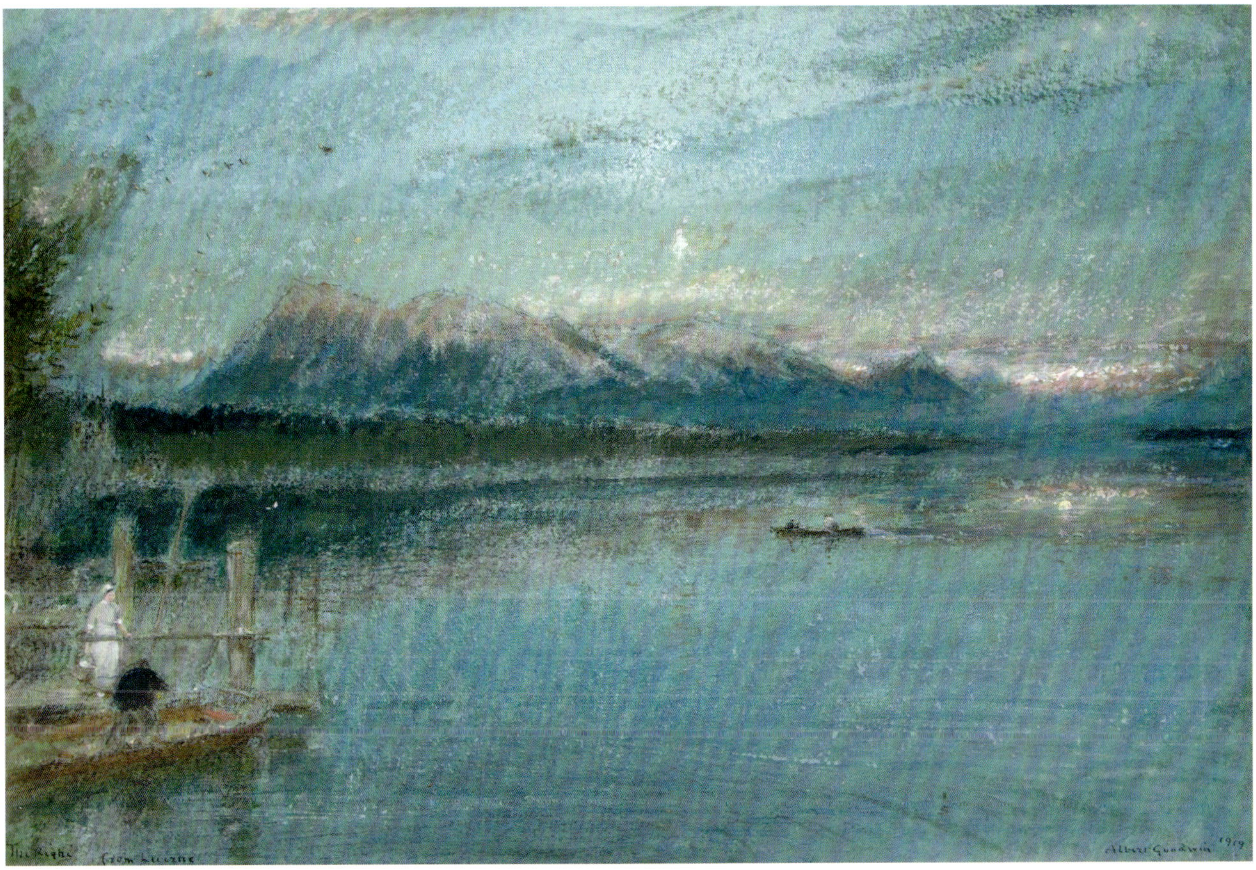

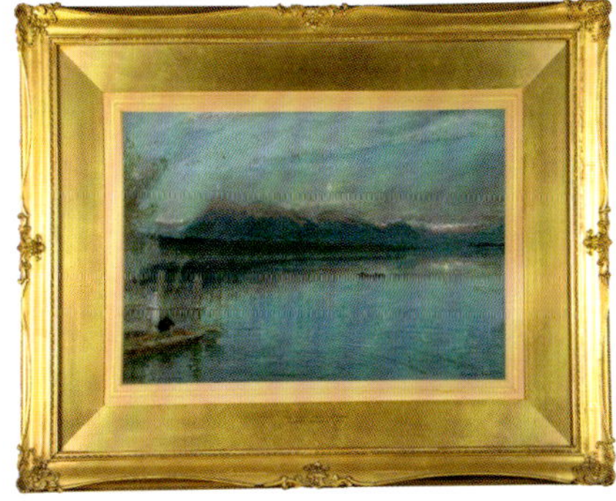

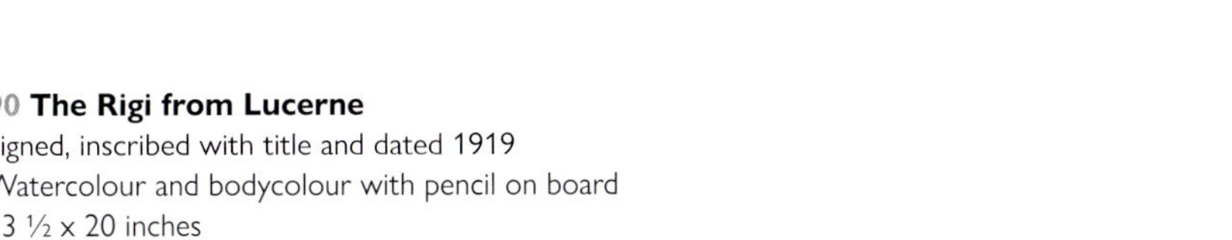

90 The Rigi from Lucerne
Signed, inscribed with title and dated 1919
Watercolour and bodycolour with pencil on board
13 ½ x 20 inches

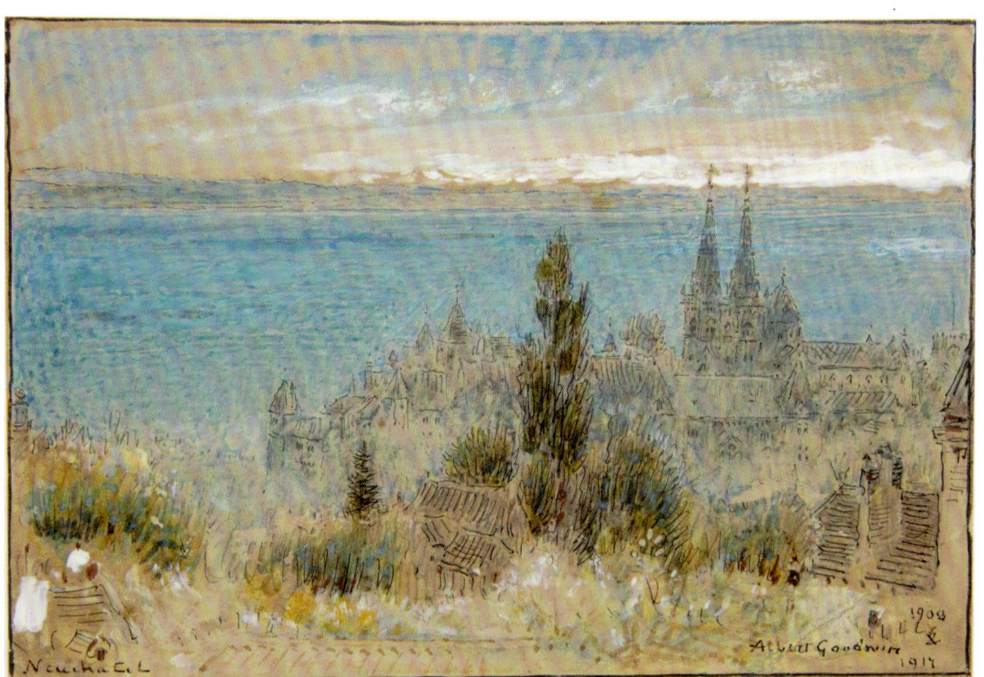

91 Neuchatel
Signed, inscribed with title and dated 1908 and 1917
Watercolour with pen ink and bodycolour
4 x 6 inches
A work of this title was exhibited in 'Drawings and Pictures by Albert Goodwin, RWS', Leggatt Brothers Gallery, London, 1919, as No 32.

92 The Blue Lake, Kanderstag
Signed, inscribed with title and dated 1907
Signed and inscribed 'The Blue Lake' on supporting sheet
Watercolour enclosed by a decorative border
5 ½ x 7 ½ inches

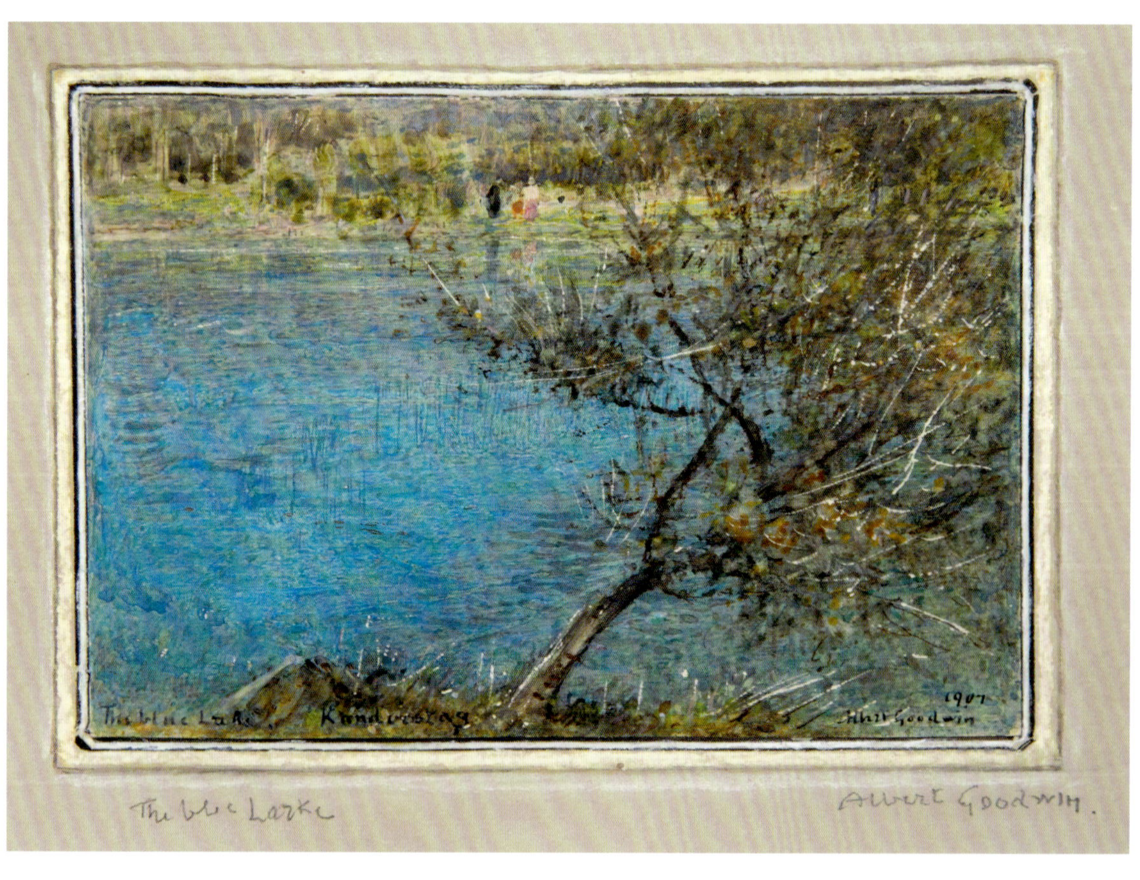

93 Trafoi in Tyrol
Signed and inscribed
with title
Watercolour with
bodycolour enclosed
by a decorative border
3 ¾ x 5 ½ inches

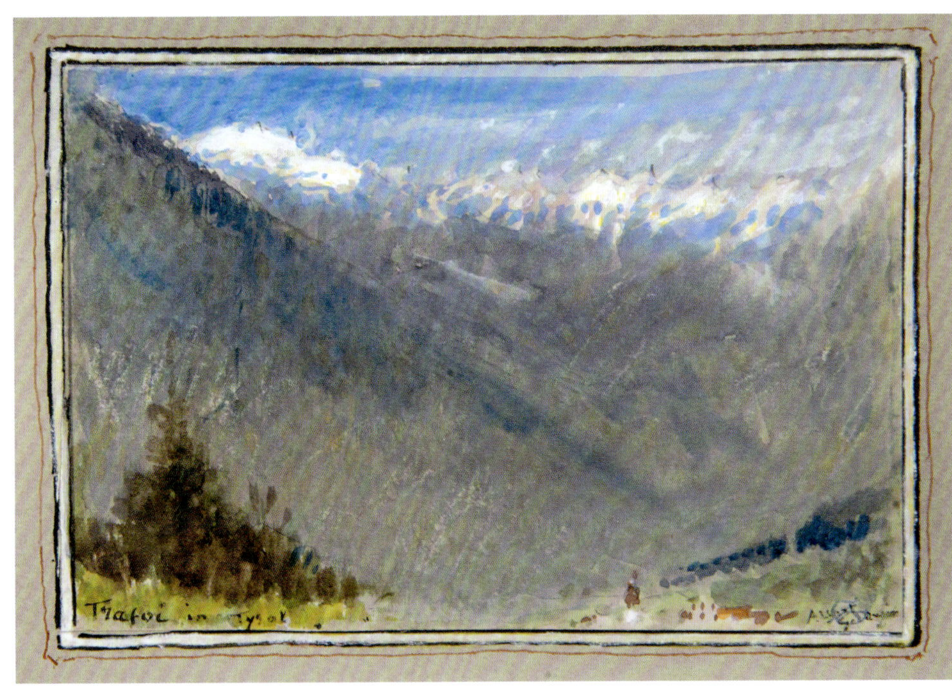

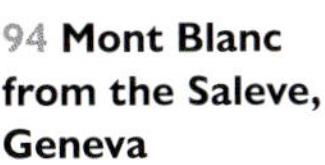

94 Mont Blanc from the Saleve, Geneva
Signed and inscribed
with title
Watercolour,
bodycolour and
oil on paper
10 x 14 inches

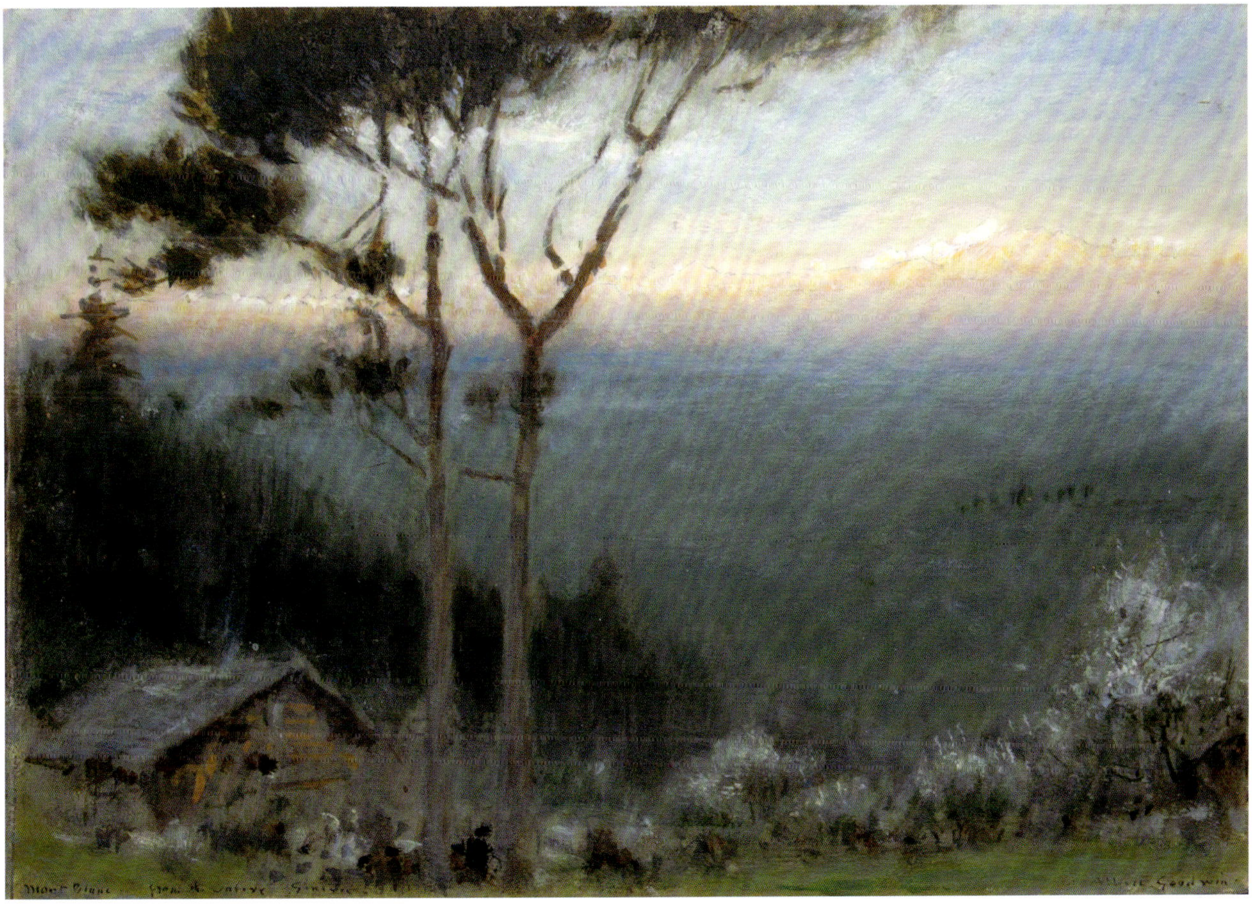

The Island of the Sounding Cymbals, 'Arabian Nights'

This work is one of many by Albert Goodwin that was inspired by his reading of *The Arabian Nights*. When it was exhibited at the Fine Art Society in March 1896, its listing in the catalogue was accompanied by the following comment:

Sinbad merely mentions the island in one of his voyages, but the title is a very suggestive one. The huge wild bees' nests hanging from the roof of the cavern are a very common object in India.

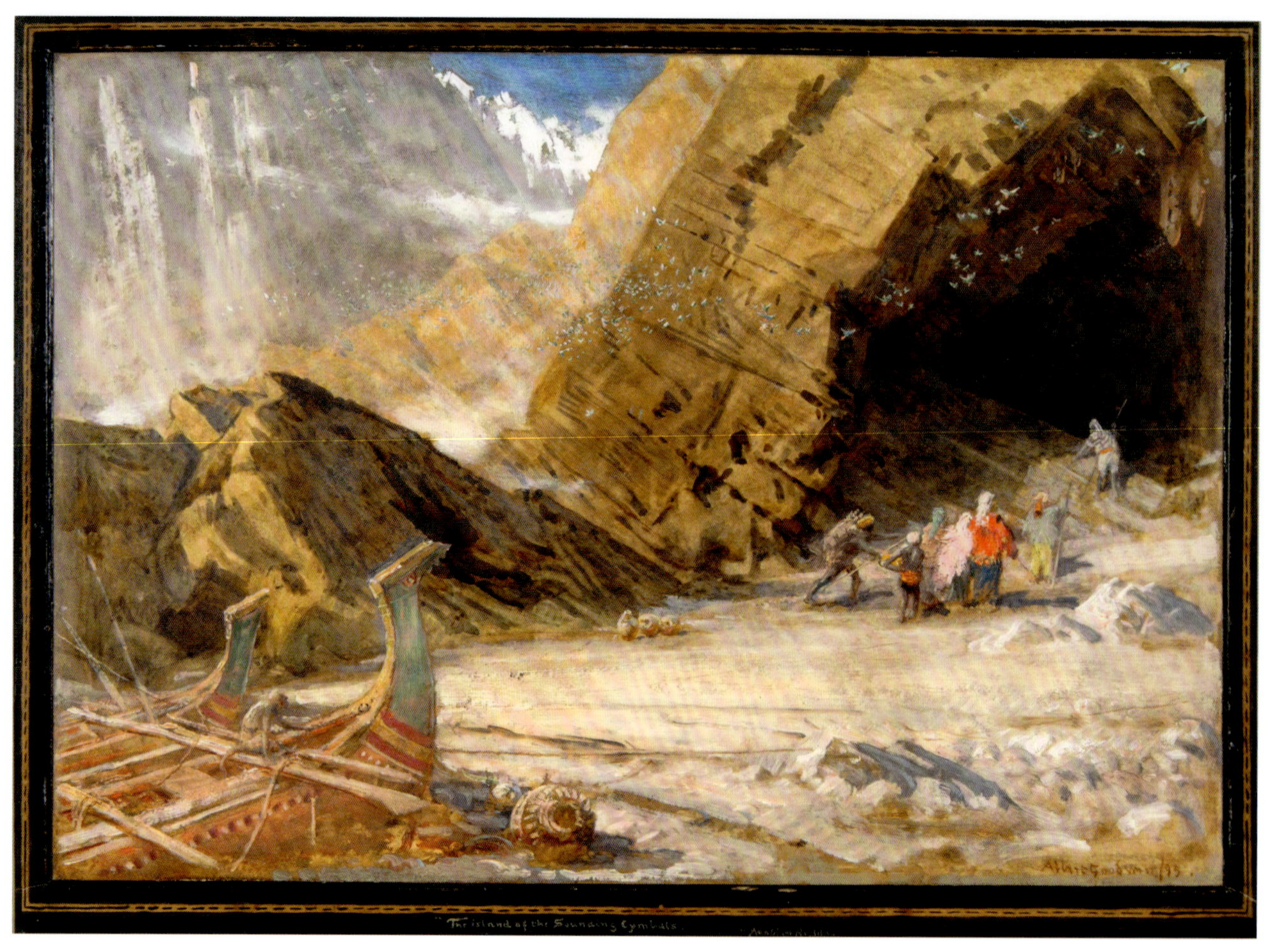

95 The Island of the Sounding Cymbals, 'Arabian Nights'
Signed and dated /95
Inscribed with title on decorative border
Oil, watercolour and varnish on paper
15 ¼ x 22 inches
Provenance: 'The Collection of Works by Albert Goodwin, RWS, RWA. The Property of Matthew Biggar Walker, Esq, of 1 Park Crescent, Wolverhampton', Christie, Manson & Woods, London, 9 March 1928, No 130
Exhibited: Royal Society of Painters in Water-Colours, Summer 1891, No 114;
'A Collection of Pictures and Drawings of Imaginative Landscape in Europe and Asia by Albert Goodwin RWS', Fine Art Society, London, March 1896, No 53;
'An Exhibition of Oil Paintings, Water Colour Drawing, etc by Albert Goodwin, RWS RWA, Loaned by M B Walker Esq', Municipal Art Gallery and Museum, Wolverhampton, December 1925, No 18;
'An Exhibition of Oil Paintings, Water Colour Drawing, etc by Albert Goodwin, RWS RWA, Lent by M B Walker Esq', City of Birmingham Museum and Art Gallery, 1926, No 134;
'Albert Goodwin RWS (1845-1932), An Exhibition of Watercolours to commemorate the fiftieth anniversary of the artist's death', Southgate Gallery, Wolverhampton, May 1982, No 23

The Unknown Land

This work was almost certainly inspired by Albert Goodwin's voyage to Australia and New Zealand in 1916-17. To Goodwin, the title would have suggested the call of God to Abraham to 'Get thee out of thy country … unto a land that I will show thee' (Genesis, xii 1). However, he may also have been thinking of the afterlife, as was Edmund Blair Leighton five years earlier when he used the phrase, 'To the Unknown Land' as the title of one of his most famous paintings, showing an angel transporting a dead child by boat.

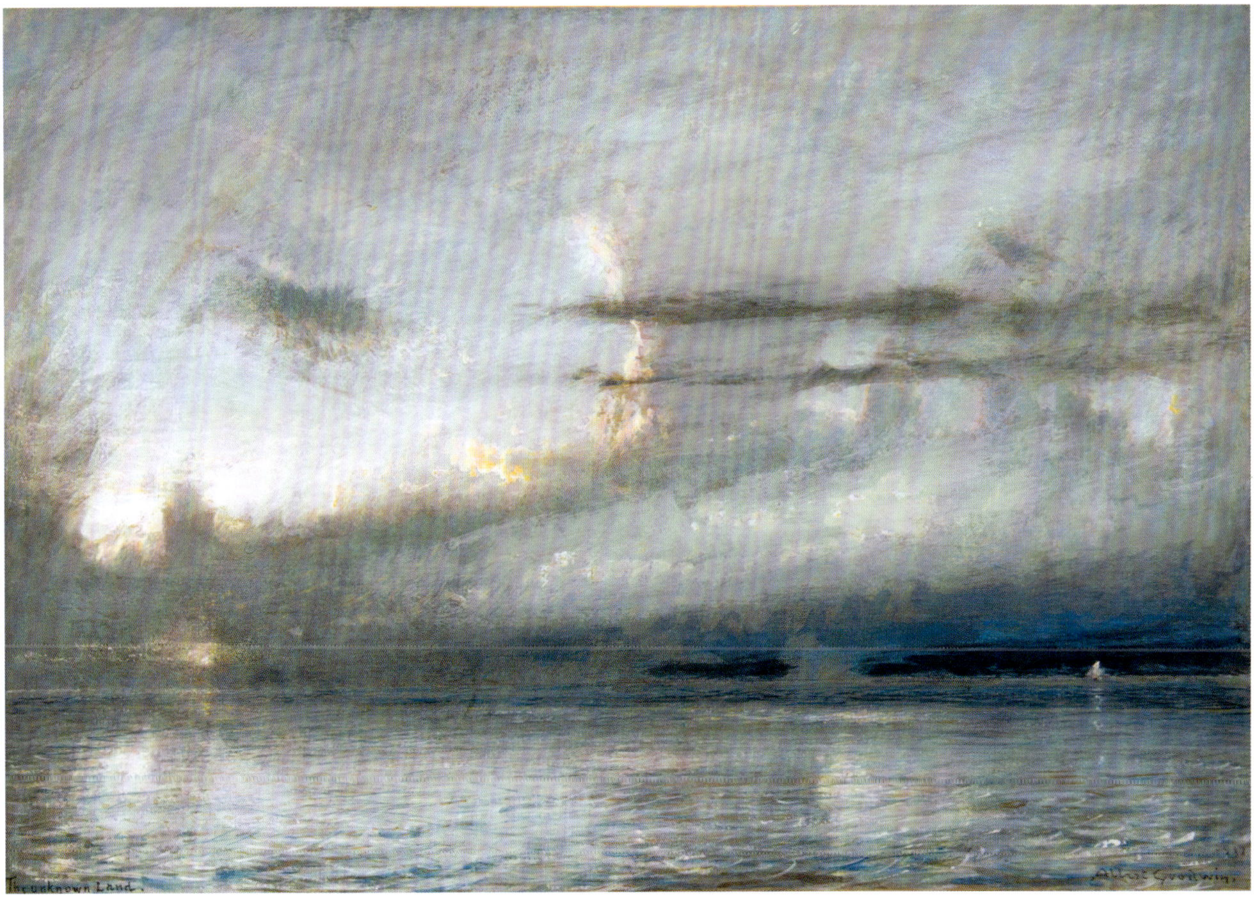

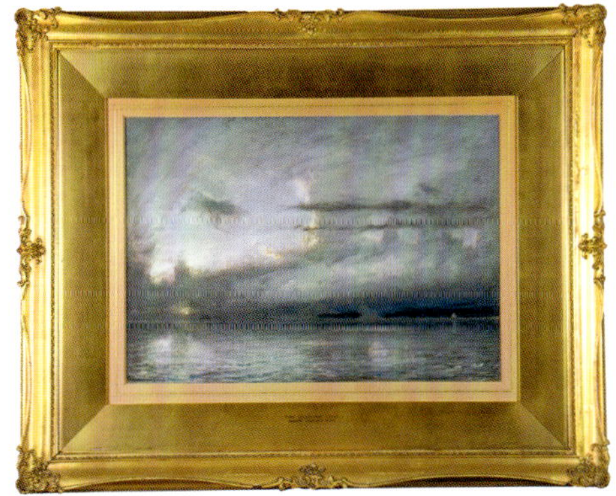

96 The Unknown Land
Signed, inscribed with title and dated 1917
Watercolour and bodycolour
14 x 20 ¼ inches
Exhibited: Royal Society of Painters in Water-Colours, Summer 1918, No 8

Biographies

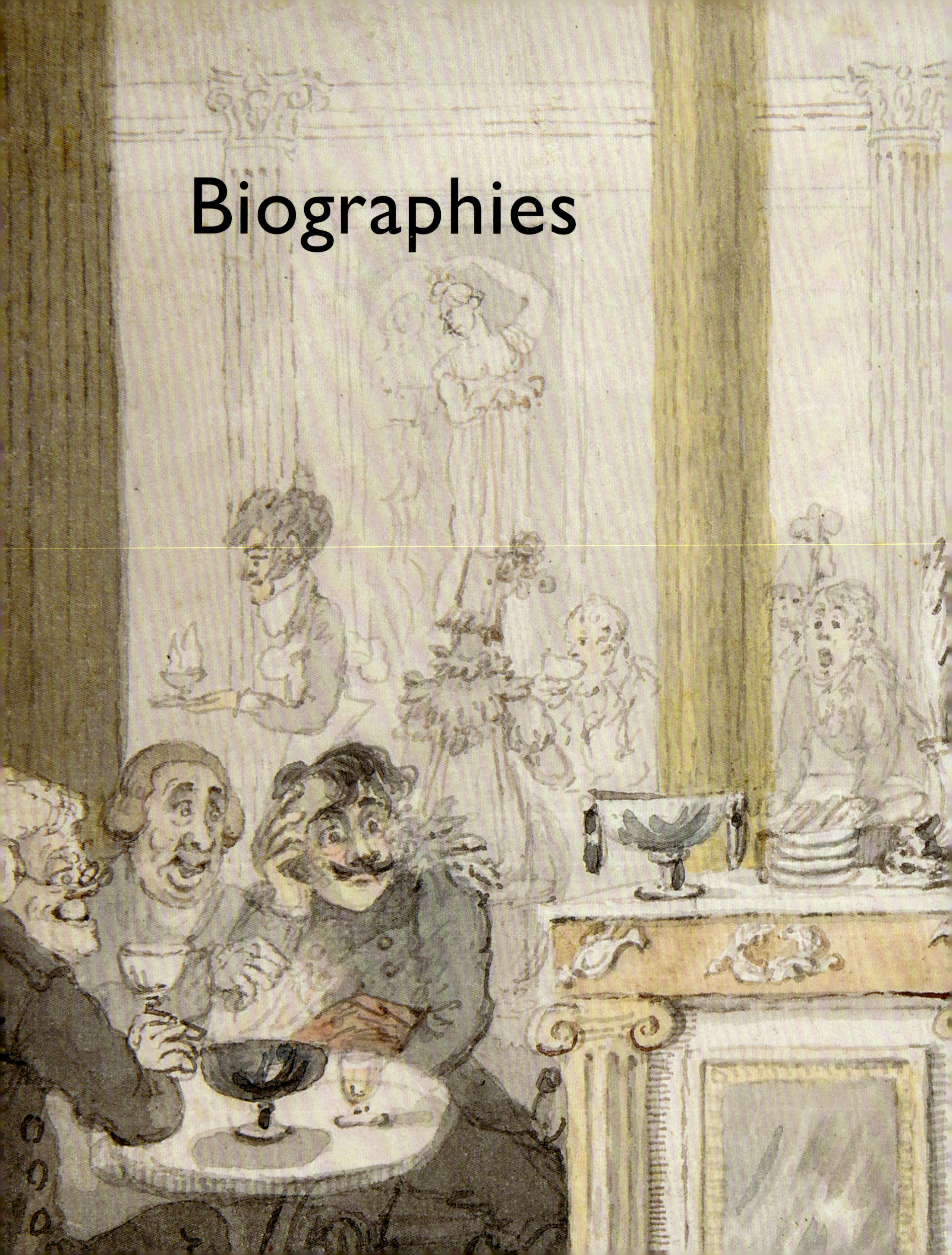

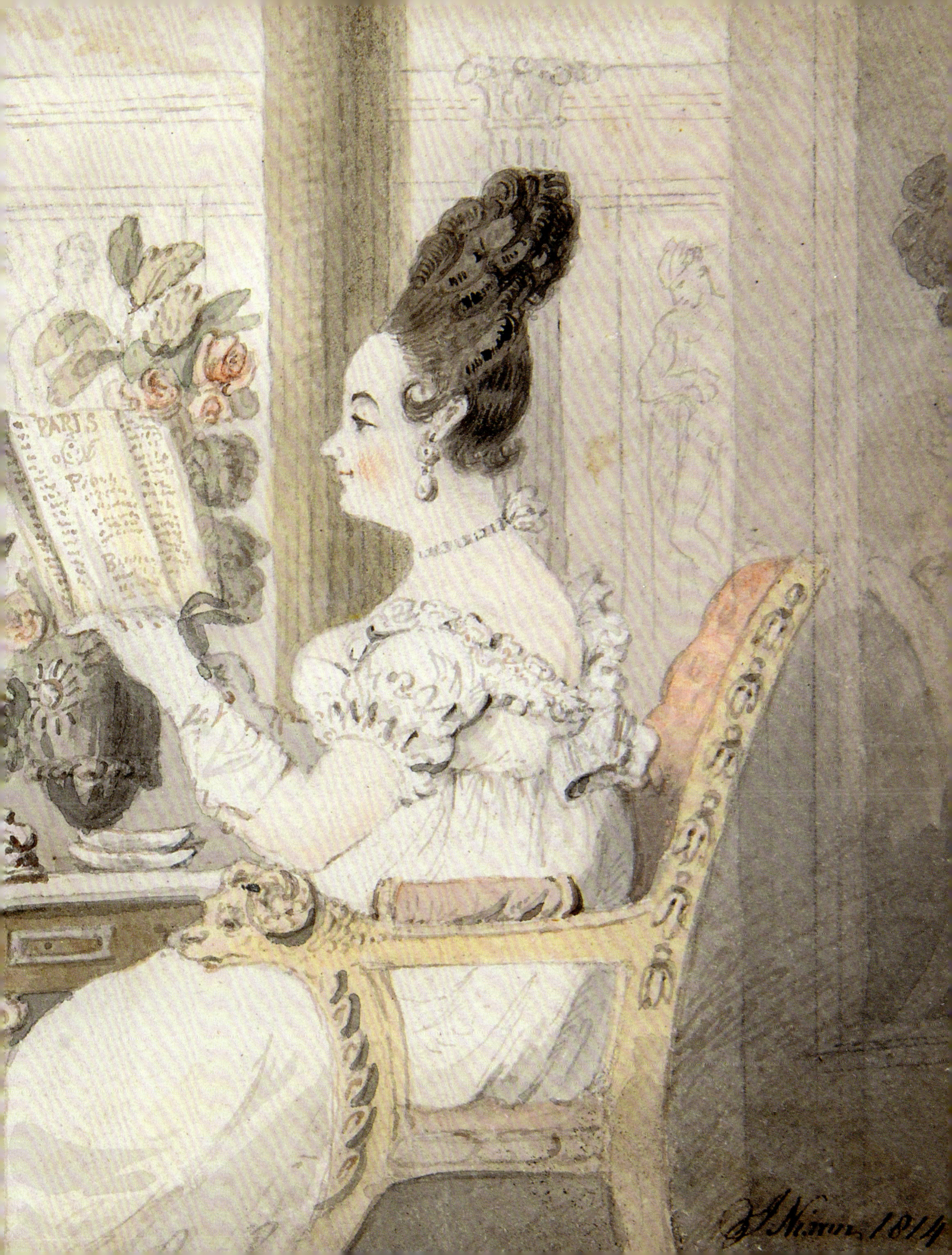
PARIS
J. Nixon 1814

JAMES GILLRAY

James Gillray (1756-1815)

Having developed the skills of draughtsman and engraver, James Gillray established himself as the first professional caricaturist in Britain, and dominated the field. Breaking free of the rigid symbolic language of amateur caricaturists, he employed his rich imagination, and exaggerated the features of his targets, to powerful political ends.

James Gillray was born in Chelsea, which was then in the county of Middlesex, on 13 August 1756. He was the only surviving child of a disabled Scottish ex-soldier who joined the extreme protestant sect of the Moravian Brethren, and became sexton of its burial ground in Chelsea. In 1762, at the age of five, Gillray was sent to the Moravian school in Bedford, but returned to his parents two years later, when the school was closed for financial reasons. It is uncertain what further general education, if any, he received, but he certainly developed a talent for drawing while still young. By 1770, he was apprenticed to Harry Ashby, the writing engraver and publisher, based at Russell Court, Covent Garden. However, he soon became bored and left 'to join a company of strolling players' (as reported by a German journalist in 1798, and quoted by Anita McConnell and Simon Heneage in their entry on Gillray in the *Oxford Dictionary of National Biography*, 2004, page 298).

By 1775, Gillray had returned to London, and was engraving satirical prints for the publisher, William Humphrey, who was then based at Gerrard Street, Soho. Those that he designed as well as engraved were greatly influenced by the work of John Hamilton Mortimer. His work as an engraver enabled him to support himself through his studies at the Royal Academy Schools, which he entered in 1778. He is likely to have attended the lectures of the engraver, Francesco Bartolozzi, and may also have received some lessons from the pioneering stipple engraver, William Wynne Ryland. While producing a range of illustrations, miniature portraits and reproductive engravings during this period, he developed his own distinctive style of caricatures, and over the next six years gradually established his reputation as the leading caricaturist in Britain.

During the 1780s, Gillray focussed on English party politics, attacking both the Whigs and the Tories, and also members of the royal family, including George, the Prince of Wales. Of the three great stipple engravings that he produced in 1792, *A Voluptuary under the Horrors of Digestion* caricatures the results of the Prince of Wales' debauchery in a particularly explicit way.

Regarding his attitude to international affairs, Gillray was initially pleased when the ancien régime fell in France in 1789. However, he altered his opinion as events turned more bloodthirsty, and produced some horrific satires of the revolutionaries, including *Un Petit Souper à la Parisienne* (1792), in which Sans Culottes are shown dining on the remains of their enemies. The rise of Napoleon inspired a further group of incisive caricatures, including *The Plum Pudding in Danger* (1805), in which Napoleon and the Tory leader, William Pitt, divide a globe-like pudding between them. Having attacked the response of the Whig Opposition to the revolution, he accepted a pension from Pitt in 1797.

Alongside the political subjects, Gillray produced a large number of social caricatures, often based on designs or ideas by such amateur artists as the Rev Brownlow North, the Rev John Sneyd and Charles Lorraine Smith.

Before the mid 1780s, Robert Wilkinson, of 58 Cornhill, published many of Gillray's caricatures while, after that date, they were issued by Samuel Fores, of 3 Piccadilly, and significantly by Hannah Humphrey, of 51 New Bond Street. The younger sister of William Humphrey, Hannah became his sole publisher in 1791, and his landlady from 1793, by which time she had moved to 18 Old Bond Street. She continued to offer him steady support, and he would move with her to 37 New Bond Street in 1794, and then 27 St James's Street in 1797.

A decade later, in 1807, his physical and mental health began to decline. Exhibiting signs of insanity in 1810, he attempted to commit suicide in the following year. Eventually, he died on 1 June 1815, in his room above Mrs Humphrey's shop in St James's Street, and was buried at St James's Church, Piccadilly.

His work is represented in numerous public collections, including the British Library, the British Museum, the National Portrait Gallery and Tate; and the Library of Congress (Washington DC).

Further reading:

'Gillray, James (*b* London, 13 Aug 1756; *d* London, 1 June 1815)', Jane Turner (ed), *The Dictionary of Art*, London: Macmillan, 1996, vol 12, pages 639-641;
Richard T Godfrey, *James Gillray: the art of caricature*, London: Tate Publishing, 2001;
Draper Hill (intro), *James Gillray (1756-1815): Drawings and Caricatures*, London: Arts Council, 1967;
Draper Hill, *Mr Gillray the Caricaturist: a biography*, London: Phaidon, 1965;
Anita McConnell and Simon Heneage, 'Gillray, James (1756-1815)', H C G Matthew and Brian Harrison (eds), *Oxford Dictionary of National Biography*, Oxford University Press, 2004, vol 22, pages 298-305;
Thomas Wright, *Historical and Descriptive Account of the Caricatures of James Gillray*, London: Henry G Bohn, 1851;
Thomas Wright, *The Works of James Gillray: the caricaturist, with the story of his life and times*, London: Chatto and Windus, 1873

JOHN NIXON

John Colley Nixon (before 1759-1818)

One of the most notable amateur artists working in London in the late eighteenth century, John Nixon became best known for his caricatures of urban society.

John Nixon was the son of Robert Nixon, a successful Irish merchant. With his brother Richard, he too developed a mercantile career, living and working at Basinghall Street, near Guildhall Yard in the City. He was a special juryman at the Guildhall and a Captain of the Guildhall Volunteers. Yet at the same time, he moved in leading artistic and fashionable circles, acting as honorary secretary of the Beefsteak Club and producing a number of landscape paintings, caricatures and illustrations.

Nixon exhibited at the Royal Academy of Arts between 1781 and 1813, while another of his brothers, the Rev Robert Nixon (1759-1837), was an honorary exhibitor between 1790 and 1808. As curate at Foots Cray, Kent, Robert played host to J M W Turner, who painted his first oil while staying with him in 1793, and gave him his first lessons in landscape painting. He also received lessons in figure painting from Stephen Rigaud. In 1798, Robert accompanied Turner and Rigaud on a sketching tour of Kent. Yet another brother, James, was a miniature painter.

John Nixon combined business and pleasure by both trading and sketching on the frequent tours that he made to Ireland in the 1780s and 1790s; he was accompanied on one such Irish trip by topographer and caricaturist, Captain Francis Grose (1791), and in turn went with Thomas Rowlandson to Bath (1792).

As a result of extensive travels, across Britain and on the Continent (1783-84; 1802 and 1804), Nixon became a topographical illustrator; his drawings were included in *Seats of the Nobility and Gentry* (1779-86) and he illustrated Thomas Pennant's *Journey from London to the Isle of Wight* (1801) and a *Guide to Watering Places* (1803). He also exhibited a set of illustrations to Laurence Sterne's *Tristram Shandy* at the Royal Academy (1786). Throughout the period, he drew popular caricature prints, often published by William Holland and usually satirising social preoccupations, such as *A Country Dance*.

Nixon was a member of the set of Elizabeth Craven (Lady Craven), Margravine of Ansbach at Brandenburg House, Hammersmith, and proved a notable amateur actor in its theatrical productions.

Visiting the Isle of Wight regularly from 1789, Nixon died there, in Ryde, in 1818. Before he died he was bequeathed the estate of Upland, Ilford, Essex, by his great uncle Richard Eastland.

His work is represented in numerous public collections, including the British Museum and the V&A.

Further reading:

Frank S Brown, *A Georgian Comedy of Manners: Humorous Watercolours of Life in Bath, the West Country and London by John Nixon*, Bath: Holburne Museum, 1994;
L H Cust (rev Douglas Fordham), 'Nixon, John Colley (*b* before 1759; *d* 1818)', H C G Matthew and Brian Harrison (eds), *Oxford Dictionary of National Biography*, Oxford University Press, 2004, vol 40, pages 936

JOHN WILSON CARMICHAEL

John Wilson Carmichael (1799-1868)

The Newcastle artist, John Wilson Carmichael, has gained a particular reputation for his impressive marine subjects, which were informed by his own experience as a sailor and ship builder. However, he was a wide-ranging painter of landscapes and townscapes, especially early in his career, when he collaborated closely with leading local architect, John Dobson.

John Wilson Carmichael was born at Ouseburn, Newcastle upon Tyne, on 9 June 1799, the eldest of the three children of the shipwright, William Carmichael, and his wife, Mary (née Johnson), the daughter of a mariner. During his teens, he spent three years at sea, working on a ship that sailed between Spanish and Portuguese ports. He then followed his father's trade, and was apprenticed to the ship builder, Richard Farrington & Brothers, of North Shore, Newcastle. The Farringtons were also cabinet makers, upholsterers, gilders and carvers, and were engaged in the cultural life of the town. As a result, they recognised and encouraged Carmichael's artistic talent, Joseph Farrington buying him his first box of watercolours. In time, he also became a friend and pupil – however informally – of Thomas Miles Richardson Senior, the leading artist in Newcastle at the time. From the early 1820s, he collaborated closely with the architect and developer of Newcastle, John Dobson, working up his perspective drawings into arresting watercolours, complete with figures.

In 1825, Carmichael stopped working as a carpenter, and set himself up as a landscape painter and drawing master. In the following year, he married Mary Sweet in Ryton, a little west of Newcastle, and they settled at New Road, in Newcastle itself. (By 1846, they had eight children.) His later residential and studio addresses in Newcastle comprise Blackett Street, Percy Street, Grainger Street, and Hood Street.

In 1827, Carmichael was, with T M Richardson and Henry Perlee Parker, instrumental in founding the Northern Academy of Arts, and it would become the main local showcase for his work. His increasing abilities as a painter and illustrator of landscapes and marines soon attracted influential local patrons, both private and civic, including Major George Anderson and Trinity House, Newcastle (a charitable guild of seafarers). With the arrival of George Balmer in North Shields in 1831, Carmichael gained a friendly rival and, eventually, intimate friend, and they would collaborate on several paintings. His interest in developing infrastructure led, among other projects, to a further collaboration, that with John Blackmore on the the illustrated book, *Views on the Newcastle and Carlisle Railway* (1836).

From 1835, Carmichael exhibited in London, at the Royal Academy of Arts (21 works, 1835-59) and the Society of British Artists (6 works, 1838-47). Successes at these venues led him to move to the capital a decade later in 1846, and he and his family settled at 20 Howland Street, Bloomsbury. In 1853, they moved to 8 Milton Street (now Balcombe Street), Marylebone. Carmichael continued to work hard and ambitiously, producing large-scale historical and contemporary subjects, which he exhibited at the British Institution (21 works, 1846-62) as well as the Royal Academy.

In 1855, *The Illustrated London News* commissioned him to go to the Baltic to record the events of the Åland War, a naval conflict between Russia and the allied nations of Britain and France, which related to the Crimean War. The trip resulted not only in the drawings that were engraved for publication in *The Illustrated London News* but also several paintings. The Baltic was probably the furthest extent of his travels during his years as an artist, and his Mediterranean subjects are likely to have been based on sketches by others. His abilities as a technician were exploited by Winsor and Newton when it commissioned him to produce two handbooks: *The Art of Marine Painting in Watercolours* (1859) and *The Art of Marine Painting in Oil Colours* (1864).

Following the death of a son in 1862, Carmichael left London and settled at 18 Mulgrave Terrace, Scarborough. He continued to paint, and produced a number of watercolours of the northeast coast. Dying in Scarborough on 2 May 1868, he was survived by his wife and most of his children. His studio sale was held at Christie, Manson & Woods, in London, on 24-25 November 1870.

Carmichael's eldest daughter, Margaret, was the mother of the artist, Herbert Gustave Schmalz.

Another daughter, Annie, married the wood-engraver, William Luson Thomas, who founded the illustrated weekly newspaper, *The Graphic*, in 1869, as a rival to *The Illustrated London News*.

His work is represented in numerous public collections, including the National Maritime Museum (Greenwich) and the V&A; and Brighton and Hove Museums and Art Galleries, Grimsby Fishing Heritage Centre, Hartlepool Museums and Heritage Service, Laing Art Gallery (Newcastle), Shipley Art Gallery (Gateshead), Sunderland Museum & Winter Gardens and York Art Gallery.

Further reading:

Andrew Greg, 'Carmichael, John Wilson (1799-1868)', H C G Matthew and Brian Harrison (eds), *Oxford Dictionary of National Biography*, Oxford University Press, 2004, https://doi.org/10.1093/ref:odnb/4703;
Andrew Greg, *John Wilson Carmichael: Painter of Life on Sea and Land*, Tyne and Wear Museums, Newcastle upon Tyne, 1999;
Diana Villar, *John Wilson Carmichael 1799-1868*, Portsmouth: Carmichael and Sweet, 1995

JAMES BAKER PYNE

James Baker Pyne, VPSBA (1800-1870)

Though he seems to have taught himself to paint, James Baker Pyne developed into a significant landscape painter, first as a member of the Bristol School, and then as a spirited follower of J M W Turner.

James Baker Pyne was born in Bristol on 5 December 1800. In accordance with his parents' wishes, he was articled to an attorney, but abandoned law at the age of 21 to pursue his interest in art. Apparently self-taught, he absorbed the influence of other Bristol painters, especially Francis Danby, whose characteristic dark, poetic tones reappear in Pyne's early landscapes of the local area.

Pyne's artistic development was supported by an increasing local interest in the visual arts. The Bristol Institution for the Promotion of Literature, Science and the Fine Arts, in Park Street, was founded in 1823, and held inaugural exhibitions of Old Masters and contemporary artists in 1824. The contemporary exhibition – called in some sources the 'Bristol Gallery of Arts' – was organised by a number of leading artists, including Edward Villiers Rippingille and Samuel Jackson, the latter taking responsibility for its hanging. A landmark in the establishment of a Bristol School of Artists, it also provided Pyne with his first opportunity to show his work in public.

By the late 1820s, Pyne was living at 6 Dove Street, Kingsdown, near the centre of Bristol, and supplementing his income by working as a drawing master and, possibly, a picture restorer. In 1827, William James Müller became his apprentice, and had lessons in oil and watercolour, though amicably cancelled his indentures after two years (and never took another teacher). At some point, Müller's friend, George Arthur Fripp, also took lessons in oils from Pyne.

Though 'he enjoyed little of the social life of Bristol's other artists' (Greenacre, in Matthew and Harrison 2004, vol 45, page 643), Pyne briefly shared a studio with Samuel Jackson in 1829, and three years later spent six weeks in France with E V Rippingille.

In 1831, when he first exhibited in Liverpool, Pyne was living at 11 Wellington Place, Stapleton Road, Bristol. Two years later, he gave his address as 33 New Church Street, Edgware Road, Paddington, London, and exhibited for the first time at both the British Institution (until 1844) and the Society of British Artists. Between 1836 and 1841, he also exhibited seven works at the Royal Academy of Arts. During this period, he moved fairly frequently, living at 89 Milton Street, Dorset Square (1836) and 6 Earl's Court Terrace, Old Brompton (1840), before settling at York Cottage, North End, Walham Green, Fulham, in 1841. This probably coincided with his marriage.

From the 1830s, Pyne's works showed the influence of J M W Turner, through their use of dramatic effects and increasingly restricted palette, often dominated by pale yellow. The artist passed this influence onto his pupil, James Astbury Hammersley, who would have an important role in the artistic life of Manchester. From 1839, Pyne followed Turner in producing the first of a series of volumes of lithographed illustrations, *Windsor, with its Surrounding Scenery*.

In 1842, Pyne was elected a member of the Society of British Artists, and soon showed exclusively at its gallery in Suffolk Street, off Pall Mall East (206 pictures in all). For some years, he also acted as its Vice-President. Occasionally, he collaborated with other artists, notably William Shayer SBA, who added figures to his landscapes, and Thomas Sidney Cooper RA, who added animals.

In 1846, Pyne travelled through Germany and Switzerland to Italy, in order to gather material to work up into finished pictures. The initial results appeared at the Suffolk Street Galleries in the following year: two views of the Rhine and three of the Italian Lakes. It is perhaps these pictures that prompted the Manchester art dealer, William Agnew, to commission Pyne to paint the English Lake District, between 1848 and 1851, and then to revisit Italy, between 1851 and 1854 (partly in the company of the watercolourist, William Evans of Bristol). His paintings of the Lake District resulted in an exhibition in 1852, and two volumes of lithographs: *The English Lake District* (1853, published by Agnew, lithographed by W Gauci) and *Lake Scenery of England* (1859, published by Day & Son, lithographed by Thomas Picken). He also contributed frequently to the *Art Journal* between 1856 and 1870. Several of his Continental subjects were included in the Manchester Art Treasures Exhibition in 1857.

By 1855, Pyne had moved from Fulham to Camden Town, living first at 43 Camden Villas and, by 1863, at 203 Camden Road. He died at this last address on 29 July 1870. His sons, James Baker Pyne, a photographer, and Charles Pyne, an artist, survived him.

His studio sale took place at Christie's on 25 February 1871.

His work is represented in numerous public collections, including the British Museum and the V&A; Manchester Art Gallery and Wolverhampton Art Gallery; and Indianapolis Museum of Art.

The V&A also holds his Picture Memoranda, two manuscript volumes recording the oil paintings that he produced between 1840 and 1868.

Further reading:

David Cordingly, 'Pyne, James Baker (*b* Bristol, 5 Dec 1800; *d* London, 29 July 1870)', Jane Turner (ed), *The Dictionary of Art*, London: Macmillan, 1996, vol 25, page 759;
Francis Greenacre, 'Pyne, James Baker (1800-1870)', H C G Matthew and Brian Harrison (eds), *Oxford Dictionary of National Biography*, Oxford University Press, 2004, vol 45, page 643

JOHN SKINNER PROUT

John Skinner Prout, NWS (1805-1876)

John Skinner Prout's talent as a landscape painter led him to develop a fascinating career. Having first established himself as a 'Picturesque Antiquarian' in emulation of his uncle, Samuel, he then migrated to Australia, where he gained a pioneering position as both a topographical artist and a teacher and lecturer. On his return to England, he capitalised on his antipodean experience by presenting entertaining and educative dioramas and panoramas, while also producing a substantial body of watercolours of British and European scenes, which he exhibited as a leading member of the New Society of Painters in Water Colours.

John Skinner Prout was born in Plymouth, Devon, on 19 December 1805, a son of John Prout and his wife, Maria (née Skinner), and a nephew of the watercolour painter, Samuel Prout. He was educated at Plymouth Grammar School. He was mainly self-taught as an artist, though he emulated the work of his uncle, in style and subject matter. In 1827, he moved to Penzance, Cornwall, where he worked as a drawing teacher. A year later, he married the harpist and music teacher, Maria Heathilla Marsh, in Colaton Raleigh, Devon, and they spent the early years of their marriage in Penzance. They would have five daughters and five sons.

In 1831, Prout moved with his growing family to Bristol, and he established himself as a topographical watercolourist and lithographer, exhibiting with the Bristol Society of Artists from its first exhibition in 1832. Early in 1833, he helped found the Bristol Sketching Club, alongside William Evans, Samuel Jackson, W J Müller, T L Rowbotham and William West. He went on numerous sketching tours with Jackson and Müller, across southern England, and to Wales and Ireland. Back in Bristol, he prepared his first volume of lithographs, *Picturesque Antiquities of Bristol*, which was published by George Davey in 1834. Further sketching tours yielded the volumes, *Antiquities of York, Antiquities of Chester* and *Castles and Abbeys of Monmouthshire*. In 1838, he and his family moved to London and, in the same year, he was elected a member of the New Society of Painters in Water Colours. Across his career, it would become the main showcase for his work.

In 1840, Prout and his family migrated to New South Wales, in Australia, where relatives of his had already settled. During the next eight years, he excelled in the country as an artist, teacher and promoter of the fine arts. Settling first in Sydney, he was elected a member of the Sydney Mechanics School of Arts in June 1841, and in the same month gave its members the first two of a number of lectures on painting. He imported a lithographic press from England and, in 1842, began to undertake series of lithographic views, beginning with *Sydney Illustrated* (1842-44), which was produced in collaboration with John Rae. In the same year, he also worked as a scene painter at the Olympic Theatre and as a drawing master at Sydney College, and began the first of several sketching tours in New South Wales. In October 1843, an exhibition of his work was held at Cetta & Hughes's shop in George Street, and his paintings continued to appear in local loan exhibitions through the decade, courtesy of their owners.

In January 1844, Prout and his family moved to Hobart on the island of Van Diemen's Land (which would be officially renamed Tasmania in 1856). While there, he befriended the expatriate artist, John Glover, and his family. As the result of sketching tours in Tasmania and Victoria, many made in the company of Francis Simpkinson, he achieved two further lithographic projects: *Tasmania Illustrated* (1844-47) and *Views of Melbourne and Geelong* (1847). During his visit to Melbourne, he delivered lectures on art at the local Mechanics Institute.

Following their return to England in 1848, Prout and his family settled in London, and from then on lived at various addresses in the area of Camden Town and Kentish Town. He was re-elected as associate (1849) and member (1862) of the New Society of Painters in Water Colours, and exhibited with it regularly and frequently. He made a name for himself with his Australian subjects, including much admired studies of giant tree ferns and at least two particularly ambitious works: *A Grand Diorama of Australia* (shown at the Western Literary Institution, in Leicester Square, in 1850) and the imaginary panorama, *A Voyage to Australia, and a Visit to the Gold Fields* (shown at 309 Regent Street, in 1852).

From 1854 until his death, Prout continued to make summer sketching tours in Britain and on the Continent. The many works that he produced during this later period of more than two decades were executed in a style that absorbed the influences of J M W Turner and John Duffield Harding, as well as of fellow artists of the Bristol School.

John Skinner Prout died at his home, at 4 Leighton Crescent, Kentish Town, on 29 August 1876. His studio sale was held at Christie, Manson & Woods on 26 February 1877.

His work is represented in numerous public collections, including the British Museum and the V&A; The Fitzwilliam Museum (Cambridge); Yale Center for British Art (New Haven, CT); and the National Library of Australia (Canberra) and the State Library of New South Wales (Sydney).

Further reading:

Tony Brown, 'John Skinner Prout', *Design & Art Australia Online*, 2001; Tony Brown & Hendrik Kolenberg, *Skinner Prout in Australia 1840-1848*, Hobart: The Tasmanian Museum and Art Gallery, 1987; Huon Mallalieu, 'Prout, John Skinner (1805-1876)', H C G Matthew and Brian Harrison (eds), *Oxford Dictionary of National Biography*, Oxford University Press, 2004, https://doi.org/10.1093/ref:odnb/22843;
Scott Wilcox, 'Prout Family (2) John Skinner Prout (*b* Plymouth, 1806; *d* London, Aug 29, 1876)', Jane Turner (ed), *The Dictionary of Art*, London: Macmillan, 2003, https://doi.org/10.1093/gao/9781884446054.article.T069857

EDWARD ANGELO GOODALL

Edward Angelo Goodall, RWS (1819-1908)

A member of a well-known family of artists, Edward Angelo Goodall established his individuality by recording the places and people that he encountered on wide-ranging travels. These included an early expedition to British Guiana (1841-44) and a commission from *The Illustrated London News* to cover the Crimean War (1854-55). Increasingly, he became associated with scenes of the Mediterranean, from Gibraltar to Constantinople, and especially Venice, which he visited on 15 occasions. His work is restrained, meticulous yet often luminous.

Edward Angelo Goodall was born in London on 8 June 1819, the eldest of the ten children of the Yorkshire-born engraver and painter, Edward Goodall, and his wife, Eliza (née Le Petit). Four of his siblings also became artists: Alfred, Eliza, Walter and, most famously, Frederick. At the time of his birth, the family was living at 20 Arlington Street (now Arlington Road), Camden Town. In 1823, it moved to 11 Lower Platt Place, also in Camden Town, and then, in 1827, to Mornington Grove Cottage, Mornington Grove, Hampstead Road (which Edward Goodall had especially built).

Edward Angelo Goodall was educated at University School, London, and then began an apprenticeship in engraving with his father. He painted in his spare time, and was encouraged by such visitors to his home as J MW Turner, David Roberts and – a close neighbour – Clarkson Stanfield (all of whom had their work engraved by Edward Goodall). Stanfield was particularly impressed by his watercolour of the landing of the Lord Mayor at Blackfriars Bridge, which he produced in 1836, at the age of 17, and which was awarded a silver medal by the Society of Arts. As a result, his father allowed him to pursue a career as a painter.

In 1841, Goodall began to exhibit (initially showing views of Caen in Normandy) at leading London galleries, including the British Institution, the Royal Academy of Arts and the Society of British Arts. However, in July of that year, he joined the Schomburgk Guinea Boundary Expedition, led by Robert Schomburgk, which intended to map the boundaries of British Guiana, in South America. He replaced W L Walton as the expedition's official artist, Walton having pulled out when Schomburgk's brother, the botanist, Richard, contracted yellow fever. Over the following three years, he produced watercolours of both botanical subjects (which would be exhibited in Berlin) and indigenous tribes (which were shown in London and Paris). The watercolours were later donated to the Colonial Office (and are now in the collections of the British Library, along with letters and a journal).

On his return to England in 1844, Goodall took up oil painting, and from 1845 exhibited an oil annually at the RA, the first being *Landing Place to an Indian Village, British Guiana, South America* (No 582), which was admired by Turner. He made many sketching tours in Europe and North Africa, sometimes in the company of other artists, and took in France, Spain, Portugal, Gibraltar, Italy, Greece, Turkey, Egypt and Morocco. Venice was a favourite destination, and he visited it 15 times.

In 1854, Goodall was commissioned by *The Illustrated London News* to visit the Crimea, and record the events of the war between Russia and the alliance comprising Britain, France, Sardinia and the Ottoman Empire. Arriving in the December, he spent a year in the region attached to the Naval Brigade Headquarters, and recorded key events in 65 watercolours. On departing, he went to Rome to paint.

In 1858, Goodall married Frances Chittenden, the daughter of the gentleman farmer, Andrew Chittenden, of The West Court, Detling, Kent. They settled at 24 St George's Square (now Chalcot Square), Primrose Hill, and would have four sons and seven daughters. When the family moved to 57 Fitzroy Road, by 1865, Goodall retained his St George's Square address as a studio. He was elected an associate of the Society of Painters in Water Colours in 1858, and a member in 1864, and it increasingly became the main showcase for his work. He continued to undertake sketching tours and to exhibit well into the 1880s.

Edward Angelo Goodall died in London on 16 April 1908, and was buried at Highgate Cemetery. A studio sale was held at Christie, Manson & Woods on 30 November 1908.

His work is represented in numerous public collections, including the British Library and the V&A.

Further reading:

Richard Goodall, *The Goodall Family of Artists*, www.goodallartists.ca;
Michael St John-McAlister, 'Edward Angelo Goodall (1819-1908): An Artist's Travels in British Guiana and the Crimea', *Electronic British Library Journal*, 2010, Article 5

ALFRED WATERHOUSE

Alfred Waterhouse, PRIBA RA (1830-1905)

Alfred Waterhouse was one of the most important and successful of Victorian architects and designers. He was also admired for his architectural perspectives and landscape watercolours.

Alfred Waterhouse was born in Aigburth, Liverpool, on 19 July 1830, into a comfortable mercantile Quaker family, as the eldest of seven children of the cotton broker, Alfred Waterhouse, and his wife, Mary (née Bevan). He was educated at the Quaker boarding school, Grove House School, Tottenham (then in Middlesex). He then served an apprenticeship with Richard Lane and P B Alley, a Quaker practice in Manchester, and many of his own early commissions would be for Quaker relatives and friends. Returning from the first of several Continental tours in 1854, he set up his practice in Manchester, working in a Neo-Gothic style, influenced and admired by John Ruskin. He established his reputation by winning the prestigious local competitions for the Assize Courts (1859-64) and the Town Hall (1868-77, including its furniture and fittings). In 1860, he married Elizabeth Hodgkin, the daughter of the Tottenham barrister and Quaker minister, John Hodgkin. They would have three sons and two daughters (the elder of whom married the poet, Robert Bridges).

In 1865, Waterhouse moved to London, and lived and worked at 8 (later 20) New Cavendish Street. The innumerable commissions that followed tested his planning skills and professionalism, and encouraged him to broaden his stylistic range to take in Romanesque and French Renaissance. He also achieved distinction as a technical pioneer, in employing terracotta on an extensive scale in his work on the Natural History Museum, London (1873-81), and on numerous offices of the Prudential Assurance Company (from 1877). Other major works included churches (he was baptised into the Anglican Church in 1877), country houses and institutional buildings.

Exhibiting designs and landscape watercolours regularly at the Royal Academy of Arts, Waterhouse was elected an associate, in 1878, and full Royal Academician, in 1885. He was awarded a Gold Medal by the Royal Institute of British Architects (1878), and a decade later was elected its President (1888-1891). He was also a founder member of the Society for the Protection of Ancient Buildings and a life trustee of Sir John Soane's Museum, London.

In 1878, Waterhouse bought an estate at Yattendon, Berkshire, and designed its house, Yattendon Court (which has since been destroyed). He died there on 22 August 1905.

His work is represented in the collections of the Royal Institute of British Architects and the V&A.

Further reading:

Colin Cunningham and Prudence Waterhouse: *Alfred Waterhouse: Biography of a Practice*, Oxford: Clarendon Press, 1992;
Colin Cunningham, 'Waterhouse, Alfred (1830-1905)', H C G Matthew and Brian Harrison (eds), *Oxford Dictionary of National Biography*, Oxford University Press, 2010, https://doi.org/10.1093/ref:odnb/36758;
Colin Cunningham, 'Waterhouse, Alfred (*b* Aigburth, Liverpool, July 19, 1830; *d* Yattendon, Berks, Aug 22, 1905)', Jane Turner (ed), *The Dictionary of Art*, London: Macmillan, 2003, https://doi.org/10.1093/gao/9781884446054.article.T090810

ETTORE ROESLER FRANZ

Ettore Roesler Franz (1845-1907)

Ettore Roesler Franz was an Italian painter in oil and watercolour, of landscapes and genre scenes, who exhibited regularly in London during the late nineteenth century. He remains best known for his immediate and atmospheric views of Rome and its environs, including places and practices that have since been lost to redevelopment and social change. In recent years, his pioneering work as a photographer has also attracted attention.

Ettore Roesler Franz was born in Rome on 11 May 1845, the son of Luigi Roesler Franz, who was of Bohemian descent, and Teresa (née Biondi). He was educated at the Christian schools of the Trinità dei Monti and, from 1863, studied art at the Accademia di San Luca. There he befriended the sculptor, Ettore Ferrari.

Between 1864 and 1872, Franz worked at the British Consulate, where he met the consul and artist, Joseph Severn, who had been a close friend of the poet, John Keats. On the death of Severn in 1879, he and his brother, Alessandro, contributed to a funerary plate in his memory, and Alessandro took his place as consul. Alessandro married the Englishwoman, Julia Teiser, and went to live with her in England, so providing Ettore with an entrée into the society and art market of Britain and its empire.

Franz was probably the first artist to devote himself to depicting the working class areas of Rome, many of which were coming under the threat of destruction, as the city was developed, from 1870, as the capital of the newly unified Italy. Devoting himself to his art from 1872, he began to exhibit at the Società degli amatori e cultori di belle arti, in Rome, in 1873, and the Società promotrice di belle arti di Torino, in 1874.

In 1875, Franz became the first President of the Società degli Acquarellisti di Roma, which he had helped found with nine other artists, including Vincenzo Cabianca, Onorato Carlandi, Nazzareno Cipriani, and Cesare Maccari, and which was modelled on the British Society of Painters in Water Colours. From the same year, he began to exhibit regularly in London, at venues that included the Dudley Gallery, and in 1878 participated in the Exposition Universelle in Paris. Such international exposure would lead to his gaining some significant patrons, including three kings of Italy and members of the Danish, German and Russian royal families.

In 1881, Franz visited various European cities, including Oxford, Paris and Cologne. By that year, he had begun to create the first of his three famous series of watercolours, which had the encompassing title of 'Roma Pittoresca' (but is better known in English as 'Vanishing Rome'). So he held a non-selling solo show at his studio at 96 Piazza San Claudio of works that formed the nucleus of the first series. Two years later, in 1883, the first set of 40 watercolours was exhibited in the Esposizione nazionale di belle arti di Roma, at the Palazzo delle Esposizioni. However, the second and third series of the cycle were not exhibited until 1897, in the foyer of the Teatro Drammatico Nazionale in Via Quattro Novembre.

Among other honours, Franz was appointed Knight of the Order of the Crown of Italy (1890) and an honorary citizen of Tivoli (1903).

His friend, the Futurist, Giacomo Balla, painted a famous portrait of him, which was exhibited at the Venice Biennale in 1902.

Ettore Roesler Franz died in Rome on 26 March 1907.

His work is represented in the collections of the Museo di Roma.

EDWARD THEODORE COMPTON

Edward Theodore Compton (1849-1921)

An active member of the British Alpine Club, as well as that of Germany and Austria, E T Compton based himself in Bavaria, and became one of the first artists to devote himself to depicting the remote and inaccessible heights of the Alps. Nevertheless, he travelled widely, from Scandinavia to North Africa, in search of subject matter for his brush.

Edward Theodore Compton was born in Stoke Newington, London, on 27 July 1849, the son of Theodore Compton, a Quaker insurance agent and amateur artist, and his wife, Elizabeth (née Harrison), the daughter of a Quaker barrister. In 1867, the family migrated to Darmstadt, Germany, which was then an important centre for the arts, so that Edward could complete his education. It is said that both Edward and his father went on to give lessons in art, and that Edward numbered among his students Alice, the daughter of the Grand Duke and Duchess of Hessen und bei Rhein. While living in Darmstadt, Edward went on a sketching tour of the Rhineland, Mosel and Eifel areas of Germany (1867-68), and, with his entire family, on a tour of the Bernese Oberland (July 1868). As a result of these travels, and especially his sight of the peaks of the Eiger, Mönch and Jungfau, he decided to become a painter of mountains. He would become one of the first artists to devote himself to the remote and inaccessible Alpine heights.

In 1869, Compton moved to Munich, in Bavaria, which was another artistic centre, and two years later, he began to exhibit at the city's Glaspalast. In 1872, he married the young Munich painter, Auguste Amalie Plötz (who was also known as Gusti von Romako). Together they would have three sons and two daughters, including the mountain painters, Edward Harrison Compton and Dora Keel-Compton, and the still life painter, Marion Compton. For two years, he and Auguste travelled through the Tyrol, Carinthia, Italy and Switzerland, and then, in 1874, settled at Feldafing, on Lake Starnberg, southwest of Munich. There, in the years 1877-78, they would build a comfortable home, the Villa Compton.

Retaining contact with Britain, Compton became a member of the Alpine Club in 1880 and, from that year, regularly contributed to such London exhibitions as those of the Royal Academy of Arts. In 1907, he and his son, E H Compton held a joint exhibition at the Fine Art Society. He also illustrated books for British publishers, including *The Picturesque Mediterranean* (Cassell, 1891, with others), his father's *A Mendip Valley* (Edward Stanford, 1892) and J F Dickie's *Germany* (A & C Black, 1912, with E H Compton). In addition, he produced guides for the Deutscher und Österreichischer Alpenverein, of which he was a member.

As a climber, Compton made some notable ascents, including Torre di Brenta and Cima di Brenta, both in 1882; and Aiguille Blanche de Peuterey, in 1905, and tours of the Silvretta Mountains, in 1909, both with the mountaineer, Karl Blodig. Away from the Alps, he travelled and painted in Scandinavia, Spain, Corsica and North Africa.

During the First World War, Compton was invited by the Austrian Army Command to paint pictures of the mountain front. However, despite approval from Berlin, the Bavarian High Command forbade him to do so. He was also excluded from the artists' association, Münchener Künstlergenossenschaft, because he was English.

Following the end of the war, Compton climbed Austria's highest mountain, the Grossglockner, on the occasion of his seventieth birthday, in 1919. He died in Feldafing on 22 March 1921.

His work is represented in the collections of the Alpine Club.

Further reading:

Philip Alan Tallantire, *Edward Theodore Compton (1849-1921): Mountaineer and Mountain Painter*, P A Tallantire, 1996

GEORGE SAMUEL ELGOOD

George Samuel Elgood, RI ROI (1851-1943)

George Samuel Elgood is best known for his watercolours of gardens, which were informed by a combination of observation and knowledge, and epitomise a classic genre of the Edwardian age. However, his range encompassed landscapes and interiors, as suggested by the works included here.

George Samuel Elgood was born in Oxford Street, Leicester, on 26 February 1851, one of ten children of a wool merchant. Brought up in Suffolk, he was educated privately and, for a year, from 1865, at Bloxham School, near Banbury. For financial reasons, the family returned to Leicester soon after that date. He studied at Leicester School of Art, and sketched the surrounding countryside with his teacher, Wilmot Pilsbury; his brother, Thomas Elgood; and his future brother-in-law, John Fulleylove. Another brother, Richard, would found the Leicester firm, Elgood Brothers, Art Metalworkers.

Elgood specialised in architecture at the National Art Training School, South Kensington (which later became the Royal College of Art). However, the death of his father in 1874, forced him to return to Leicester to take over the family yarn agency. Though able to paint only in his spare time, he managed to produce images of Leicestershire and elsewhere, and began to exhibit them at the Walker Gallery, Liverpool and in London at the Dudley Gallery and the Baillie Gallery.

Following his marriage to the artist, Mary Clephan, in 1881, Elgood painted full time. They based themselves at Rose Cottage, Markfield, Leicestershire, and also spent several months each year in Italy. He exhibited at London and provincial societies, and at dealers, including the Leicester Galleries and especially the Fine Art Society, where he held 13 solo shows. He was elected to the membership of the Royal Institute of Painters in Water Colours (1881) and the Royal Institute of Oil Painters (1883).

After the turn of the century, Elgood worked increasingly as an illustrator of books, including *Some English Gardens* (1904, with Gertrude Jekyll), *Some Italian Gardens* (1907), and two books by Alfred Austin: *The Garden that I Love* (1905) and *Lamia's Winter Quarters* (1907). He worked as a landscape gardener, specialising in the laying out of formal gardens, and becoming an authority on Renaissance gardens in England, Italy and Spain. From 1908, he lived with Mary at Knockwood, Tenterden, Kent, dying there on 21 October 1910. His wife survived him by 15 years.

His work is represented in the collections of the Art Gallery New South Wales (Sydney).

Further reading:
Diana Baskervyle-Glegg, 'Elgood, George Samuel (1851-1943), H C G Matthew and Brian Harrison (eds), *Oxford Dictionary of National Biography,* Oxford University Press, 2010, https://doi.org/10.1093/ref:odnb/62311;
Eve Eckstein, *George Samuel Elgood: His Life and Work 1851-1943*, London: Alpine Fine Arts Collection, 1995

LOUISA ANNE BERESFORD, MARCHIONESS OF WATERFORD

Louisa Anne Beresford, Marchioness of Waterford (née Stuart) (1818-1891)

Though largely untutored, Louisa Anne Beresford, Marchioness of Waterford, became one of the best-known amateur painters of her time. Working mainly in watercolour, she produced images that, ranging in mood and scale, reflected her interests in religion and philanthropy. She was influenced by artists of the Italian Renaissance, and encouraged by John Ruskin and members of the Pre-Raphaelite Brotherhood.

The Honourable Louisa Stuart was born at the Hôtel de Charost, Paris, on 14 April 1818, the daughter of Sir Charles Stuart, the Ambassador to the French Royal Court, and his wife, Lady Elizabeth Margaret (née Yorke), daughter of the 3rd Earl of Hardwicke.

Sir Charles was recalled from Paris in 1824, and settled with his family at Bure, in Hampshire (now in Dorset), on the remaining portion of Highcliffe, the estate developed by his grandfather, the 3rd Earl of Bute. However, in 1828, he was created Lord Stuart de Rothesay, and again appointed Ambassador to Paris, serving office until the 1830 Revolution. The family then shared their time between their Hampshire estate, much of which had been repurchased and restored, and their London home, at 4 Carlton House Terrace. Launched into society, Louisa and her elder sister, Charlotte, were noted as beauties, and so became much feted and much painted. Portraits of her include those by George Hayter (with her mother and sister, 1830, Government Art Collection) and Francis Grant (1859-60, National Portrait Gallery).

Louisa was described by a contemporary as 'perfectly devoted to her paint box at ten years old' (see Joicey and Nunn, 1983, page 28). She had occasional teachers, including a Mr Shepherdson and a Mr Page, but, in the main, she taught herself to paint by copying prints and family portraits, and by making studies from nature. Though she made some use of oils at an early age, she worked mostly in watercolour. A long visit with her parents to Rome and Naples, in the winter of 1836, broadened her horizons and decisively affected her artistic development; for she not only copied the work of old masters, but emulated their emphasis on mythological and religious subjects.

In 1839, Louisa met her future husband, Henry de la Poer Beresford, 3rd Marquess of Waterford, while attending the Eglinton Tournament, in Scotland, with her mother. They married at the Royal Chapel, Whitehall, on 8 June 1842, and then divided their time between Curraghmore, in Ireland, and Ford Castle, Northumberland. The Marquess tempered his formerly notorious sporting life in order to satisfy his bride. His notable generosity enabled her to fulfil her deep religious principles in a life of service. His encouragement helped her in the improvement of her art. Thus she was desolated when, in March 1859, he was killed in a hunting accident.

Following her husband's death, Louisa based herself at Ford, where she continued her work, and from where she occasionally went abroad. From the early 1850s, she had been acknowledged by leading figures in the art world. John Ruskin had encouraged her to seek tuition, while Pre-Raphaelite painters invited her to join a sketching club. Now she fulfilled her earlier promise. She decorated the village school, which she had built at Ford, with murals depicting the Lives of Good Children of the Bible (1862-83). In 1867, she inherited Highcliffe, and from then on divided her time between the two properties.

From the late 1870s, Louisa also exhibited her work in London, at the Grosvenor Gallery, the Dudley Gallery and the Society of Women Artists. As a result, she became one of the best-known amateurs of her time, befriended by Edward Burne-Jones and George Frederick Watts, and admired for her strong imagination, her mastery of composition and her use of rich Venetian colouring.

Following her death at Ford on 12 May 1891, retrospectives of her work were mounted in Ford itself (1891, 1892) and at Carlton House Terrace (1910).

Her work is represented in the collections of the British Museum, the National Portrait Gallery, Tate and the V&A; and The Fitzwilliam Museum (Cambridge).

Further reading:

Augustus Hare, *The Story of Two Noble Lives, being memorials of Charlotte, Countess Canning, and Louisa, Marchioness of Waterford*, London: George Allen, 1893 (3 vols);
Michael Joicey and Pamela Gerrish Nunn, *Lady Waterford Centenary Exhibition*, Ford: Lady Waterford Hall, 1983;
Charles Stuart, *Short Sketch of the Life of Louisa, Marchioness of Waterford*, London: printed by Spottiswoode, 1892;
Virginia Surtees, *Sublime & Instructive. Letters from John Ruskin to Louisa, Marchioness of Waterford, Anna Blunden and Ellen Heaton*, London: Michael Joseph, 1972;
Charlotte Yeldham, 'Beresford [née Stuart], Louisa Anne, Marchioness of Waterford (1818–1891)', H C G Matthew and Brian Harrison (eds), *Oxford Dictionary of National Biography*, Oxford University Press, 2004, https://doi.org/10.1093/ref:odnb/45749

SPY

Sir Leslie Ward, RP (1851-1922), known as 'Spy'

For almost forty years, the caricaturist, Leslie Ward, was synonymous with the society paper, *Vanity Fair*. His 'character portraits' were invariably well observed and witty, but rarely cruel.

Leslie Ward was born on 21 November 1851 at Harewood Square, London (on the site of what is now Marylebone Station). He was the son of the history painter, Edward Matthew Ward, and his wife, Henrietta Ada Ward, a fashionable portrait painter. His mother came from a long line of artists, most notably her paternal grandfather, James Ward. He learned to draw, paint and sculpt within this environment.

Ward was educated at Chase's School, Salt Hill, near Slough, and then at Eton. While there, he drew caricatures of his masters and fellow pupils, and exhibited a bust of his brother, Wriothesley, at the Royal Academy Summer Exhibition of 1867. In 1869, his father placed him with the architect, Sydney Smirke, a family friend. Yet he really wanted to paint, and this was made possible by the intervention of W P Frith.

Soon after he entered the Royal Academy Schools in 1871, Ward began to exhibit portraits in oil and watercolour, and could easily have made a career in that field. (Indeed, he would be elected to the Royal Society of Portrait Painters in 1891.) However, in 1873, another family friend, John Everett Millais recommended that Ward take his caricature of the zoologist, Professor Richard Owen, to Thomas Gibson Bowles, the owner of *Vanity Fair*. As Bowles had temporarily fallen out with his regular caricaturist, Carlo Pellegrini (who signed as 'Ape'), he invited Ward to join the staff, and suggested his pen name, 'Spy'. For the next fifteen years, the two artists shared between them most of the weekly coloured cartoons that featured in *Vanity Fair*. Then, on the death of Ape in 1889, until he left in 1911, Spy dominated. Latterly he also contributed 'character portraits' to *The Graphic*, *Mayfair* and *The World*.

Three years after he published his autobiography, *Forty Years of Spy*, in 1915, Ward was knighted. He died suddenly of heart failure at 4 Dorset Square, Marylebone, London, on 15 May 1922.

His work is represented in the collections of the National Portrait Gallery.

Further reading:

Peter Mellini, 'Ward, Sir Leslie [pseud. Spy] (1851 1922)', H C G Matthew and Brian Harrison (eds), *Oxford Dictionary of National Biography*, Oxford University Press, 2004, vol 57, pages 325-326

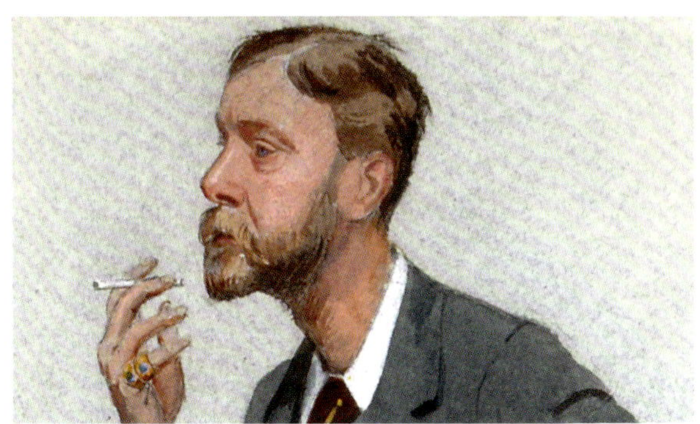

Detail of *Mr Walter Herries Pollock* [62]

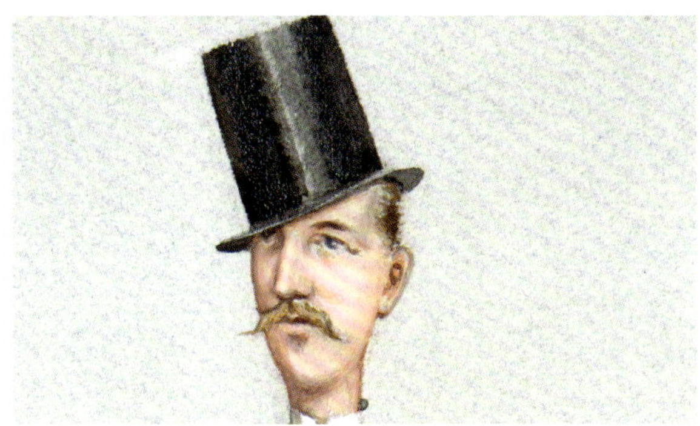

Detail of *HM George, King of Greece* [63]

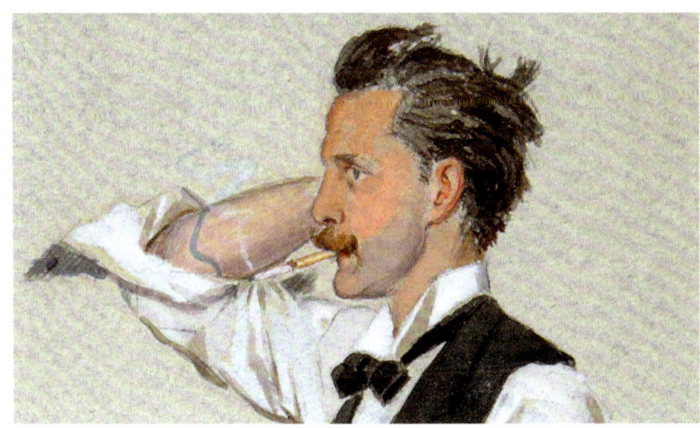

Detail of *Mr H J Cockayne-Cust, MP* [65]

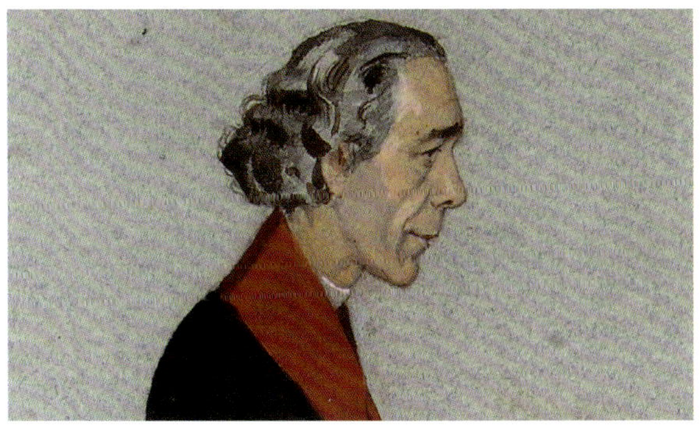

Detail of *Joseph Armitage Robinson, Dean of Westminster* [64]

WILLIAM HENRY MARGETSON

William Henry Margetson, RI RMS ROI (1861-1940)

Best known as a figurative artist, William Henry Margetson was equally successful as a painter and an illustrator. He became popular as an illustrator of adventure stories and fairy tales in the 1890s, and then gained a reputation as a painter of beautiful young women, sitting or standing in contemplation, at home or in the garden.

William Henry Margetson was born at 21 Grove Hill Terrace, Denmark Hill, London, on 1 December 1861, the younger son of the Yorkshire-born export merchant, Edward Margetson, and his Lancashire-born wife, Eleanor (née Bradshaw), the daughter of an engraver. In 1871, the family was living at 194 Camberwell Grove, and in 1881 at 210 Camberwell Grove.

Margetson was educated at Miss Pace's School, 122 Camberwell Grove, and Dulwich College, leaving the latter in 1877. He studied at the National Art Training School, South Kensington, and then, from 1878, at the Royal Academy Schools, winning the first of several prizes that August. In 1881, while still a student, he began to exhibit works at the principal London galleries, including two paintings at the Society of British Artists. Having established a studio at Ormond Chambers, 28 Great Ormond Street, by 1885, he exhibited genre scenes, portraits and other works regularly at the Royal Academy of Arts between 1885 and 1901 (and then occasionally until 1922).

In the mid 1880s, Margetson also began to contribute illustrations to periodicals. This included a collaboration – in *The English Illustrated Magazine* in 1885 – with the journalist and novelist, Joseph Hatton, and his elder daughter, Helen, who, like Margetson, had studied at the RA Schools, and was establishing herself as an artist. The piece was

> based on the diaries of Hatton's son Frank, an explorer and geologist who had died in 1883 in an accidental shooting in Borneo. (These were subsequently published in *North Borneo: Explorations and Adventures on the Equator*, published by Sampson Low.)
> (Robert J Kirkpatrick, 2017)

The first books that Margetson illustrated were also by Joseph Hatton, including *The Lyceum 'Faust'* (1886), a critique of Henry Irving's production of Goethe's *Faust*. He would go on to illustrate the sixth volume of 'The Henry Irving Shakespeare' (published by Gresham) and design Irving's production of Watts Phillips' *The Dead Heart* for the Lyceum Theatre (both 1889).

Margetson married Helen Hatton at St Mark's Church, Marylebone, in 1889 (when he was living or keeping a studio at 1 Lennard Place, St John's Wood – now the top section of Cavendish Avenue). By 1891, they and their first-born child, Hester, were boarding with the butler, George Gravatt, and his wife, at 7 St Anns Terrace, Marylebone. At that time, Margetson was working from 7 St Paul's Studios, Talgarth Road, West Kensington. The Margetsons' second child, Oliver, was born in West Kensington in 1892.

During the 1890s, Margetson established himself as an illustrator of adventure stories and fairy tales. These included four books by G A Henty (1893-98) and *The Village of Youth and Other Fairy Stories* (1895), by his sister-in-law, Bessie Lyle Hatton.

By the middle of the decade, Margetson and his family moved to Southeast London, living first in Deerhurst Road, Streatham, and later at 24 Hopton Road, Streatham, and 107 Thornlaw Road, West Norwood. The Margetsons' third child, Beryl was born at the latter in 1899. Margetson also maintained a studio in the area, at Farnham Road, Streatham. In 1894, he joined the Art Workers' Guild and, in 1896, was elected to the Royal Society of Miniature Painters. At some point after that date, he became an instructor in drawing at the Central School of Arts and Crafts at Morley Hall, Regent Street.

Following the turn of the century, Margetson continued to work as an illustrator, adding Biblical stories to his range of subjects, for such publications as *Hurlbut's Story of the Bible Told for Young and Old* (1904). However, he concentrated increasingly on his paintings, and especially those of beautiful young women. He was elected to the Royal Institute of Oil Painters, in 1901, and the Royal Institute of Painters in Water Colours, in 1909.

In 1902, the Margetsons left London and settled at Bohams, Westbrook Street, Blewbury, near Didcot, in Berkshire (now Oxfordshire). By 1911, they had moved within the village to The Homestead, London Street (now Corrydon House, London Road). In about 1925, they moved a few miles east to Priory Cottage, High Street, Wallingford. He died on 2 January 1940. He was survived by his wife and all three children. His eldest child, Hester, became a painter and illustrator, and married the actor, Michael Martin Harvey.

Further reading:

Robert J Kirkpatrick, 'W H Margetson', bearalley.blogspot.com, 2017 (including a list of 'books illustrated')

GEORGE COLE

George Cole, VPSBA (1810-1883)

Essaying a number of genres early in his career, and most notably animal portraiture, George Cole concentrated on landscape painting from about 1850. His most characteristic works show the rivers, coasts and – especially – the downs of Southern England, enlivened by farm workers and their livestock, and enhanced by atmospheric effects. He and his son, George Vicat Cole, strongly influenced each other, and rivalled each other in popularity.

George Cole was born in London on 15 January 1810, the second child and only son of James Cole and his wife, Elizabeth (née Parker). By the time that his mother died, in 1819, he had moved with his family to Portsmouth. Tim Barringer cites Cole's grandson, the painter, Rex Vicat Cole, in stating that 'George Cole's father dissipated a fortune', and a James Cole did die in a poor house in Portsmouth in 1847. Because of this financial loss, Cole is said to have begun 'his life with no formal education' and served an apprenticeship as a house and ship painter.

An edition of Michael Bryan's *A Biographical Dictionary of Painters and Engravers*, published in 1878, while Cole was still alive, provides convincing detail of his beginnings as an animal painter:

> Having a taste for drawing animals, he devoted all his leisure hours to study, but without the advantage of instruction from a master, or even seeing any pictures of excellence. A travelling menagerie coming to Portsmouth Fair, young Cole being much struck with the painted cloths exhibited in front of the caravans, was most anxious to be allowed to make studies from the living wild animals. An opportunity immediately offered, as Wombwell, the proprietor of the menagerie, applied to Cole's master for colour, canvass, &c, and a convenient room for a travelling artist to paint one of these cloths in. Cole here had an opportunity of seeing a real living artist at work, and soon found out the method of applying the colours. After some careful studies from the life, he immediately set to work for himself, and his first performance so much pleased Mr Wombwell, that he at once commissioned 'A Tiger Hunt in the Jungle with Elephants, &c.' This picture, which was an immense undertaking, being twenty feet square, was finished and exhibited for the first time at Weyhill fair, where it created much sensation … this painted cloth brought many commissions to Mr Cole's master from other menagerie proprietors, and our young artist was considered a great genius by these people … Conscience told him that he was helping others in deceiving the public, and, if he wished to be a real artist, he must be more truthful to nature … After serving the full time of his apprenticeship he quitted his master's business but still remained in Portsmouth, where he was greatly respected, and was for some time successful as an animal portrait painter. (pages 31-32)

In 1831, Cole married Eliza Vicat, a member of a Portsmouth Huguenot family. By a decade later, they were living at 1 Green Row, Portsmouth, with their three sons. Two of these – George Vicat Cole and Alfred Benjamin Cole – would follow in their father's footsteps.

During the 1830s and 40s, Cole worked in a number of genres in addition to animal portraiture, including human portraiture, still life and landscape. In 1838, he began to exhibit in London, and would do so most frequently at the Society of British Artists. Soon after this debut, he took some lessons from the Scottish painter, John Wilson. Then, in 1845, he attracted much attention with his *Don Quixote and Sancho Panza with Rosinante in Don Pedro's Hut*, when he showed it at the British Institution. Success led him to move with his family (by then comprising four children) to Montague Lodge, a large house in Buckland, just outside Portsmouth.

By 1849, when he first exhibited at the Royal Academy of Arts, Cole had begun to concentrate on landscape in emulation of works by artists of the Dutch School, which he had probably seen in the collections of his Portsmouth patrons. He made several sketching tours in Britain, often accompanied by his son, George, and, in 1851, they travelled together to the Moselle and Meuse. However, following a temporary estrangement in 1855, their working relationship came to an end. Cole was elected a member of the Society of British Artists in 1850 (and became its auditor in 1856, and its Vice-President in 1867).

From 1852, Cole and his family lived in London, first at 2 Lewis Place, Fulham (where a fifth child was born), and, from 1854, at 2 The Crescent, Kensington. A decade later, in 1863, he was able to purchase the larger neighbouring house, 1 Kensington Crescent, and also Coombe Lodge, near Liss, Hampshire.

During the 1850s and 60s, Cole travelled widely in Britain, taking in such popular motifs as Loch Katrine, in Scotland, and Bettws-y-Coed, in North Wales. However, at the heart of his subject matter lay the countryside of Southern England. As his career developed, he responded to his popularity by working on an increasingly large scale while also selling many smaller paintings directly to dealers.

George Cole died at his home at 1 Kensington Crescent, London, on 7 September 1883, five months after his wife.

His work is represented in numerous public collections, including Brighton and Hove Museums and Art Galleries and Portsmouth Museums.

Further reading:

Tim Barringer, 'Cole, George (1810-1883)', H C G Matthew and Brian Harrison (eds), *Oxford Dictionary of National Biography*, Oxford University Press, 2004, https://doi.org/10.1093/ref:odnb/5849

EDMUND GEORGE WARREN

Edmund George Warren, RI ROI (1834-1909)

Edmund George Warren was perhaps the best known of all Victorian watercolourists to specialise in arboreal landscapes and woodland scenes. He painted minutely detailed views of shady glades and the forest floor, and delighted in describing the effects of sunlight breaking through the canopy of leaves. He also enjoyed painting harvest scenes in the company of George Vicat Cole.

Edmund George Warren was probably born at Vine Cottage, Thistle Grove, north of the Fulham Road, in London. He was one of at least four sons – and possibly one daughter – of the painter, Henry Warren, to follow in their father's footsteps. The others were Albert Henry (1830-1911), Bonomi Edward (active 1860-79) and Henry Clifford (born 1843) – and also Fanny C Warren (active 1865-66), who was a member of the Warren household in 1866. Henry was a genre and landscape painter who specialised in Arabian subjects, and became closely associated with the New Society of Painters in Water Colours, as a member from 1835 and President from 1839.

Edmund George Warren began to exhibit works in 1852, the year in which he was elected an associate of the New Society of Painters in Water Colours. This was his principal venue for exhibition, and he would become a full member there four years later. He focussed on the southern counties of England, sometimes in the company of the fellow painter, George Vicat Cole. However, from early in his career, he also travelled widely across Britain, going as far as the Isle of Arran in the north and the River Wye in the west in search of rural subjects, and later extending his range to include Ireland.

The Warren family lived at Hortulan House, on the King's Road, in the 1850s, and at 24 Upper Phillimore Place, on Kensington High Street, in the 1860s. By 1868, Edmund had moved along the road to 29 Upper Phillimore Place and, by 1872, round the corner to 1a Phillimore Gardens. Then, in the 1880s, he lived further north at Flat 6, 1 Colville Mansions, Powis Terrace, Talbot Road, Bayswater. While there, he became a member of the Royal Institute of Oil Painters (1883-1903), though he continued to work in watercolour until the end of his career.

In the early 1890s, Warren began to have some financial problems, and was listed as a bankrupt in 1895. In that year, he moved to Ridge Cottage, Chudleigh, Devon, on the eastern edge of Dartmoor, though he had been painting in the area since the mid 1850s. Still living in Chudleigh in 1908, he died in Edmonton, Middlesex, in August 1909.

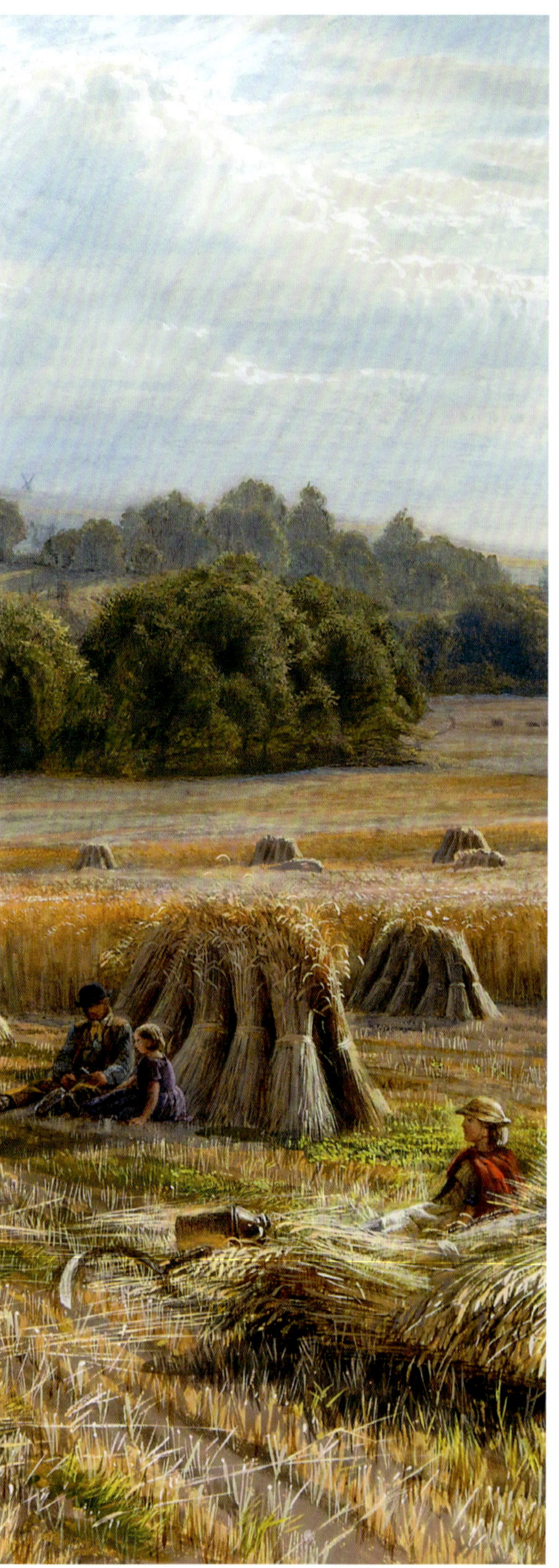

Detail of *High Summer Harvest* [68]

HECTOR CAFFIERI

Hector Edward Philippe Caffieri,
RBA RI ROI (1847-1931)

Though he is best known for his sensitive, atmospheric studies of fisherfolk – in ports that include his adopted home of Boulogne – Hector Caffieri was a wide-ranging painter of landscapes and genre scenes in the tradition of French academic naturalism.

Hector Caffieri was born at 3 Portland Place, Cheltenham (near the currently existing North Place), the second of eight children of Hector St Cyr Caffieri (1817-1890), a Roman Catholic wine merchant of French descent, and his wife, Mary (née Clow) (1820-1888). When his parents died, in Boulogne, they were styling themselves 'Caffieri de Beauvallon'. During his youth, the family lived at various addresses in Cheltenham, including 7 Painswick Lawn and 24 Montpelier Walk. He began to exhibit at the Society of British Artists in 1869, while living at the second address. (The society gained its royal charter in 1887.)

Following a brief period in the navy, Caffieri studied art in Paris under Gustave Boulanger and, at the Académie Julian, under Léon Bonnat and Jules Lefebvre. By 1873, he had settled in London and, by the following year, he had taken a studio at 8 Camden Studios, Camden Street. From there, he began to exhibit at the Royal Academy of Arts and the Society of British Artists, and he was elected a member of the latter in 1876. It is said that he was a correspondent during the Russo-Turkish War of 1877-78.

While continuing to live in Camden Town through the early 1880s, Caffieri made a number of sketching trips in England and France. Painting grounds included Burnham Beeches and the Thames at Cookham – and also Boulogne-sur-Mer. His parents retired to Boulogne, and settled at 8 Rue de La Tour Notre Dame, which became for him a second home. As a result, the port and its life would inspire his most recognisable subject matter.

From 1887, Caffieri lived at 30 Great Russell Street, Bloomsbury. Showing his work at an increasing number of venues in London and Paris, he was elected to the Royal Institute of Painters in Water Colours in 1885 (retiring in 1920) and the Institute of Oil Painters in 1894. (The Institute of Oil Painters gained its royal charter in 1909.) He held solo shows at the Continental Gallery, in New Bond Street, in 1900 and 1902.

Caffieri settled permanently in Boulogne in 1897, and became an active member of the Société des Beaux-Arts et des Arts Décoratifs du Boulonnais. His later addresses include Sentier Poure, Route-de-Calais (in 1916, along with 29 Chalcot Crescent, Primrose Hill, London) and 85 Rue des Vieillards. He died in Boulogne on 26 December 1931.

Detail of *Children Gathering Firewood* [73]

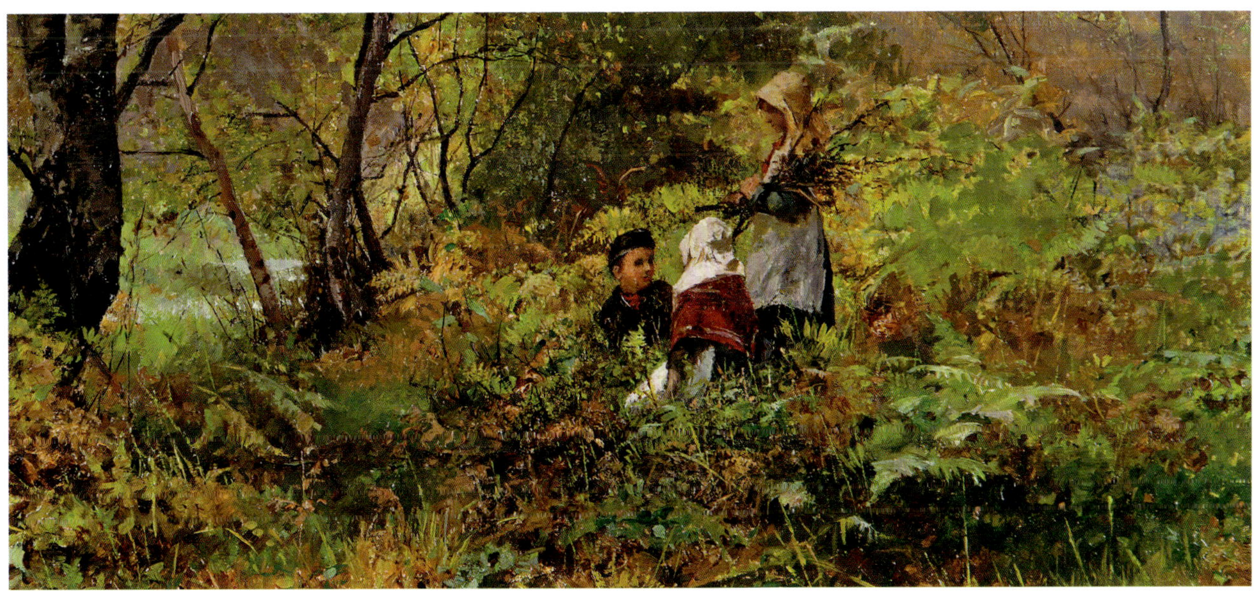

WALTER TYNDALE

Walter Frederick Roope Tyndale, RBC RI (1855-1943)

Walter Tyndale was one of the most popular and influential topographical watercolourists working at the turn of the century. He was also one of the first to benefit from the printing revolution of 1901 when his publishers, A & C Black, pioneered the use of three colour half-tone plates. The ensuing publishing boom led to a wealth of commissions for Tyndale for illustrated travel books, which took him from the Wessex countryside to Europe and the Far East.

Walter Tyndale was born at the Château Schapsdael, near Bruges, on 10 August 1855, to John Nash Tyndale (1814-1868), a Barrister-at-Law in the Middle Temple, and Charlotte Flora Hulme (born 1816). He was educated in Bruges and, at the age of 16, attended drawing classes at the city's academy. Following the outbreak of the Franco-Prussian War, the Tyndale family retreated to England and in 1871 settled in Bath. However, three years later, Walter Tyndale returned to Belgium to study at the Antwerp Academy; his assiduousness resulted in a silver medal for drawing from the antique with promotion to the life class. His ambition led him to Paris, where he studied at the Atelier Bonnat and worked in the studio of the former Antwerp student, Jan van Beers. In 1878, he returned again to England where, two years later, he took a studio in All Souls Place, in London. However, in 1881 he voyaged to the Cape to visit his brother, Arthur, who ran an ostrich farm. Though he married Evelyn Barnard in Bath in 1883 and settled with his family in Haslemere at the end of the decade, such peripatetic activities would characterise his career.

Tyndale was inspired by Claude Hayes and his friend Helen Allingham to turn exclusively to watercolour, the medium ideally suited to his topographical bent. The range of his travels is indicated by the titles of solo shows that he held at the Dowdeswell Galleries: 'Cairo, The Lebanon and Damascus' (1898), 'Cairo, Jerusalem and Sicily' (1899), 'Italy' (1901) and 'Rothenburg' (1902). His 1904 show, 'Fruit and Flower Stalls,' revealed how he could extend topography into the realms of still life and genre.

In the same year, Tyndale was commissioned by A & C Black to produce a book on 'Hardy's Wessex'. The commission resulted in a shift of allegiance: in 1905, the illustrations were exhibited at the Leicester Galleries, and later work, for other publishers, would be shown at the same venue. The most famous of these include *Below the Cataracts* (1910), *An Artist in Egypt* (1912) and *An Artist in the Riviera* (1913). From 1914, he held five solo shows at the Fine Art Society; he also continued to show regularly at the Royal Institute of Painters in Water Colours, which had elected him a member in 1911.

Following the outbreak of the First World War, Tyndale accepted a commission as D A Censor to the British Expeditionary Force and in 1915 sailed to Le Havre. At the age of almost 60, he was introduced as 'the oldest second lieutenant in the British Army'. By the end of the war, he held the rank of Captain and the position of Head Censor at Boulogne. During a period of leave, in 1918, he was elected an associate member of the Royal British Colonial Society of Artists; he became a full member in 1926. He spent many of his later years in Venice, but died at home at 29 Brunswick Gardens, Kensington, London, on 16 December 1943.

ERNEST ALBERT CHADWICK

Ernest Albert Chadwick, RBSA RCamA RI NSA
(1876-1956)

The landscape watercolours of E A Chadwick are detailed, realistic and carefully composed, but also gentle in both handling and mood. His best known works depict rural life in his native Warwickshire and surrounding counties, but he travelled widely by bicycle across England and Wales in order to discover suitable subjects.

Ernest Albert Chadwick was born in the village of Marston Green, Warwickshire, on 29 February 1876, the second of three children of the draughtsman and wood engraver, John William Chadwick, and his wife, Emily (née Woolley). Probably at that time, and certainly by 1881, the family was living at 2 Culey Place. A decade later, it had moved a few miles south to Back Lane, Hampton in Arden, and the 15-year-old Ernest was describing himself as a 'draughtsman'. He almost certainly studied under his father before he attended Birmingham Municipal School of Art. Initially, he worked as an engraver, and in the Census of 1901, described himself as such, while his sisters were identified as a teacher and a photographer.

Chadwick began to exhibit at the Royal Birmingham Society of Artists in 1896, and, as he began to specialise in landscape watercolours, it would become the main showcase for his art, displaying more than 400 of his works across his career. He was elected an associate member of the society in 1907 and a full member in 1912.

By the turn of the century, Chadwick was also exhibiting further afield. In 1900, he contributed for the first time to the exhibitions of the Royal Academy of Arts, in London, and did so almost annually until 1919. During the same period, his work began to be reproduced in periodicals, including special numbers of *The Studio*. As an example, *The Studio Yearbook for Decorative Art* for 1908 contains his images of two gardens – in Lichfield and near Lancaster – designed by Thomas H Mawson.

In 1911, Chadwick married Ethel Maud Barrows, the daughter of a wine merchant and Justice of the Peace, and they settled at 'Waterside', Alderbrook Road, Solihull (a few miles west of Hampton in Arden). Around 1918, they moved along the road to 'Caerleon'. Chadwick produced portraits of both his wife and his father-in-law, rare exceptions to his work as a landscape painter.

On the eve of the First World War, in 1914, Chadwick had a solo show of watercolours at the Graves Gallery in Birmingham, and during the war continued to exhibit occasionally. However, it is not known whether he undertook active service.

During the 1920s, Chadwick widened the geographical range of his subjects. He had adapted a bicycle to carry his painting equipment, and would travel hundreds of miles in search of suitable motifs. He made sketching tours of North Wales and Cornwall, and late in the decade visited Brittany. He is also known to have painted in Capri.

This increased variety was reflected in his activities as an exhibitor. In 1924, he was elected a member of the New Society of Artists (only three years after the society was founded to give artists living outside of London the opportunity to exhibit in the capital). In 1925, he was invited to become a member of the Lake Artists Society. And, having shown regularly at the Royal Cambrian Academy, in Conway, through the decade, he was, in 1929, elected an Academician. A decade later, in 1939, he was elected a member of the Royal Institute of Painters in Water Colours. Nevertheless, he also remained loyal to his locality, and became the Secretary of the Birmingham Art Circle.

In addition to exhibiting with societies, Chadwick held a number of solo shows, including those in London at the Greatorex Galleries (1924) and Walker's Galleries (1927, 1928, 1937 and 1938), and also as a special feature of an autumn exhibition of the RBSA (1931).

By the early 1930s, Chadwick was living in Henley-in-Arden (which lies between Solihull and Stratford-upon-Avon). Residing latterly at 'The Studio' in the High Street, he continued to work and exhibit almost until his death on 2 March 1956.

His work is represented in the collections of Birmingham Museum and Art Gallery.

JAMES AUMONIER

James Aumonier, RI ROI NEAC (1832-1911)

Though he did not take up painting professionally until he was over 30, James Aumonier soon distinguished himself with his peaceful landscapes of Southern England, and especially his pastorals and river scenes.

James Aumonier was born in Camberwell, London, on 9 April 1832, the second of the six children of Henry Collingwood Aumonier, a jeweller of French descent, and his wife, Nancy (née Stacy). He grew up with his family in North London, at addresses in Highgate and Barnet. Following the death of his father in 1848, he, and his mother and siblings, settled with his uncle, the jeweller, William Stacy, at Clifton Cottage, Willesden.

Aumonier showed an early interest in art and, while working as a paper stainer (by 1851), he took evening classes in drawing, at the London Mechanics' Institute (the forerunner of Birkbeck College); the Department of Science and Art, Marlborough House; and the National Art Training School, South Kensington. As a result of his studies, he became a designer of printed calicos for use in furnishings at a London factory, while spending much of his spare time teaching himself to paint from nature. He was living with three of his siblings at 31 Beaumont Street, Marylebone, in 1861, and, when he married Amelia Wright, the daughter of a gold beater, in 1863, she would live there too. They would have two sons and two daughters, including Louise Aumonier, who became a flower painter. (His nephew, Stacy Aumonier, became a landscape painter and writer of short stories.)

In 1864, Aumonier began to exhibit regularly, first showing at the British Institution and the Society of British Artists (which would gain its royal charter in 1887). During the 1860s, he and his family lived at addresses in New Wandsworth and Hornsey Rise, and, in the 1870s, in Kentish Town.

Not long after he started to exhibit at the Royal Academy of Arts in 1870, Aumonier made the acquaintance of William Morison Wyllie and Lionel Percy Smythe (the father and half-brother of William Lionel Wyllie), and they gave him advice and encouragement. He soon gained artistic recognition, though continued to work at the textile factory for a few more years. Working with equal success in oil and watercolour, he was elected an associate of the Institute of Painters in Water Colours in 1876, and a full member in 1879. (It received its royal charter in 1885.) He was one of the founder members of the Institute of Painters in Oil Colours in 1882, and also a member of the British Society of Pastellists, during its short life between 1890 and 1893. By that date, he and his family were living at Oxford Villas, Southdown Road, New Shoreham, Steyning, and, while they also had a London address at 115 Gower Street, Bloomsbury, he made much of being surrounded by the Sussex countryside during the decade.

Though he made only one trip abroad, to Venice and the Dolomites in 1891, Aumonier contributed to major international exhibitions, including those in Paris, Brussels, Munich, Berlin and Adelaide, and was awarded a number of medals. In 1900, the leading arts magazine, *The Studio*, published an article about him, written by Nancy Bell.

In his seventies, Aumonier continued to paint, and exhibited the results in a series of solo shows, beginning with one devoted to his watercolours at the Leicester Galleries, London, in 1908. However, he died just three years later, on 4 October 1911, at 97 South Hill Park, Hampstead, London. A memorial exhibition was held at the Goupil Gallery in 1912.

His work is represented in numerous public collections, including Manchester Art Gallery, Museums Sheffield and Russell-Cotes Art Gallery & Museum (Bournemouth).

Further reading:

P G Konody, rev Paul Cox, 'Aumonier, James (1832-1911)', H C G Matthew and Brian Harrison (eds), *Oxford Dictionary of National Biography*, Oxford University Press, 2012, https://doi-org/10.1093/ref:odnb/30501

INDEX

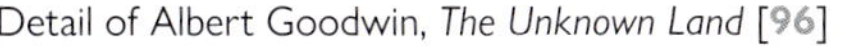

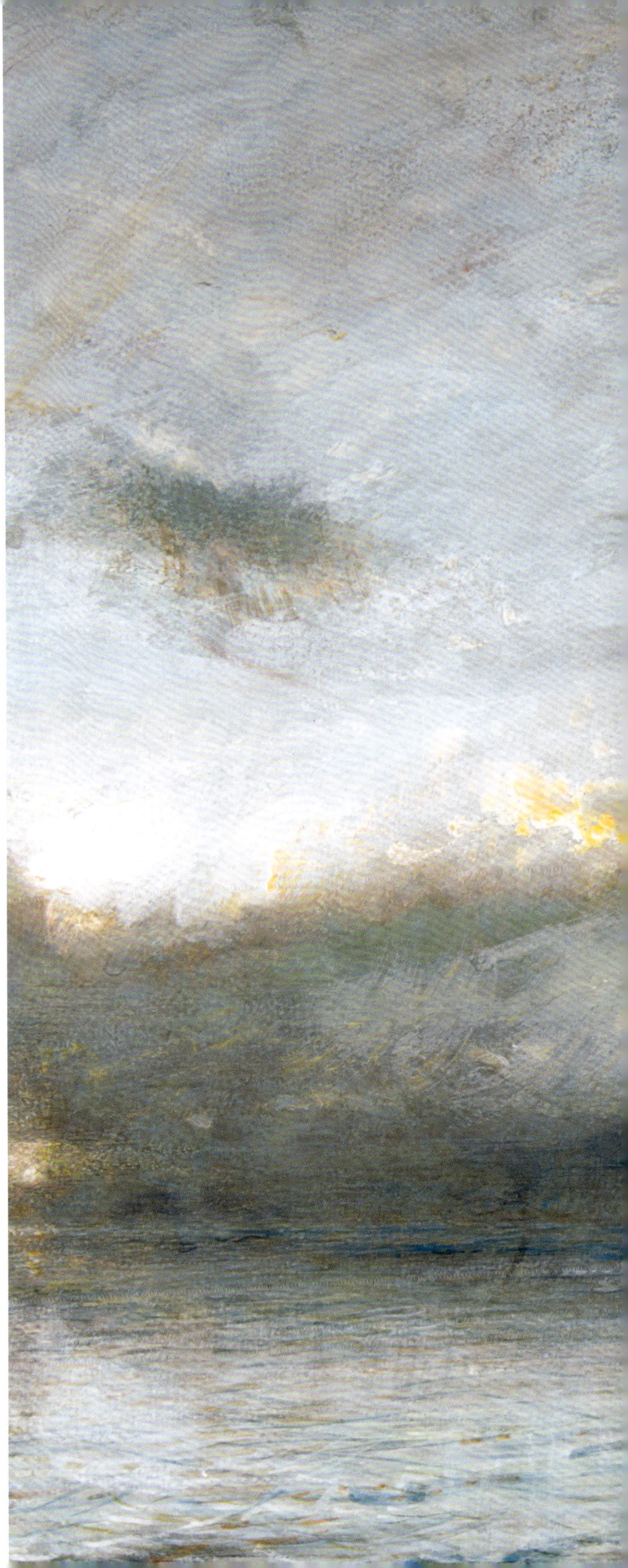

Detail of Albert Goodwin, *The Unknown Land* [96]

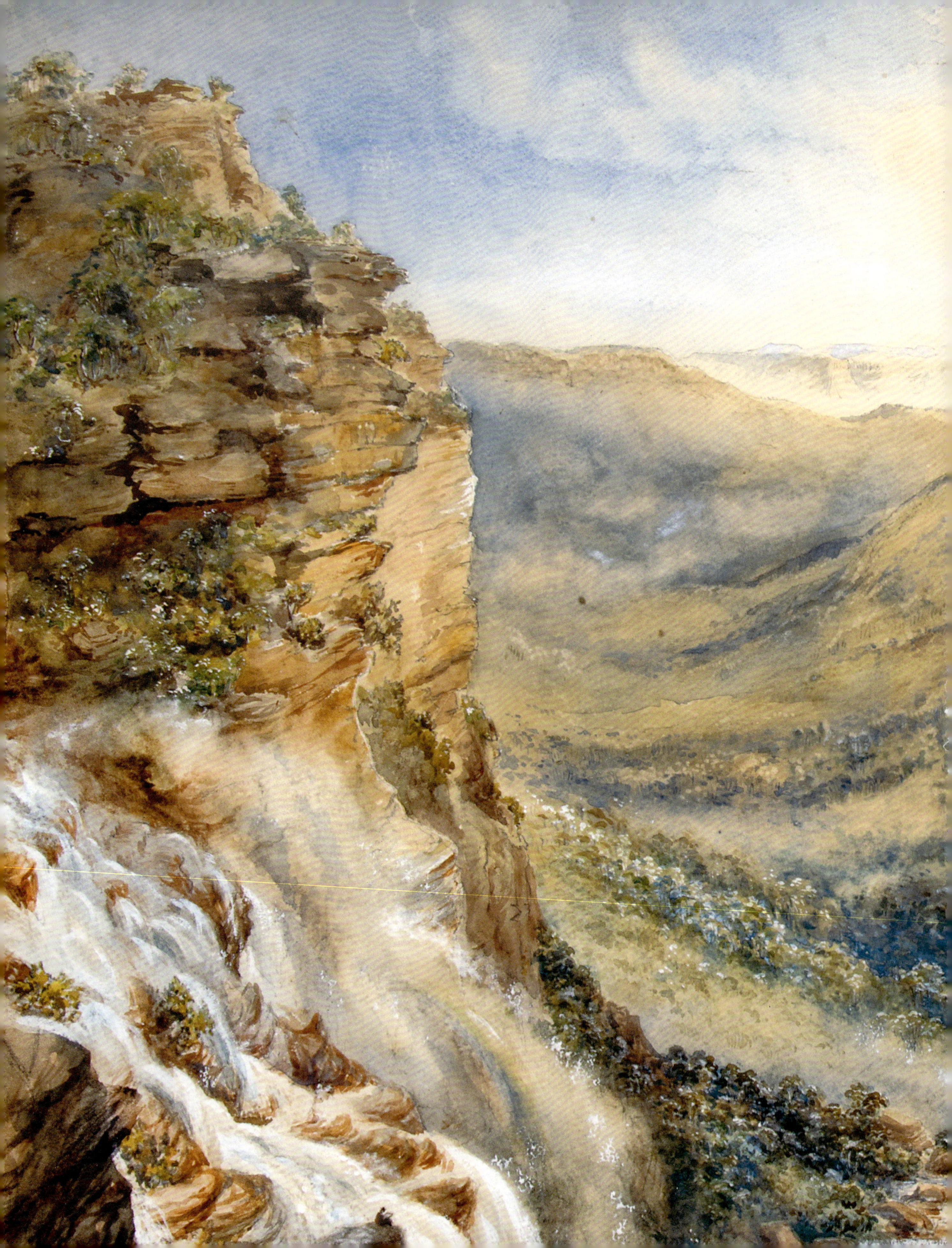